D1572377

THE PALACE GATES

Parables for the High Holy Days

THE PALACE GATES

Parables for the High Holy Days

compiled by
Rabbi Shalom Wallach

Translated by
Avraham Sutton

FELDHEIM PUBLISHERS
Jerusalem/New York

Originally published in 1993 in Hebrew
as *Sha'arei Armon,* by Tevunah Publishers.

First published 1994
ISBN 0-87306-694-1
Copyright © 1994 by Shalom Wallach and Feldheim Publishers

All rights reserved.
No part of this publication may be
translated, reproduced, stored in a retrieval
system or transmitted, in any form or by any
means, electronic, mechanical, photocopying,
recording, or otherwise, without permission in
writing from the publishers.

FELDHEIM PUBLISHERS
POB 35002 / Jerusalem, Israel

200 Airport Executive Park
Spring Valley, NY 10977

Printed in Israel

10 9 8 7 6 5 4 3 2

CONTENTS

Mashal v'Nimshal
Proverbs and Parables and their Morals

by Rabbi Shalom Wallach

Shelomo *Ha-Melech*, wisest of all men, said, "If you have become wise, it is for your own benefit" (*Mishlei* 9:12). Nevertheless, he was not satisfied in keeping his wisdom to himself. He spread his wisdom far and wide, as it is written, "And besides being the wisest of all men, he taught everyone; he taught them to weigh and probe the words of the wise, by devising many parables" (*Koheles* 12:9; Sforno *ibid.*). Shelomo *Ha-Melech* taught with parables.

Our Sages explained the value of parable with... parables: "And besides being the wisest of all men... he taught them to weigh (אזן) and probe the teachings of the Torah." That is, he made handles (אזן) with which to hold the Torah. We thus learn that until Shelomo arose, no man had ever used *mashal*—proverbs, metaphors, and parables—to explain the teachings of the Torah...

R. Yosei said: [The Torah can be likened to] a large basket full of luscious fruits, but with no handles. No one could pick it up to carry it until a wise man came and attached handles to it. In the same way, until Shelomo arose, no man really understood the teachings of the Torah.

R. Shila said: [The Torah can be likened to] a large cauldron full of boiling water, but with no handles. No one could pick it up to carry it until a man came and attached handles to it.

R. Chanina said: [The Torah can be likened to] a deep well whose waters are cool and sweet. No one could drink from it until a man came and bound ropes and cords to a bucket. Everyone was then able to draw forth water from the well. In the same way, Shelomo bound one concept to another and one *mashal* to another, until he grasped the deepest secrets of Torah. It is thus written, "The Proverbs (*Mishlei*) of Shelomo, son of David, King of Israel: To grasp wisdom and moral instruction, to discern words of profundity" (*Mishlei* 1:1)—by devising proverbs and parables, Shelomo understood the teachings of the Torah.

The Sages said: Never take a *mashal* lightly, for it is through a simple *mashal* that one can grasp and understand the teachings of the Torah. The following *mashal* will illustrate: A king once misplaced a precious treasure of gold and pearls. Does he not search for it and find it by lighting the tiny wick of a candle? In the same way, a seemingly simple *mashal* can help you understand the precious teachings of the Torah... (*Shir Ha-Shirim Rabbah* 1:1:8).

The Sages listed the *mashal* as the twenty-sixth of the thirty-two methods used in Torah exegesis:

The verse says, "The trees went out to anoint a king over them. They said to the olive tree, Reign over us!" (*Shoftim* 9:8). Do trees seek a king?! Rather, the children of Israel went to Osniel ben Kenaz, [and later] to Devorah, and [later] to Gidon, asking them to reign over them. They refused. Similarly, we find, "And Yeho'ash, king of Israel, sent to Amatzyah, king of Yehudah, saying: The thistle that was in the Levanon sent to the cedar that was in the Levanon, saying: Give your daughter to my son as a wife. But a wild beast that was in the Levanon passed by and trampled down the thistle..." (II *Melachim* 14:9). Can a thistle marry a cedar? Rather, Shechem, the son of Chamor, was a thistle in comparison to Ya'akov *Avinu*... You thus find *mashal* used everywhere throughout the prophetic writings... (The Thirty-Two *Middos* of R. Eliezer, son of R. Yosei *Ha-Gelili, Maseches Berachos*).

The wiser the teacher, the greater his responsibility to bind rope to rope, *mashal* to *mashal*, to go out to his people, to enlighten them from the depths of his understanding. "And [Shelomo] told three thousand parables" (I *Melachim* 5:12).

Shelomo composed three thousand parables for every concept in the Torah (*Eruvin* 21b). Similarly, it was said about R. Meir: He composed three hundred fox-parables... He also divided his discourses into thirds: one third *mashal*, one third Halachah, one third *aggados* (*Sanhedrin* 38b; Rashi, *ibid.*). When R. Meir died, the Sages bemoaned his passing by saying: "Gone are the masters of parables!" (*Sotah* 49a). No one matched him in his ability to make things clearly understood, to guide [his listeners] through the gates of understanding (Rashi, *ibid.*).

This is the value of a *mashal*: to guide others and ourselves through the gates of understanding. *Binah* (understanding) is related to the word *bein* (between). It is therefore always associated with the ability to "understand one thing from another" (*Chagigah* 14a; *Sanhedrin* 93b). A *mashal* should never stand in the way of the deeper meaning it wishes to communicate. It should facilitate a process of *binah*, of understanding one thing from another. In the words of the Baal Shem Tov, "A *mashal* is a vessel for the pure enlightenment of the mind" (*Keser Shem Tov*), a tool for bringing the abstract into the concrete. Numbers, for example, are abstract. When asked, What is the number four? most of us would think of four somethings—four apples, four tables, etc. We grasp the abstract spiritual concept in concrete physical terms. When David *Ha-Melech* says, "God is good to all" (*Tehillim* 145:9), we think of the light of the sun, the magnificence of creation, good health, and good livelihoods. This allows us to feel His goodness in our lives. David *Ha-Melech* thus wrote "*U'malchuso ba-kol mashalah*—[Hashem's] kingdom rules over all" (*Tehillim* 103:19), which the holy Tchernobiler Rebbe understood on two levels: In its entirety, the whole world is a *mashal*—a parable for how He *mashalah*—rules over all! (*Me'or Einayim, Ha'azinu*). Similarly, the Talmud consistently deals with abstract concepts in terms of concrete objects and circumstances: "two held on to a *tallis*," "a bull that gored a cow," "he sold him wheat and he only admitted buying barley"...

But there is an additional function to the *mashal*. By nature, man does not see, and has a very hard time admitting, his own faults (*Mishnah Nega'im* 2:5; *Sifrei Bemidbar* 12:12). It is a general principle in jurisprudence: "A man never considers himself wicked" (*Yevamos* 25b); "A man never considers himself liable" (*Shabbos* 119a). The wisest of men declared, "A man's every way is right in his own eyes" (*Mishlei* 21:2). How will a man ever correct himself without seeing the light of truth? And where is the right key that can open a man's heart to see that truth?

The *mashal* is the key. This is brought out most dramatically in the story of David *Ha-Melech*, when he wanted to marry Bas-sheva. David sent a note to Yoav, his commander-in-chief, to make sure Bas-sheva's husband, Uriyah, would be properly taken care of: "And in the morning, David wrote a letter to Yoav, saying: Send Uriyah to the front lines in the heat of the battle; then withdraw from him so that he will be hit and die" (I *Shemuel* 11:15). David then waited until Bas-sheva had risen up from mourning for Uriyah. Without delay, he sent for her and married her, and she bore a son. This entire strategy which David had conceived did not please Hashem, and He therefore sent Nasan *Ha-Navi* to David, to tell him the following parable:

> There were two men in one city, one rich and one poor. The rich man had vast numbers of flocks and herds. The poor man had nothing except one tiny lamb which he had bought and reared. And this lamb grew up together with him and his children. It ate from his bread and drank from his cup. It lay in his bosom, and was like his own daughter. [One day] a wayfarer came to the rich man. Unable to bring himself to take from his own flocks and herds in order to prepare a meal for the guest, he took the poor man's lamb and prepared a meal for the man (II *Shemuel* 12:1-4).*

---

* Delving deep into Nasan *Ha-Navi's* parable, the Sages (*Sukkah* 52b) identify the wayfarer in this verse as none other than the *yetzer ha-ra*, the notorious Evil Inclination. They point out that the three

Hearing this, David was temporarily caught off guard. Thinking that Nasan was talking about someone else, David became indignant and enraged at the evil that had been perpetrated by the "rich" man. He said to Nasan: "As Hashem lives, the man that has done this deserves to die. He shall also restore the lamb fourfold because he did this thing and because he had no pity" (*ibid.* 5-6).

The opening had been made. Nasan now turned the key: "And Nasan said to David: You are the man! Thus says Hashem, God of Israel: I anointed you king over Israel... why have you despised Hashem's command and done evil in His sight, slaying Uriyah the Chiti with the sword, taking his wife for yourself...?!" (*ibid.* 7-9).

We mentioned the fox-parables of R. Meir: "Rabi Meir composed three hundred fox-parables, of which we have only three." Rav Hai Gaon wrote the following about these profound parables in which animals play the leading roles:

> Know that each of these parables contains a profound moral. One of them tells of a fox which was about to be eaten by a lion. In order to save itself, the shrewd fox says: "I am all skin and bones. What satisfaction could you possibly get from eating me? Come with me and I will show you a plump human being, from whose carcass you can get real satisfaction!"
>
> The lion followed the fox until they arrived at a spot where a man was sitting on the far side of a deep ditch. The man was praying. When the lion saw him, he said to the

_____

used to designate the wayfarer in this verse represent a clear progression. As Rashi comments: The Evil Inclination is likened here to a passing wayfarer [who shows no indication of wanting to stay longer than a few moments]. Then he is likened to a guest or visitor, who takes up temporary residence. In the end he is likened to the man of the house. Such is the way of the Evil Inclination. He begins as a wayfarer, enjoys all the advantages of being a guest, and finally takes his place as permanent master of the house.

fox, "I am afraid of the power of his prayers. Perhaps in their merit I shall be thwarted."

The fox replied, "Neither you nor your son need be afraid! Only your grandson will have to suffer. For the present, satisfy your hunger. You have plenty of time until your grandson's turn comes."

Tricked by the fox, the lion tried jumping over the ditch, but fell in. The fox came over to him, stood on the edge of the ditch, and peered in. Said the lion, "You promised me that I would be spared any punishment! Only my grandson would have to suffer!"

The fox replied, "Your grandfather probably had some sin whose consequences you were destined to suffer."

Said the lion, "Shall the forefathers eat sour grapes and the grandchildren's teeth be set on edge?" (*Yirmeyahu* 31:28; *Yechezkel* 18:2).

The fox replied, "Why didn't you think of such a possibility from the outset?"

How much there is to learn from this parable!

One of the students of the Alter of Kelm copied the above text for his Rebbe. The Alter of Kelm never ceased being fascinated by its wisdom and depth. As recorded in his *Chochmah u'Musar* (1:113), just one of the many deep lessons he gleaned from this particular parable goes like this: The lion is the king of the animal kingdom. He is intelligent and wise, and fully understands the concept of reward and punishment. As a result, he fears pouncing on the man who is *davening*. How, therefore, did he fall for the fox's promise that punishment would surely be postponed for his grandson? Why didn't he understand that his own teeth would be set on edge as a result of the sour grapes eaten by *his* grandfather? Rather, as is usually the case, a bribe blinds the eyes of the wise. His dream of enjoying such plump prey deluded him. The same is true of a person who thinks he is graced with the three fears: fear of Heaven, fear of sinning against his Creator, and fear of being punished. When the moment of truth arrives, these three fears are conveniently suspended, his conscience is put to rest with some trite excuse, and he jumps straight-away into the ditch...

A good *mashal* is interesting; it pulls you into itself. But it never stands alone. Behind the scenes waits the *nimshal*, the moral and the meaning of the parable. It peers through the curtain of the *mashal*, anticipating the moment when we will get the point, when we will "understand one thing from another," find ourselves in the *mashal*, and say to ourselves, "I am that person." The *nimshal* peeks out between the cracks of the *mashal*, waiting to enter the heart of the reader or the listener.

The name of this book, *The Palace Gates*, is taken from the moving liturgical poem sung during the *Kedushah* of *Ne'ilah* on Yom Kippur. It is at this time that the Heavenly gates open above, and it is at this time that the gates of our hearts, our inner sanctuaries, must open as well. The parables contained in *The Palace Gates* are sure to help us open our hearts...

Rabbi Chayim Kanievsky of Bnei Brak told the story of how the Dubner Maggid was asked why he always used parables. True to form, the Maggid replied with a parable:

> A young boy once became very ill. The doctor was desperate: although he held a spoonful of the right medicine in his hand, the boy refused to open his mouth to swallow it. The boy's father, who had been standing at his bedside, suddenly dashed out of the room. Before long he was back, accompanied by a clown. The clown told such a funny story that the boy could not help opening his mouth wide with laughter. Quickly, the doctor poured the medicine down the boy's throat.
>
> "I am like that clown," explained the Maggid, "and the parables I tell are like the jokes that make us open our hearts. It is then that the truth they contain can enter and heal our souls."

This is the power of a parable. It can make an opening in our hearts and thus tear down the walls that separate us from our Father in Heaven. Even if the opening is the size of a tiny pinhole, we are promised that He will open the gates of His palace wide to shower us with blessings and goodness.

* * *

The parables in the present volume were selected from Rabbi Shalom Wallach's compilation, *Sha'arei Armon* (Bnei Brak, 5753). As in the original Hebrew, they are arranged in the order of the prayers, beginning with the *Selichos* of Elul to the closing words of *Ne'ilah* on Yom Kippur. Some of the parables are introduced by a sentence or verse taken from the prayers. For the most part, the translations of these (as well as of verses and quotations appearing in the text) are original, based on the present translator's forthcoming translation of the *Siddur*. The bracketed material and the footnotes are the translator's. With Hashem's help, a companion volume of parables (on the Pesach *Haggadah*) compiled by Rabbi Wallach is scheduled to appear in translation.

THE
Gates
OF
Elul

The Purpose of Elul:
Freedom from Servitude

Why is it important to prepare for the Days of Awe throughout the month that precedes them, the month of Elul? True,
these are the days when our supplications are most likely to
be heard, and such preparation is certainly essential if we
wish to make a proper *cheshbon ha-nefesh*—"accounting of the
soul," or moral stocktaking—before Hashem. The Maggid of
Dubno, of blessed memory, suggests another dimension to the
role of Elul, in the following parable:

A thief once noticed that a certain shop was always filled
with customers. "They must have quite a cash turnover," the
thief told himself, and he began to plan the robbery.

He decided that he would observe how each day's earnings were transferred from the store to the bank every evening. Soon enough he noticed that just before closing time, a
young man would walk out of the store·with a full briefcase
and head straight for the nearest branch of the bank with it.

Now, the thief knew that the streets were always full at
this hour, and it was not yet dark, so he had almost no hope
of getting away with grabbing the briefcase. He was about to
give up his plan when he noticed that there was a clothing
store that the young man always passed on his way to the
bank. A brilliant idea popped into his head.

The next afternoon, a few minutes before closing time, the
thief showed up at the clothing store and introduced himself
to the owner. "I work for a very wealthy man, and my boss is
interested in buying an exquisitely tailored suit. The price is
absolutely inconsequential. He insists only on the highest
quality material and tailoring. Do you have something for
him?"

"You've certainly come to the right place," the owner
answered with enthusiasm. "Just tell your boss to come in and
we'll fit him with something that will satisfy him. I assure
you, he'll leave here pleased."

"So will I..." the thief thought to himself. "But that's just the problem," he went on to explain. "He doesn't have time to come in and get fitted. He's a very busy man. That's why he sent me to bring him a suit to try on."

"But how can I determine his size?" the owner asked.

The thief acted as if he were stumped, and then suddenly answered, "I know! Let's stand outside on the street, and I'll tell you when I see somebody who's his size—you can try the suit on him!"

The two went outside and watched all the people passing by. When the thief spied the young man walking towards them, on his way to the bank with the briefcase in his hand, he pointed and called out, "See that fellow there? He's the same size as my boss!"

The owner made his way through the crowd and approached the young man. "Excuse me, but could I trouble you to come into my store for a minute?" he asked politely. "I would like to try a very expensive suit on you."

An expensive suit! thought the youth. Why not?

He accompanied the owner into the store, placed the briefcase near his feet, and tried on the beautiful suit. Stepping up to the full length mirror, he took a look and admired himself in the new suit. Then, before he knew it, the thief bent down, grabbed the briefcase, and faster than lightning, was out of the store and running.

"Thief! Thief! Grab him!" the young man cried out. As he was about to dash out of the store after the thief, the owner grabbed his shoulder. "Not so fast, mister! You're not going anywhere as long as you're wearing my suit. Take it off first, and then go your way."

"But he'll get away!" the young man pleaded.

"I'm sorry, but that's none of my business. Just take off the suit first." And as the distraught young man was taking it off, the thief swiftly disappeared into the crowd.

The lesson of this parable is as follows:

We are responsible for a "briefcase full of money," and we have been instructed to make sure that this briefcase arrives at its destination. Our task is to learn Hashem's Torah and keep its commandments. We are to fill our days with these precious commodities, and make sure that we bring them with us when we appear before God on Rosh Hashanah, New Year's Day, God's Day of Judgment.

But that cunning thief, the Evil Inclination, tries to prevent us from carrying out this all-important task. He lures us into a store that is not our own, to try on a suit that is not our own. He cons us into enjoying ostensible pleasures that afford no benefit to our bodies, and certainly not to our souls. He persuades us to waste precious time on worthless pursuits so that he can then drop his disguise, rise up and stand before Hashem's throne, and expose us for falling into his trap....

But there is still a chance. Even after we have fallen for his crafty tricks, we can still chase him, crying, "Thief!" We can still retrieve the stolen goods. How? By repenting for all the time we have wasted, and by regretting all the wrong we have done. Only then will we be able to make a penetrating *cheshbon ha-nefesh*. Only then will we be able to realize what it means to stand before our Creator on the Day of Judgment and speak to Him from the depths of our hearts. Only then, with true tears welling up from the very depths of our souls, will we make an opening in the Heavenly gates. For even if all other gates have been closed, the gates of heartfelt tears remain open.

But the frightening possibility exists that when the Day of Judgment arrives, and we wish to stand in fervent prayer and completely return to God—we will not be able to. Like the young man in the parable, we will still be dressed in that wretched suit. We will still be bound up in our vanities, wrapped up in our own foolish pastimes, unable to see beyond our own illusions, unable to see that we have lost our way.

How happy our young man would have been if, even after

he had gotten lured into the store, tried on the suit, and taken a good look at himself in the mirror, a friend had come up to him and whispered in his ear, "Watch out! The fellow standing next to you is a known thief!" If he had been warned before it was too late, he could have taken off the suit before the thief could get his hands on the money. How grateful he would be to such a friend.

Dear reader, that friend is none other than the month of Elul!

Ohel Ya'akov, *Balak*

Why Didn't the Shofar Do Its Job?

The Maggid of Lublin, of blessed memory, also emphasized the importance of preparing ourselves during the month of Elul, as a prerequisite for appearing before the Divine Throne on the Day of Judgment. To drive this point home, he quoted the following questions posed by the prophet Amos and asked how they were connected: "Can two walk together without having agreed?... Will a snare spring up from the ground, if it has captured nothing? If a shofar has been sounded in the city, shall the people not tremble?" (*Amos* 3:3-6).

Amos' intention, the Maggid explained, is to answer a very bothersome question: We know that blowing the shofar on Rosh Hashanah (which represents our own desire for inner transformation) helps to fluster the power of evil and prevent the Heavenly Prosecutor from leveling charges against us and the entire people of Israel. We know, furthermore, that the shofar helps us find favor in Hashem's eyes (for He beholds our sincere attempts to draw close to him), so that we actually picture Him rising up from His Throne of Judgment in order to sit on His Throne of Mercy. If so, if the shofar possesses this power, why are not all Jews immediately inscribed in the Book of Life on Rosh Hashanah? How is it that the Divine Accuser still has the ability to level charges against us? Why do we see so many tragedies all around us, so many people falling ill, wounded, dying? Why do so many lose their money and become impoverished? How can all this happen after we have blown the shofar? "Will a snare spring up from the ground, if it has captured nothing?" Has the shofar lost its power?

Our Sages explain that the power of evil dresses up in many disguises. As they put it, "The Evil Inclination [in a man's heart] is none other than the Prosecutor [on high]. And the Prosecutor [on high] is none other than the Angel of Death. [As the evil inclination,] he comes down [into a person's thoughts] and tempts him to sin. He then [dresses up as the Prosecutor,] goes up to Heaven, and accuses. [Finally, taking off all his disguises,] he comes down and takes a man's soul" (*Bava Basra* 16a). In very simple terms, we learn from this that the sin, the accusation of guilt, and the punishment are so inextricably intertwined as to be different aspects of the same thing.

We can now understand that the special efficacy of the shofar to fluster and confuse the Heavenly Prosecutor is not just some kind of magical spell or hex. Far from it. By blowing the shofar, we confuse and disarm the Evil Inclination within us. We break his power over us by revolting against his supremacy in our lives. When we do this down here below, the Heavenly power of the Accuser above is correspondingly weakened. For, as we have seen, they are merely different faces of the same power. At the same time, any judgment or punishment that was hanging over us [because we were unable to face the truth that we had in effect given up till now and played completely into the hands of all that contradicts truth] is sweetened and mitigated...

The sequence of two of our verses is now clearer. Why has "a snare sprung up from the ground, if it has captured nothing"? The only explanation is that "a shofar has been sounded in the city, but the people did not tremble."

But another question still remains. Why and how is it that

the shofar did not succeed in penetrating people's hearts and causing them to tremble? The answer to this is given in the first verse quoted: "Can two walk together without having agreed?"

The explanation is as follows: A flame more easily takes hold of a wick which has already been singed with fire than one which has not. The same is true of our ability to fear Hashem and feel the awe of His Presence. This fear and awe is likened to fire, as per the verse, "My heart grew hot within me; when I contemplated [Your awe], I became inflamed" (*Tehillim* 39:4). For this same reason, it is written, "Happy is the person who fears [You] at all times" (*Mishlei* 28:14). For only after we have already made this fear part of our inner makeup is it easily ignited when we need it. If we have not "prepared the wick," it is much more difficult to "light the flame"...

This can be likened to two men traveling on a journey. Traveling is certainly more pleasant when in the company of a friend. But what if the two men have never met before and do not recognize each other? What if they are total strangers?

This is the prophet's answer: You asked why the shofar did not do its work in Heaven above? Because you didn't help it do its work below in your own hearts. And why didn't it work in your hearts? Because you failed to prepare yourselves during the entire month of Elul! You didn't prepare the wicks of your hearts so that the fire of fearing and loving God could grab hold. You didn't bother to make friends with that feeling of awe that is so necessary when you wish to come before Hashem. You have therefore remained total strangers...

Ohel Ya'akov

The Advantage of Preparing for Judgment Day

The Maggid of Dubno found yet another advantage in preparing for the Day of Judgment. He explained that there is an immense difference between someone who prepares for its advent and someone who just happens to be there when the day finally comes around. The one who prepares himself through Torah study and mitzvos, will not arrive empty-handed. Even if everything he has done does not amount to much, and on Rosh Hashanah he ends up impoverished before Hashem, there is still a great difference. Unlike the person who just floats along and finds himself sitting in the synagogue on Rosh Hashanah, the one who has tried to prepare for the awesome day has at least done something. The Maggid illustrated this difference with the following parable:

A rich man once heard someone knocking on his door. He looked down from his office window and saw one of the members of his community. The door opened downstairs, and he heard his servant asking the man why he had come.

"I have come to ask a favor of your master..." was the answer.

"My master is occupied at the moment, and does not wish to be disturbed," the servant replied.

"When can I meet with him then?"

"Try coming back around four o'clock this afternoon."

The man left, and the rich man returned to his work.

At four o'clock, he again heard knocking at the front door. As he looked down from his office window, he saw the man waiting again. The door opened, and the servant informed him that the master of the house was still occupied.

"I will wait out here," the man offered. "I only ask that you inform me when your master can receive me. It is a very urgent matter."

The door closed, and the rich man returned to his work, but after an hour his curiosity got the best of him. He glanced down and saw the man pacing nervously on the front walk. The rich man's mercy was aroused, and he instructed his servant to show the man in.

He entered and immediately told the rich man that he was in dire need of financial assistance, explaining why he needed a short-term loan. He brought out a contract which he had already prepared and on which the signatures of two co-signers already appeared. He told the wealthy benefactor how much he would appreciate his assistance.

The rich man reasoned to himself that, after all, it is a mitzvah to lend money to a man in need, and he had the money to lend. He presented his visitor with the sum he had requested, and extended the date of repayment even beyond the date the man had suggested.

Later that evening, as the rich man entered the synagogue for the *Minchah* and *Ma'ariv* prayers, one of the congregants turned to him and said, "Oh, as long as we've met, maybe you can lend me a few thousand rubles for a few days?"

The rich man responded by saying that he wasn't carrying such a sum of money, and he redirected the conversation into other areas.

The question is, why didn't he respond to this second *man's request as generously as he did to the first?

The answer is simple. The first borrower went to the trouble of coming to his house in the morning, and then returning in the afternoon. When he was again told to wait, he stood outside until the right time. He put so much effort into getting the loan that it was only right for the rich man to respond in kind by making the effort to fulfill his request.

The second man, on the other hand, did not go out of his way and made no effort. He met the rich man in passing and turned to him for help in a rather haphazard way. This was certainly an indication that he could not have been in such dire straits. Since he obviously didn't need the money that much, why should his request deserve the same treatment as the first man's?

God spoke to the prophet Yirmeyahu about this kind of situation when He said, "Do not pray for this people. Do not lift up your voice in supplication and prayer. Do not *encounter* Me" (*Yirmeyahu* 7:16). "Do not encounter Me," i.e., do not just meet Me by accident. If you want an answer, prepare yourself and knock sincerely on the Heavenly gates, as it is written, "Thus says the God of Hosts, the God of Israel... 'When you call upon Me, *you must go* and pray *to Me.* Then I will hearken to you'" (ibid. 29:12). That is, if you will make a special effort to walk towards Me, if you will prepare yourselves, this is a sign to Me that you take the matter seriously, that it is one of importance to you, in which case I will surely hear, for I am merciful...

This preparation, this approach, this going towards God—this is the work of Elul!

Kochav Mi-Ya'akov, *Haftarah* to *Ki Sissa*

THE
Gates
OF
Selichos

שְׁמַע קוֹלֵנוּ ה׳ אֱלֹקֵינוּ חוּס וְרַחֵם עָלֵינוּ

"Hashem, only You are our God, hear our call! Pity us, have compassion on us!"

In his work *Sidduro shel Shabbos*, Rabbi Chayim of Tchernovitz (author of *Be'er Mayim Chayim*) explained this plea with a parable.

How great the love of a father and mother for their infant. When he begins to say, "Abba," they smile at him lovingly, pick him up, play with him, hug and kiss him, and generally cannot stop showing their affection to him. The child eventually grows up, however, and his parents' expectations of him grow in proportion. Now, they require that he behave himself properly. When he comes of age, he must go to school. He must pay attention to his studies and learn all that his teachers teach him. He is expected to exhibit good character traits and good manners. He is expected to show reverence for his parents and esteem them. If he fulfills these expectations, he will be a source of pride and comfort to them. They will shower their love upon him in return.

There was once a child like this. He embodied all that his parents could ask for and they loved him dearly. But one day, the child fell ill. While he wasn't entirely bedridden, he nevertheless became very weak and fatigued. He could no longer show honor to his parents as he used to. His desire to learn also ebbed. His brilliance vanished. He would sit in the corner and just daydream. His parents' grief knew no bounds.

One day, the boy's face lit up and he said to his father, "It's true that I can't do the things I used to do, that earned me your love in the past. But if you could think of me as an infant, completely dependent on your mercy, couldn't you love me again just for calling you 'Abba'?"

Our relationship to Hashem resembles that of this boy and his parents. Once, long ago, we "grew up." We dwelt in our Holy Land and we earned our Father's love by serving Him in the Holy Temple. While our *Kohanim* performed the holy service and our *Leviyim* sang their sacred songs, our ancestors stood praying from the depths of their hearts. Our Sages sat in the Sanhedrin to judge us, and our Prophets transmitted Hashem's words to His beloved children. Even after the Temple was destroyed, we were blessed with masters of the spirit, sainted individuals, in every generation.

Now we have regressed ten times over. Our energy has been drained. We have so few good deeds to our credit. We seem to have lost the ability to please our Maker. What is left? What can we do?

We can call, "Abba!" We can ask Hashem to remember the love He had for us before... It is when we are unable to fulfill His expectations, that we need His love more than ever before. This is an exact parallel to our relationship with our children.

Indeed, this is exactly what our intentions should be when we call out, "Hashem, only You are our God, hear our call!" Despite the fact that we are unworthy, hear how we are calling You. Hashem, You are beyond any conception we can have of you, but You are our God. Hashem, You alone are our Provider. And for this alone, "Pity us, have compassion on us," for we have fallen to such a low estate.

Sidduro shel Shabbos

"Hashem... hear our call!"

The Maggid of Rotzky told a similar parable: Imagine a boy who has disappointed his father and caused him untold grief. When he comes to ask forgiveness, how shall he begin, other than to entreat his father to arouse his mercy? But if the father has banished the boy from home, the boy must first knock on the door and ask to be allowed back in. He must first cry out, "Abba, my dear father, please hear my voice!" Only after the door has opened, and his father has agreed to listen to him, may he ask forgiveness. Only then may he continue and ask, "Pity me, have compassion on me!"

Akleda d'Rachamei

הֲשִׁיבֵנוּ ה׳ אֵלֶיךָ וְנָשׁוּבָה, חַדֵּשׁ יָמֵינוּ כְּקֶדֶם

"Hashem, return us to You. Then we shall surely return. Renew our days [of redemption], as of long ago."

Our Sages tell us of an ongoing debate, as it were, between God and the Jewish people (*Eichah Rabbah* 5:21). God tells us through His Prophet Malachi, "Return to Me and I shall surely return to you" (*Malachi* 3:7). We respond by saying, "Hashem, You return us to You. Then we shall surely return!" (*Eichah* 5:21).

But wait a moment. Do we even have a foot to stand on? After all, God adds, "Return O reckless children, and I will heal your backsliding" (*Yirmeyahu* 3:22). [It seems that our own claim is considerably weakened. How can we continue to ask for help from Above if we are errant in taking the necessary steps to correct the situation below?]

The Maggid of Dubno was once asked this question. This was his answer: On the contrary, our claim in this ancient debate is completely justified. It is God's side which has been considerably weakened. Everyone, even God, agrees that our claim has now prevailed! Why? A parable will help to clarify this.

There was once a very wealthy man, whose son was forced by circumstances to travel to a distant city. Before he left, the young man came to his father to bid him farewell. As he spoke, his eyes filled with tears. "My beloved father, as long as I sat at your table, I did not lack a thing. Now, however, I will be a stranger wherever I go. Who will care for me and attend to my needs?"

"What kind of question is this, my son!" the father replied. "You surely have a pen and paper. If you write me often, and make a list of all your needs, I will attend to them in detail with great joy."

"I will certainly do so, Father," the son promised. "But I request that you not wait to receive a letter from me. Inquire about my well-being from the merchants who travel between the two cities, because—who knows?—I might become deathly ill and completely unable to write a letter. It is also possible that I will find myself under tremendous pressure, and, overwhelmed by life's vicissitudes, I may forget to write. I therefore ask, dear Father, that you always judge me favorably, and make a point of actively inquiring about my well-being!"

This is the meaning of David *Ha-Melech*'s plea, "My God, I call out to You! My Rock, do not turn a deaf ear to me. If You remain silent, I will be likened to those who have fallen into the pit" (*Tehillim* 28:1). Yes, under normal circumstances, we have always called out to God. But David *Ha-Melech* was praying for future generations, when circumstances would overwhelm us, when our minds would be confused, when we would feel faint at the sight of so many of our People becoming estranged from their Jewishness. At times like these, we would be unable to call on God as usual. At times like these, we plead that He not turn a deaf ear towards us. On the contrary—we ask that He inquire of our well-being, lest we be left on our own, and fall deeper and deeper into the pit of hopelessness, God forbid.

In such a situation, everybody agrees that God must initiate the redemption as He did when He brought us out of Egypt. He must redeem us quickly, before it is too late. Our call to Him is therefore justified: "Hashem, return us to You. Then we shall surely return. Renew our days [of redemption], as of long ago!"

Ohel Ya'akov, *Vayelech*

אַל תַּשְׁלִיכֵנוּ מִלְּפָנֶיךָ, וְרוּחַ קָדְשְׁךָ אַל תִּקַּח מִמֶּנּוּ

"Do not cast us away from Your Presence. Do not take Your Holy Spirit away from us!"

The Maggid of Dubno told a parable to explain this plea.

The residents of a certain city rebelled against their king. In order to squelch the uprising, the king was forced to amass a sizable army. To protect themselves, the inhabitants of the province gathered behind their city walls and sealed all its gates. The king decided to besiege the city until the people would be forced to surrender. Boasting among themselves of the strength of their fortifications, the people claimed, "The king will never be able to breach our walls. We have nothing to worry about."

Little did they understand that the king did not consider them important enough to fight against. He would merely set up a siege and wait for them to surrender.

It wasn't long before the siege began to have its effect. As food supplies dwindled, and the people were hungry for bread, demonstrations of self-sufficiency and the spirit of rebellion soon gave way to worry and anxiety.

The people decided to meet and confer on a future course of action. With their last remaining strength, they came together and concluded that their rebellion had backfired and failed miserably. The king had prevailed. If the siege continued, they would all die of hunger. They had no choice but to surrender immediately and suffer the consequences of their actions.

Who among them would represent them before the king? They were all ready to go, but not one of them had the strength to stand on his feet...

As they sat weak and drained, the sound of a trumpet blast was heard. The king had decided to put an end to the siege that had apparently failed to bring the people to their knees. He was now going to storm the city with the full might of his troops, and everyone knew that the king's men would breach the walls and enter the city. Not one of them had the strength to stand on his feet. They would all be slaughtered mercilessly. Not a single soul would be left!

They heard the large battering ram crashing into the gates. Within minutes the gates would give way. Gathering all their strength, the people crawled towards the gates and lifted up their weak voices: "Stop! Our king! We have already returned to your service. We just did not have the strength to tell you! Give us a little nourishment so that our strength will return. And then we will be able to stand before you and accept your sovereignty over us!"

The lesson of this parable is clear: God awaits our return. But it is long overdue. The danger exists, therefore, that He will decide to take critical steps, to punish us... We must therefore hasten to call out, "Do not cast us away from Your Presence!" Do not take such drastic steps, Hashem! We want to do what You want! It is just that we have no strength left to return. Our spirits have simply dried up. Therefore, "Do not take Your Holy Spirit away from us!" Do not deprive us of Your holy inspiration! Restore it to us, and we will show You how we will return to You with complete sincerity.

This is what David *Ha-Melech* meant when he said, "Send forth Your light and Your truth. They will lead me. They will bring me home to the mountain of Your Sanctuary... I will then thank You eternally to the accompaniment of a harp, O God, my God!" (*Tehillim* 43:3-4).

Ohel Ya'akov, *Ki Savo*

מִי שֶׁעָנָה לְאַבְרָהָם אָבִינוּ בְּהַר הַמּוֹרִיָּה, הוּא יַעֲנֵנוּ

"He Who answered Avraham our forefather on Mount Moriah, He will answer us."

The Maggid of Dubno asked a penetrating question about this plea. He also provided an amazing answer. Both the question and the answer were given in the form of a parable.

There was once a store owner who lived in a certain village. All the residents of that village bought their supplies from him.

When the son of the *gevir* (lord of the village) got married, the store owner sent him an expensive wedding present, worth fifty rubles. A few weeks later, one of the village peasants married off his son. The store owner sent him a wedding present as well—but this gift was disgraceful in comparison to the first. It wasn't worth more than two or three rubles.

The peasant came to the store owner and complained. "Where is the justice here? Is this fair? I buy my supplies in your store just as the *gevir* does. But to the one who is *already* blessed with such wealth, to *him* you send such an elegant gift! And for me—the proverbial poor man who is always visited with poverty—for me you have a disgraceful gift!"

"Listen," the store owner replied, trying to calm the man down, "I can understand why you're upset. But just listen for a minute and you'll see that I haven't disgraced you in the least. True, both you and he buy all your supplies here. But can you compare your purchases to his? He buys large quantities of my best stock, and on top of that he pays cash! It wouldn't be an exaggeration to say that half my livelihood comes from him. You, on the other hand—what do you buy? A salted fish tail?! A handful of matches? And on top of it you charge it! What profit do I make from you? With the little gift I gave you I returned a whole year's profits—the profits I make from your purchases for a whole year!"

The meaning of this parable explains the question.

How can we come before God and ask to be answered like our father Avraham? What do we have in common with him?! How can we possibly compare ourselves to him? He is the *gevir*—the lord of our People. Hashem made good profits from the mitzvos Avraham fulfilled and the good deeds he performed. On Mount Moriah, he was prepared to offer his only son to Hashem! It was the most difficult test he had ever undergone. Of course Avraham has the right to come before Hashem in the merit of such self-sacrifice.

We, on the other hand, are like poor beggars who buy very little and who hardly pay for what we buy. We are lethargic and lifeless whenever we do perform a mitzvah. How, then, can we be so arrogant? How can we come before Hashem and ask Him to answer us as He answered Avraham after the most difficult test of his life?!

The answer to this question will be understood from the following parable.

A Jew once lived in a certain village. He was what we call a *boor ve'am ha'aretz* (an unrefined and ignorant man), but he was graced with tremendous wealth and with an extremely bright son. The boy studied in a yeshivah and excelled in his learning. He was always poring over the sacred books, and he was considered to be brilliant, head and shoulders above all the other students in the yeshivah...

The day came when the *Rosh Yeshivah* passed away. The leaders of the community deliberated over who should be chosen to take his place. Some of them claimed that no better candidate could be found than the young genius, the wealthy man's son, while others argued that the son of an ignorant villager should not be appointed as *Rosh Yeshivah*. Neither side could convince the other, and in the end, they compromised:

They would appoint the young man as the new *Rosh Yeshiva* if his father would agree to finance the yeshivah for ten years. The proud father thought about it and agreed. In the following years, he saw his son become an eminent teacher, greatly revered by his students. He also saw his grandchildren following in his son's path and one of them stood out as a potential genius...

The years went by, and the villager passed away. More years went by, and his son, the *Rosh Yeshivah*, also passed away. It was unanimously agreed to appoint his son, the genius, in his place.

An elder of the community stood up and spoke. "I remember that when the *Rosh Yeshivah*, of blessed memory, was appointed to his position, his father was asked to support the yeshivah for ten years. It would be fitting for this young man to be asked to do so as well."

All present found this quite amusing. "There is no comparison!" they replied. "The only reason the *Rosh Yeshivah's* appointment was dependent on his bringing in such a sum was that *he* was the son of an ignorant villager. *His* son, on the other hand, had a father who was outstanding in Torah! It is in the merit of his honorable father that he is being appointed *Rosh Yeshivah* now."

The lesson: It is certainly true that no one can compare to our father Avraham. We should, however, not forget what kind of father *he* had. His father was Terach and he came from Charan... We, on the other hand, are Avraham's children. It is therefore sufficient that Hashem answer us in his merit...

Mishlei Ya'akov

עֲשֵׂה לְמַעַן עוֹלָלֵנוּ וְטַפֵּנוּ
"Act for the sake of our babies and our growing children."

The Maggid of Lublin told the following parable about this:

There was once a man who worked very hard in order to provide bread for his young children. The time came when the factory where he was employed closed down, and along with it, the source of his livelihood. As he sat at home, his hungry children asked him for bread.

"What can I do, my dear children?" he replied. "I have no bread to give you. You have no choice but to go from door to door and beg for food."

They said to him, "But if this is to be our new livelihood, then you must be the one to do it. Just as you went out in the past, you must go now."

"You are mistaken, my dear ones," he answered them. "As long as the work involved effort and sweat, intelligence and experience, I was capable of doing ten times more than you and the responsibility was surely mine. Now, however, the source of our livelihood has been taken from us and we are forced to accept charity. In this, you will have seven times more success than I, for the Almighty will surely bless you. Because you are children, you will find favor and arouse pity in people's eyes."

The meaning of the parable is this: If we attempt to come before Hashem on the basis of our own merits, the good deeds of the righteous (*tzaddikim*) among us would be worth more. After all, they serve Him with pure intention, with a devoted heart, and every ounce of their soul. For this reason, their deeds are pleasing to Him and He intervenes on their behalf.

Our service, on the other hand, is half-hearted. Our deeds are very poor indeed. We are therefore forced to rely on Hashem's graces. When it comes to finding grace in Hashem's eyes, the supplications of children are particularly precious. Their prayers are pure, and are therefore able to rise up and break through all the gates that *our* prayers were unable to enter. In the merit of their children, parents will be inscribed for a year of blessing and livelihood.

Ohel Ya'akov

עֲשֵׂה לְמַעַן גְּמוּלֵי חָלָב שֶׁלֹּא פָּשָׁעוּ

"Act for the sake of babies weaned of [their mothers'] milk, who have not transgressed."

The Maggid of Rotzky told the following story, that took place in Morocco.

A certain man forged the seal of the king on an official

document. He was caught and tried: his punishment was to have his hands cut off. His wife begged and pleaded before the monarch, that he reduce the severity of her husband's sentence and revoke his punishment. All her pleading was in vain.

What did she do? She bound the hands and feet of her infant son, and stood in the middle of the road waiting for the king to pass by on his horse. At the right moment she laid the infant down and immediately stepped backwards, hiding in the shadow of the buildings.

The king approached and saw the child in the middle of the road. He stopped his horse and asked sternly, "What is this?"

The woman stepped forward and replied, "Your majesty, the king! In your wisdom, you have sentenced my husband to have his hands cut off. I will not protest the righteousness of your decree, for it is certainly lawful and just. But, your majesty, I will ask of you something: that you trample this tender infant to death under the hooves of your horse. For what shall I do with him, I, poor mother and wretched widow that I am?! What shall I do after my husband, our sole source of livelihood, is taken from me?! Moreover, the child has a part in his father's offense: was it not in order to buy food for him that he did what he did? I fear for the child, and I cannot bear the thought of his suffering starvation. I have therefore placed him here on the road..."

The king's mercy was aroused for the child, for the mother, and for the father. He ordered the man released from jail immediately.

Like the mother in the parable, we also turn to God and say: Master of the universe! If not for our sake, please act for the sake of babies weaned of [their mothers'] milk, who have not transgressed!

Serigi Nefishi, *Derush Vav*

עֲשֵׂה לְמַעַן תִּינוֹקוֹת שֶׁל בֵּית רַבָּן
"Act for the sake of schoolchildren."

The Days of Awe were drawing near and the Maggid of Lublin went to the schoolhouse to speak to the children. He told them the following parable.

A father and his young son were once traveling together from their hometown to the capital city. Throughout the journey, the father took devoted care of his son, making sure he had enough to eat and drink, shading him from the hot rays of the sun, and arranging a safe place to sleep at night. When the path they traveled became tangled with brambles and thistles, he carried his son on his shoulders. When they crossed a river, he carried him on his back.

After a long and difficult journey, they finally reached their destination. To their sorrow, however, they arrived at such a late hour that the city gates were locked.

The father turned to his son and said, "My precious child, until now I have attended to all your needs. When necessary, I carried you as a nursing mother carries her baby. Now we have arrived at the gates of the city and they are locked. However, built into the city wall is a small guardhouse with tiny windows. If you can squeeze through one of them, you will find the keys to the gates, hanging on the wall. You will then be able to let us both in."

The meaning of the parable is this: Until now, dear children, your parents have attended to all your needs to the best of their abilities. They have provided you with food, clothing, and shelter. They have taught you Torah, and educated you in what is right. They have protected and shielded you from all harm and cared for your health. They have done all they can for you.

Now, the awesome days of judgment have arrived. We, your parents, are aware of the severity of Hashem's judgment of His people. We are concerned for the future. We fear lest we may not be found worthy in Hashem's eyes. Even our prayers are restricted. Since the *Beis Ha-Mikdash* (Holy Temple) was destroyed, our prayers rise up to Heaven only with great difficulty. This is the meaning of the statement, "The gates of prayer were closed on the day the *Mikdash* was destroyed" (*Berachos* 32b).

But our Sages, of blessed memory, taught us that the prayers of schoolchildren are accepted in Heaven. These prayers make it possible for the world to continue to exist, even when it is otherwise deserving of destruction (*Shabbos* 119b). It is in your power to repay your parents and do them a tremendous favor. Pray for them. On their behalf, plead for a good and blessed year for the entire Jewish People. It is in your power to squeeze through the gates, and to open the door for all our prayers to enter.

Ohel Ya'akov

מִתְרַצֶּה בְּרַחֲמִים וּמִתְפַּיֵּס בְּתַחֲנוּנִים, הִתְרַצֵּה וְהִתְפַּיֵּס
לְדוֹר עָנִי, כִּי אֵין עוֹזֵר

"[You Who become] reconciled with mercy and placated through supplications, be reconciled and placated toward [this] destitute generation, for there is no [one to plead for] help."

The Chasam Sofer explained this supplication with a parable. The residents of a certain village were behind in paying their taxes. They sought an audience with the king and requested an extension. The king responded favorably to their request and set a new date for payment.

When the day arrived, they still lacked the necessary sum. How could they ask for another extension? They turned to one of the king's closest ministers and asked him to entreat the king on their behalf. As a kindness to his minister, the king was willing to grant one more extension. Another date was fixed for payment.

This date was also drawing near, but the villagers still did not have the money. They thought of approaching the minister and asking him to speak on their behalf again, but to their disappointment, they learned that the minister had been transferred to a higher post elsewhere. What were they to do?

They gathered together and sought an audience with the king. When they were ushered into his chambers, they pleaded before him and cried, "Your majesty, behold! Our distress is manifold! Not only do we lack the money to pay you, but we cannot even find the words necessary to beseech you, and we have no one to plead on our behalf. Our king, be gracious to us and answer us, despite the fact that we have not acted properly. Act charitably and kindly toward us!"

The lesson of this parable is as follows:

Hashem first created the world with His quality of Divine Judgment and only then introduced His quality of Divine Mercy. This is reflected in the order of our High Holidays. First comes Rosh Hashanah, the Day of Judgment. Ten days later, after we have been given an opportunity to repent and mend our ways, Yom Kippur arrives. Yom Kippur parallels the concept of mercy. It is the Day of Cleansing and Atonement when we are reconciled with Hashem and He inscribes us in the Book of Life. This is the meaning of our plea to Hashem, "[You Who become] reconciled with mercy..."*

---

* This is not to say that Rosh Hashanah itself is lacking the component of Hashem's mercy. On the contrary—for once we are moved by the gravity of His Judgment on Rosh Hashanah, His Mercy is aroused. Indeed, Hashem's Judgment is nothing but an "arousal from above," to bring about an "arousal from below." If this occurs, its purpose is fulfilled, and it is no longer required. The Judgment is mitigated and becomes transformed into Mercy. As we have noted above, this contains double significance: Judgment changes into Mercy, and it is revealed that Judgment itself is the greatest mercy. This is why we blow the shofar on Rosh Hashanah and say, "Elokim rose up with the blast, Hashem with the sound of the shofar" (*Tehillim* 47:6).

In former days, when the date to settle our long overdue accounts arrived, and we were still found terribly lacking, what did we do? We appointed pious and righteous prayer leaders to placate Hashem on our behalf with heartfelt supplications. This is the meaning of, "[You Who become] reconciled with mercy and placated through supplications."

Now, however, all of our great men have left us. They have been transferred to higher posts in the Heavenly realms. We find ourselves without anyone to plead our case. It is for this reason that we all stand and cry out, "Be reconciled and placated toward this destitute generation, for there is no one to plead for help! Our Father, our King, be gracious to us and answer us..."

Derashos Chasam Sofer, II:351

כִּי הוּא יָדַע יִצְרֵנוּ, זָכוֹר כִּי עָפָר אֲנָחְנוּ
"For You know our inclinations; remember that we are but dust."

The Maggid of Horodna explained this supplication with the following parable:

A rich merchant employed a man to work in his store. The employee was loyal, faithful, responsible, upright, and honest. One day, however, the merchant fired him and hired another man in his place. The new employee was the exact opposite of his predecessor. He was a sly and deceptive man, a liar and a thief. The surprising thing was that not only did the merchant employ such a character, but he even doubled his salary!

People expressed surprise and asked the merchant, "What have you done? How could you possibly exchange good for evil, uprightness for deception, an honest man for a liar?!"

"I am aware of all this," the merchant replied, "and I did it nevertheless. You see," he went on to explain, "my previous employee was upright and loyal. He didn't have a dishonest bone in his body. He never tried to hide a penny from me. This is all true. But he was lazy and lacked motivation and incentive. He never did anything to expand the business and he never thought of any ideas to increase profits. He was a real *shlemiel* and a *shlemazel*. As long as he worked for me, business remained at a standstill, and nothing ever moved.

"But with my new worker," the merchant continued, "everything has changed. To be sure, he isn't very honest or dependable, and I have to keep my eyes on every move he makes, but he knows how a business should be run. He constantly thinks up new ideas and he knows how to get things done. Even if he does embezzle and stash a little now and then, the remaining profits will be more than enough for both of us!"

The Maggid interpreted this strange parable in the following way: Angels have no Evil Inclination. They just serve God. They have no ulterior motives, no egos, and no desire to sin. When Hashem was about to give the Torah to Moshe on Mount Sinai, it was these angels who protested, saying, "O God, our Master, Your Name is too powerful to rule on the earth. Establish it in the Heavens above... What is mortal man, that You should think of him, and even the finest human being, that You should consider him?" (*Tehillim* 8:2,5). The angels objected to lowering the Divine Torah down to the level of human beings. "Leave it with us," they said. "Man is full of deceit. Even the best of them are liars. They lie to You and they lie to themselves. Even the good they do is filled with deceit and fraud. They are constantly chasing after their desires. They think that by covering over their sins they can fool everybody, including You. But they fool only themselves. Even the wisdom they accumulate is used to dominate others. We angels, on the other hand, are loyal and dependable servants. We will never stray from the straight path by a hairsbreadth!"

The answer is: Yes, you are correct. Angels are loyal,

dependable, and honest, while man is full of deceit. But this is just the point. If, despite man's powerful urge to do wrong, he takes hold of himself and does good once in a while for unselfish motives—even if it is not completely unselfish, even if it is full of ulterior motives... If, despite the fact that he is but mortal dust, he overcomes his lethargy and performs the will of his Creator with alacrity... the proceeds are ten times more valuable. This is the meaning of the *mishnah* (*Pirkei Avos*), "Who is powerful? He who overcomes his inclination." This transforms all our disadvantages into advantages!

Divrei Haskel

THE
Gates
OF
Rosh
Hashanah

Erev Rosh Hashanah

Rising for Selichos

The Maggid of Dubno told the following parable about the importance of rising before dawn on *Erev Rosh Hashanah*.

There was once a Jew who lived in a village among gentiles. Their jealousy and hatred of him was fiercer than that of Esav for Ya'akov. When the ruler of the country made his annual visit to the village, the Jew requested an audience with him, in order to plead for a reduction on his taxes as well as a more permissive policy toward his fellow Jews. Then, when he arrived, he found that his malevolent gentile neighbors had gotten up early and preceded him, in order to slander his reputation with the ruler. After such an introduction, he wasn't received very cordially. Moreover, the ruler doubled his taxes! The man simply did not know what to do.

He returned home dejected, and his wife offered him the following advice: "Next time, when the ruler comes to the village, get up in the middle of the night and make sure you are standing at the entrance of his manor before the crack of dawn! That way, you'll be sure to be first to get in to see him, and you'll be able to awaken his mercy before your enemies arrive and connive to turn him against you!"

The lesson of the parable is this:

It is written in *Sefer Iyov*, "The day arrived when the prosecuting angels came and stood before God. The Accuser himself came in among them" (*Iyov* 1:6). The holy *Zohar* (II:32b) asks, "What day arrived?" and answers, "It was The Day, the Day of Judgment, Rosh Hashanah." And so it is every year on that day. It is then that the Chief Prosecutor in Heaven comes forth to accuse us. He rises up early and presents a long list of our transgressions before the Heavenly Throne as testimony that we are undeserving of God's mercy. "Justice demands," he says with a devilish smile, "that they be punished for all their wrongdoing."

In the meantime, down on Earth, Jews are stirring in their sleep. Elul has passed. It is Rosh Hashanah. The Day of Judgment has arrived. The prayers begin. We call out to our Father in Heaven. We begin to repent for all our misdeeds and pray for Divine Mercy.

But is it too late? Has the Prosecutor, by rising early, succeeded in blocking our penitential prayers from entering the gates of Heaven? What must we do?

We must rise early the day before Rosh Hashanah, and begin to plead for our lives, for the lives of our children, and for our People. This is what Yirmeyahu meant when he warned against imminent destruction. He exhorted us, "Arise, cry out in the night! At the beginning of every watch, pour your hearts out like water, before Hashem! Lift up your hands to Him for the souls of your young children, who faint from hunger at the head of every street" (*Eichah* 2:19). If we can pray like this, Hashem will surely accept us, and we will be inscribed and sealed in the Book of Life for a good and prosperous year.

Kol Bochim 78b

The Merchant, the Wagon Driver, and the Horses

The Maggid of Jerusalem, Rabbi Shalom Schwadron, related the following, in the name of Rabbi Chayim of Brisk:

It wasn't long ago that merchants would cross national borders, stock up on a lot of merchandise in a neighboring country, and try to make it back across the border without paying customs duties. In order to do this without being apprehended, they would hire skilled wagon drivers. Familiar with the entire countryside, these men knew the back roads and forests like the back of their hands. They could cross the border in the dark of night, ensuring a successful operation.

From the moment a deal was struck, however, a merchant

would become extremely nervous: Everything had gone fine so far, but who knew what was around the next bend in the road? Who knew if he would succeed in crossing the border? Perhaps the border guards would capture him, confiscate his merchandise, and imprison him... While the merchants were nervous and agitated, however, the wagon drivers were calm and collected. They were used to crossing the border, sneaking along unknown pathways... They were calm and untroubled, that is, until the day they actually set out on the road.

They had to travel at night, and during the course of that whole day, the drivers became bundles of nerves. They were jumpy and distraught, suspicious of everything and everybody. As they began their journey, they constantly glanced back over their shoulders to make sure they weren't being followed; they strained their ears at the slightest sound; they shuddered at every suspicious movement in the night. If they were caught, their horses and wagons would be confiscated, and they themselves would be tried and sentenced.

Only the horses remained calm and collected throughout the entire episode.

To what can this be compared? Some people begin feeling the trepidation of the Days of Awe on *Rosh Chodesh Elul*. They realize how much is at stake, how many lives are hanging in the balance, how much each person stands to lose... Even those who remain unmoved throughout the whole month of Elul, however, feel the awe of Hashem's Judgment on *Erev Rosh Hashanah*. Only a person as spiritually insensitive as a horse would begin looking for a barber on *Erev Rosh Hashanah*!

אַל תָּבֹא בְמִשְׁפָּט עִמָּנוּ, כִּי לֹא יִצְדַּק לְפָנֶיךָ כָּל חָי

"Enter not into judgment with us, for no one alive can justify himself before You."

The Yismach Moshe told the story of a foolhardy wagon driver who drove his team of horses so recklessly that they ended up running off a high mountain pass and dragging the wagon, the driver himself, and his son into a deep ravine. As they fell, the wagon overturned, and the boy was killed. When the police arrived, they found the driver wailing bitterly, crying, and pulling out his hair over the death of his beloved son. "Woe is me, woe is me! What have I done?! I have killed my only son. Oh, that I could have died in his place!"

Even when he was taken into custody and brought before the judge, he continued crying uncontrollably. "My son, my son," he wept, "nothing can ever replace you!" His piercing screams sent shivers of terror into everyone's hearts.

The judge heard the case and ordered the man released. "He has already received his punishment," the judge ruled, "with the unfortunate death of his son. No conceivable punishment could be more severe than that."

The same is true of a person who awakens to realize the severity of his transgressions. For a sin is not merely an act that was performed—it leaves a mark on the soul of the one who performed it. When a person truly regrets having done wrong, this very regret takes the place of any external punishment.

This is the meaning of our plea, "Enter not into judgment with us." For even prior to our coming into Your presence and standing *before You*, we have admitted our wrongdoing. We have suffered pangs of conscience and fully regretted our misdeeds. Why? We understand that no one can deny having done wrong and then come before You expecting to be judged innocent. "No one alive can justify himself *before You*."

The *Yismach Moshe* clarified this further with the following example:

Picture a man lending a sum of money to his friend. The borrower signs the promissory note and deposits it with the lender. When the time comes to pay the loan, the borrower does not show up; the lender goes to him to demand that he repay the loan. If the borrower denies that he borrowed the money, the lender will summon the borrower to court and force him to pay. If, on the other hand, the borrower admits his debt, and merely requests an extension because he is not presently able to pay—what will the lender gain by summoning him to court?

This is what we mean when we plead to Hashem, "Enter not into judgment with us." Do not summon us to stand before You in Your court of law. Why? For we understand that "No one alive can justify himself before You." On the contrary—we do not plead innocence before You as if we had not done wrong. We are not like a borrower who denies his debt. Rather, we admit our accountability! It is just that we are too poor to pay. What will be gained by summoning us to court? We therefore entreat You to give us an extension.

Yismach Moshe

מִלְּפָנֶיךָ מִשְׁפָּטֵנוּ יֵצֵא, עֵינֶיךָ תֶּחֱזֶינָה מֵישָׁרִים

"May our judgment come forth from before You. Your eyes alone behold the uprightness [of our deeds]."

Rabbi Levi Yitzchak of Berdichev was Israel's chief advocate. He explained this prayer with the following parable:

There was once a king whose minister disobeyed him. In his anger, the king declared, "You yourself will determine your own punishment! You will judge yourself according to the requirements of strict justice and such will be your sentence."

The minister shuddered at the thought. "This is bitter indeed, for I myself know I have done wrong, and against whom I committed a crime. I have rebelled against a great and mighty king, a good and beneficent master. Moreover, I cannot judge myself leniently (literally, beyond the requirements of strict justice). If I choose a lenient sentence, this itself

will demonstrate my lack of respect for the king and my lack of appreciation for all the good he has done me. I have no choice but to ask the king himself to pass sentence on me. He is gracious and merciful, and his generosity is unlimited
It is in his power to judge me leniently."

This is the meaning of our prayer, "Enter not into judgment with us, for no one alive can justify himself before You." We are begging Hashem, "Do not ask us to judge *ourselves*, for since we know the extent of our sins, it is not in our power to judge ourselves favorably." Rather, "Let our judgment come forth from before You." *You* pass sentence on us, for Your generosity is not limited by the requirements of strict justice. "Your eyes alone behold the uprightness [of our deeds]."*

Yismach Moshe

---

* This supplication is based on the verse, "May my judgment come forth from before You. Your eyes alone behold the uprightness [of my deeds]" (*Tehillim* 17:2). There are various ways to understand what is being said here. Rabbi Samson Raphael Hirsch sees the emphasis on the word *mi-lefanecha*—"from before You." He explains: "Let that judgment I seek in prayer be such that it corresponds to Your own evaluation of me—*mi-lefanecha*, from before You: I seek no self-deception."

Rashi explains: I know I have transgressed and therefore am surely deserving of punishment. I ask only that the judgment come forth from You, and not be brought before You by the Prosecutor, i.e., let Your mercy precede judgment, as in the verse, "Quickly let Your mercy precede us, for we have fallen very low" (*Tehillim* 79:8). Let judgment proceed from Your mercy to insure that I will not be punished according to the requirements of strict justice. Furthermore, I ask that You take into account any merits I may have to my credit.

Metzudas David explains both halves of the verse together: Do not judge me according to my sins. Rather, behold the upright deeds I have done and judge me according to those...

Rabbi Levi Yitzchak's interpretation is based on the connection between the word *meisharim* in this verse and the expression *lifnim mi-shuras ha-din* (*Berachos* 5a; *siddur*, morning prayers). In addition to reading "*Eineicha techezeinah meisharim*—Your eyes behold uprightness," he reads "*Eineicha techezeinah lifnim mishurim*—Your eyes perceive beyond the requirements of strict justice." Based on this reading, he explains that this is David Ha-Melech's prayer (and ours) to Hashem: "We ask You not to look upon our

The Day of Judgment

Making a Start

What service are we to perform on Rosh Hashanah? What is expected of us? The Maggid of Dubno answered this in connection with the *midrash* on the verse: "I will call out to the supreme God, to the awesome Power Who performs all things for me" *(Tehillim* 57:3). *"I will call out to the supreme God*—on Rosh Hashanah; *to the awesome Power Who performs all things for me*—on Yom Kippur" *(Bereshis Rabbah* 98:1).

The Maggid explained this *midrash* with a parable:

There was once a poor man whose son was outstanding in every way. How much did this father do for his son! How much did he exert himself for his sake! And what did he want in return? What did he expect? To see his son follow the right path, to see him married, and the happy father of his own children. But large sums of money are needed to marry off a son, and the poor man didn't have a penny to his name.

One day, to his surprise, he was approached by a wealthy gentleman. "I have met your son," began the gentleman. "I have spoken with him at length and I find him to be of excellent character. I have a daughter who is also outstanding in every way, and I would like your son to be her groom."

"But," the poor man stammered, "you are a wealthy man, and I am poor and impoverished."

"I know," the wealthy man replied. "I am willing to provide everything—or almost everything. I am willing to pur-

---

case and judge us according to how guilty *we* know ourselves to be. Rather, You alone judge us—for then we shall surely be found innocent. This is because Your eyes alone behold uprightness. You alone are compassionate and gracious. You alone can go beyond the requirements of strict justice to pardon our wrongs. You alone can bless us with goodness, redemption and true comfort, Amen." *(Kedushas Levi*, additions to Rosh Hashanah, immediately preceding *Parashas Vayelech*, p. 281.)

chase an apartment for the couple, with all the furnishings; I will cover all the expenses of the wedding; I will provide a fitting dowry; and I will even take it upon myself to support the couple for ten years. But..."

"But what?" the poor man queried.

"But *you* must provide a beautiful suit for the groom. This will be the suit he wears under the wedding canopy. That is all."

"That's wonderful!" the poor man cried out. "Incredible! But, I don't have a penny—I don't even have enough money to buy the material for such a suit..."

"I'm sorry, but less than this, I will not accept," the wealthy man declared. "I am providing so much—and you must give something!"

The poor man was perplexed. "What can I say? Give me ten days and I'll see what I can do. I'll try to find enough money for the suit."

"Fine," the wealthy man agreed. "Let us meet in another ten days. At that time, we will either write up a *tenaim* (an engagement contract) and your son will be rewarded with wealth and prominence, or you will show up empty-handed, and each of us will go his way."

After they took leave of each other, the poor man did not know what to do. Potential wealth and happiness awaited his son, and a heavy weight was lifted from his shoulders—but it all depended on one suit! He started going from one merchant to another, asking for a loan, but each time his request was refused. Who would lend money to such a poverty-stricken man? Where would he get enough to pay back? Heartbroken and depressed, he returned home.

A short while later, at the wealthy man's home, a servant appeared and announced to his master, "Someone wishes to speak with my lord."

"Let him in," the wealthy man answered.

The door opened, and the poor man stood at the entrance.

"So soon?" the wealthy man exclaimed. "Have you raised

the money?"

"No," the poor man replied.

"Why have you come, then? Did we not agree that I would provide everything else, if you come up with the money for the suit? And you have another ten days!"

"You're right," the poor man answered. "And that's why I've come. I would like nothing more than to show up in another ten days with the money in hand—but I can't. I've already gone everywhere, and asked everyone. They all turned me down. I am coming to you now, not as one father-in-law to another, but as a poor wretch to a wealthy gentleman with a compassionate and gracious heart. Please, I beg of you, open your hand and give me charity. Look at my broken heart, empathize with my situation. Kindly give me enough money to buy a beautiful suit for my deserving son. And then... then I will arrive here in another ten days and fulfill my part of the bargain by providing the suit! And you can then do your part... I beg you, do it from the goodness of your heart!"

Like this poor man, we too need "large sums" that we cannot possibly come up with. We are asking for pardon, forgiveness and cleansing for so many mistakes and transgressions. We are asking for a good and blessed year. The problem is, we have no good deeds with which to pay for even one single day of happiness out of the three hundred and sixty-five we are requesting.

But then comes the great offer. Incredibly, God is ready to give everything, but with one condition: We must do all in our power to open our hearts and return to Him in complete repentance. This condition is stated explicitly in the Torah (*Vayikra* 16:30) in connection with Yom Kippur, the Day of Atonement: "On this day, you will be cleansed of all your sins; you will be purified from all your sins." God will do everything, but with one condition. The verse concludes, "You must purify yourselves before God!" Before He fulfills His part of the bargain, you must fulfill yours: Purify yourselves. Prepare your hearts with repentance and honest regret.

The gates of light are opened before us. We cannot enter, however, because our hearts have been closed. And because of this closedness, this inability to pry an opening even the size of a pinhole, we stand to lose a glorious opportunity. The gates of light are wide enough for wagon-loads of goodness and blessing to pass through, and yet we cannot enter. What shall we do?

We must do exactly what the poor man did. We must approach the door of Hashem's chamber and request His assistance in opening our hearts to love and fear Him! This is what Rosh Hashanah is all about. This is why the shofar is blown, to send shivers down our spines and into our hearts, so that we can do our parts in preparation for the holiest day of the year!

This is the meaning of the *midrash*, "I will call out to the supreme God," on Rosh Hashanah; "to the awesome Power Who performs all things for me," on Yom Kippur. Yes, God is prepared to do everything on Yom Kippur, on the condition that we make a start. And for the sake of this start, we call out and express our hope to Him on Rosh Hashanah: "Draw us after You, and we shall follow!" (*Shir Ha-shirim* 1:4).

Ohel Ya'akov, *Emor*

Why Is Rosh Hashanah Before Yom Kippur?

This question was posed by Rabbi Yisrael Salanter. Why did God arrange Rosh Hashanah at the beginning of the year?

At first sight, it would seem fitting that Yom Kippur inaugurate the new year. Thus, on Yom Kippur we would return and repent, thereby meriting forgiveness and pardon, and on Rosh Hashanah we would be inscribed for a good year. The way it is, however, Rosh Hashanah begins while we are burdened by many sins, and our sentences are suspended until Yom Kippur, when we repent and are cleansed!

If Yom Kippur came first, we would fail to prepare for it properly. A man's heart cannot be opened instantly. It is a process. First, Rosh Hashanah must trigger the initial awakening. It must dawn on us that our lives are at stake. Only then will our requests for health and livelihood be serious, genuine and sincere. Only then will our hearts begin to pry open until on Yom Kippur they will be fully opened, and we can cry out to our Creator from the depths of our beings.

This is what David *Ha-Melech* meant when he said, "Hashem, You are my light and my salvation" (*Tehillim* 27:1). *"You are my light*—on Rosh Hashanah; *You are my salvation*—on Yom Kippur." God enlightens our eyes and takes us out of the dark on Rosh Hashanah. We awaken as if from a deep slumber and realize that we cannot take life for granted. We begin to ask Hashem, "Remember us for life, O King who desires life! For Your sake, O God of all that is alive!" We realize that such a request is a joke unless we resolve to desire the kind of life that Hashem Himself desires. We realize that we must return to Him by leaving our childish games and becoming aware of His Presence in all our affairs. By the time Yom Kippur comes, we are then ready to abandon all the distractions and begin our lives anew. Only then will Hashem save us and cleanse us. Once we have done our part, He will remove all the barriers that separated us from Him.

The Maggid of Rotzky was troubled by this explanation. He expressed this with the following parable:

A villager once visited a train station, where he saw a long freight train with many cars and only one steam engine at the head. "How can it pull so many cars?" he asked. He was told that the boxcars were empty and therefore it was not hard for the engine to pull them.

"But when they are full," he continued, "how will they move?" Another locomotive would be added on to the end of the train, he was told, and used to push from behind. This second locomotive was usually even larger than the first and could push an entire train on its own. He heard, and he was satisfied.

Now, the Maggid explained, according to Rabbi Yisrael, Rosh Hashanah is the first steam engine. The rest of the train is Yom Kippur. The latter will arrive at its destination empowered by the former. In other words, our "Remember us for life, O King who desires life" is the engine, and our "We have done wrong" and "We have sinned" are the cars.

But how can this be? Our "We have done wrong" and "We have sinned" are completely different than those of our ancestors. Their "boxcars" were empty, while ours are overflowing with sins! How can our engine move such a heavy load of "We have done wrong" and "We have sinned"? Our boxcars are full of lies and excuses, slander and talebearing, and a whole load of unsavory deeds.

The answer is, however, that if our Yom Kippur "boxcars" of "We have sinned" are fuller than theirs, our Rosh Hashanah "Remember us for life, O King who desires life" steam engine is much more powerful as well!

Just think for a moment. What were our ancestors asking for when they said, "Remember us for life, O King who desires life"? What did they include in such a request? Bread to eat—bread and salt! Clothes to wear—a coat for him and a dress for her! A roof of straw to live under...

But what do we have in mind when we ask to be remembered for life? Are we satisfied with a simple loaf of bread, with a few vegetables and fruits? We want meat, fish, and all kinds of delicacies. We want cakes and cookies of all sorts. Not one dress do we want, but an entire wardrobe, with dresses for every season, in all the colors of the rainbow and from the best fabrics. A warm oven is no longer enough—we want other electrical appliances, and luxuries without end. Hillel the Elder earned a coin a day, half of which he paid the guard to enter the *Beis Midrash*. Our ancestors earned a few gold pieces, and they were more than satisfied. We take loans and eat them up, until we are in need of more.

Our "Remember us for life, O King who desires life" includes our national, economic and financial security. It includes the security of our country, our region and the entire world! It is no wonder that, were we to contemplate how much we are asking, were we to realize the enormity of all we entreat on Rosh Hashanah, our hearts would open and we would cry all day long. Such a Rosh Hashanah could pull an entire freight train of regretful thoughts, speech and actions to complete repentance on Yom Kippur.

Akleda d'Rachamei 35

Rejoicing on Rosh Hashanah

A Maggid once related a parable in the name of the Chafetz Chayim:

A child was orphaned of his father, and his mother sent him to learn in yeshivah. His mother suffered inordinately at her husband's passing, and her anguish was so great that her heart gave way and she passed away as well. The child was now alone in the world, but he didn't know. He didn't know that his mother had died. He went on studying as if nothing had happened.

His rabbis discussed it among themselves. "How can we break such news to him?" they wondered. "How will he be able to stand the shock?"

They deliberated until they came up with a solution. They had a beautiful new suit made up for the boy, and in the pocket of the suit they inserted a small note with the solemn news of the boy's mother's death. When he puts on the suit, they thought, he will put his hand in the pocket and the matter will be known...

They brought the boy his suit. He rejoiced greatly. He put on the suit and took pride in it. If only he knew what was hidden in the pocket...

The Chafetz Chayim explained: We rejoice on Rosh Hashanah. We dip our apples in honey. We eat our pomegranate and fish head. This is like a new suit! But in the pocket of this new suit there is a note for each one of us. Who knows what is written on the note in our pockets?

Divrei Emunah, the Admor of Toldos Aharon, שליט"א

God's Joy Is Your Strength

In the eighth chapter of the book of Ezra we learn that many Jews who returned to Eretz Yisrael from the Babylonian Exile were ignorant of Torah. When their first Rosh Hashanah in Eretz Yisrael arrived, they gathered together in Yerushalayim and asked Ezra the Scribe to read the Torah of Moshe to them. Ezra stood on a raised wooden platform so that everybody could see him. The moment he opened the Torah scroll, all the people rose. Ezra pronounced a blessing on the Torah, and everyone answered *Amen!* As he began to read from the Torah, the people bowed their heads. Some started weeping. The more he read, the more they realized how far they were from Hashem. They grieved, and they wept.

Seeing this, Ezra and Nechemyah spoke to the people, saying: "This is a holy day to Hashem your God. Do not mourn and do not weep... Go home. Eat choice meats and drink sweet wines. Send portions to those who have nothing prepared. For this day is holy to our Lord. Do not be grieved, for *God's joy is your strength*... And all the people went their way to eat and to drink, to send portions [to those in need], and to celebrate joyously, because they understood what they had been told" (*Nechemyah* 8:9-12).

In the Laws of Rosh Hashanah, the *Tur* (*Orach Chayim* 581) quotes the Midrash: "When a criminal faces serious charges in a court of law, he is usually brought before the judge dressed in black shrouds, his hair overgrown and his nails long and unkempt—for he does not know what his sentence will be.

When the Jewish people appear before God to be judged on Rosh Hashanah, however, they come with cut hair and nails, washed and fresh, and dressed up in their finest white garments. They eat, drink and rejoice on Rosh Hashanah, and prepare extra portions, for they know that Hashem will perform a miracle for them."

The Maggid of Dubno asked how we can be so sure of ourselves and rely completely on Hashem's mercy. How can we dress up in holiday clothes? How can we eat festive meals when our very lives are in the balance, when our cases are about to be judged, when everything—health, livelihood, wealth, contentment, peace of mind—is about to be decided?! When our deeds are so lacking and we are so full of shortcomings, how can we eat and drink? How can we be happy and light-hearted? He answered with a parable.

There were once two distinguished ministers who were awarded the distinct honor of having the king's royal signet emblem placed in their possession for safekeeping. It was a large signet made of gold with which they were to stamp and seal all royal decrees.

The ministers were given the privilege of living in the royal palace with their respective families. They ate the king's bread and drank his wine. The king's tailor sewed their clothes and the royal shoemaker made their shoes. Their only duty was to safeguard the signet and stamp all decrees that were issued by the king.

Once the two ministers sat down to drink wine together, but they imbibed too much. When they wanted to crack some nuts, but couldn't find the nutcracker, they took the king's signet and began to pound the nuts with it. The signet was ruined. Suddenly, the door opened, and the king stood in the doorway...

They immediately came to their senses. They sat transfixed as the king stared right at them and through them. He glanced around the room, saw the empty bottles, the nutshells and the broken signet. He understood what had happened, and continued to stare right through them.

Then he spoke: "In four hours, your case will be judged in the royal court. You will be tried for the sin of desecrating the king's emblem and destroying royal property. The penalty for each of these charges is death. Now go and bid farewell to your families. My officers will bring you to trial at the appointed hour."

The sentence fell upon them like thunder on a bright day. With knees shaking, the ministers rose up and made their way to their quarters.

One of them immediately told his wife and children of the entire incident. Their tears and wailing were beyond description. He took advantage of his last remaining hours to prepare a will. At the last minute, he took leave of his beloved wife and children amidst a downpour of tears. He submitted himself to the custody of the king's soldiers.

On his way, he saw his friend being accompanied by a troop of guards. He could not believe what he saw. His friend's eyes were not red from crying. He was not bent down in anticipation of the worst. He did not drag his feet like a man who was sentenced to death. On the contrary, he walked straight and upright, and a faint smile could even be discerned on his lips.

Poor fellow, thought his friend. Surely his mind has gone. He approached him and asked, "Did you bid farewell to your family?"

"No," the other answered.

"It appears to me that you are unaware of the gravity of our situation," his friend remarked. "We are about to be accused of very grave sins, the penalty for which is death. And the king himself is the judge and the witness!"

"You are correct," he replied. "But this fact is a ray of light for us. While you were weeping and wailing, I sent a message to the king's minister to appear before the king and speak in our favor. He explained that the wine had gotten the better of us, and that we had acted out of lightheadedness after the wine had clouded our senses. The king was gracious and acquiesced. He agreed to forgive and pardon us if we would express our sincere regret for having acted the way we did and promise never to repeat such behavior... Now do you see why I am not dressed in black? There is no reason to weep as one who is sentenced to death! True, the charge is a charge whose penalty is death, but my fate is in my own hands! If my regret is sincere and honest, and my repentance genuine, I will be judged favorably!"

When his friend heard this, he also smiled and drew himself up to full stature....

Ohel Ya'akov, *Emor*

Rosh Hashanah Night

תִּכְלֶה שָׁנָה וְקִלְלוֹתֶיהָ, תָּחֵל שָׁנָה וּבִרְכוֹתֶיהָ

"Let the old year and its curses end! Let the new year and its blessings begin!"

Last year, as well, on *Erev Rosh Hashanah*, we sang this same *piyut* (poem), *"Achos Ketanah,"* and pronounced these very same words. We requested that the old year with its evil curses be gone and done, and that the new year with its blessings be ushered in. Apparently our prayers were not accepted. The proof of this is that we are standing here right now and repeating the same exact request, namely, that the curses of the past year be brought to an end, and the blessings of the coming year be brought to fruition!

But we can ask: How can we be sure that the coming year will be any better than last year? How can we make sure that, unlike our failure to make last year a blessed year, our prayers will have an impact this year?

The Maggid of Dubno answered this question with a parable.

There was once an eminent and skilled doctor who was known far and wide as the best in his field. People came from all over to seek his services and solicit his expertise in healing ailments without bitter medicines and painful operations. He generally required his patients to abstain from certain foods and indulge freely in others. His diets did wonders for his patients, and they were easy and pleasant to keep.

One day, a father showed up for an appointment with his ailing son. "Doctor," the father said, "this is my only son. I love him more than anything in the world. Please heal him!"

"Your only son," the doctor repeated, nodding. "He has probably been spoiled from the day he was born. He probably gets everything he wants..." He examined the child, and finally announced, "He must be extremely careful in what he eats. First of all, he must completely abstain from all sweets!"

"Abstain from all sweets?" the boy cried out. "Never! How can I live without sweets?!"

"That's not all—it's just the first thing on the list," the doctor continued. "But I want to talk privately with your father now. Would you mind leaving the room for a moment, young man?"

"My father has no secrets from me," the boy vainly announced. "I want to remain."

"Your father may not keep secrets from you," the doctor quipped, "but I do. Leave now and don't argue!"

The boy made a face and exited.

After the door closed behind him, the doctor began to speak to the father. "What I suspected is true. Your son is an angel, but a frightfully spoiled angel. He is used to having his every wish granted, and therefore it is extremely difficult for him to listen to and do what he is told. Now, you must understand that the entire success of my treatment depends on his adhering exactly to the diet I prescribe. You yourself have seen that when he heard that he may not eat sweets, he immediately protested and refused to comply. What will be when he hears the rest of the list?"

The poor father wrung his hands and sighed. "What can we do, doctor? He is sick and his condition is going to worsen!"

"Listen to what I am going to tell you," the doctor said. "Take him to another doctor who will treat him along more conventional lines. He will give him shots, and the shots will hurt. He will prescribe medicines, and they will be bitter. Let your son experience that kind of treatment first, and then give him a choice. Let him decide if he wants to continue with the other doctor or submit himself to my care. However, you must warn him. If he chooses my painless treatment, he must not stray one iota from my instructions. The success of my treatment depends on his following instructions strictly."

The father took the boy to the other doctor who immediately began treating him with painful injections and bitter medicines. The boy protested, cried, complained, whined—all to no avail. The medicines were forcibly administered, against his will, for his own good. He actually began to feel better, but a full and complete recovery was very far off.

"How much longer will I have to suffer through this?" he wailed.

"I don't know... perhaps for years," his father replied. "Unless you agree to keep the diet that the other doctor prescribes and hold to it, no matter what."

"I agree!" the boy relented. "I promise I will do whatever he tells me. Just tell me that these tortures are over and done."

This is the parable, and its lesson is clear: Hashem has a wondrous and pleasant way to heal us from all our physical aches and spiritual pain. We need only return to Him wholeheartedly and observe His commandments. We need only indulge in keeping His mitzvos and abstain from transgressing His laws. But we are weak of character and spoiled. We even fool ourselves into thinking that we can be healed while still holding fast to our old ways. He has therefore provided us with an alternative, namely, the way of affliction and sickness, God forbid. As our Sages taught (*Berachos* 5a), suffering certainly cleanses us and allows us to atone for all the sins we have committed. When we finally realize, however, that the first way is inestimably easier, we should return to Hashem and choose His preferred way.

This is the meaning of an enigmatic statement the Sages made on the verse, "It was evening and it was morning, a single day" (*Bereshis* 1:5). They said, "*It was evening* alludes to the deeds of the wicked. *It was morning* alludes to the deeds of the righteous. *A single day* alludes to Yom Kippur, the Day of Atonement" (*Bereshis Rabbah* 3:8). The Sages are teaching us here that after a person has tasted the bitterness of suffering, which is the way Hashem has prepared for those who have become enmeshed in their own evil, he is able to choose the preferred way of observing His commandments. Yom Kippur is then the day when the "wicked" of the first part of the verse are transformed into the "righteous" of the second part of the verse! [Just as evening precedes morning, and they are two aspects of one day,] they are one and the same!

In the same way, when we finally understand the lesson that the bitter curses of the previous year teach us, we can choose to change our ways during the coming year. Yom Kippur will then truly atone and the new year's blessings will begin...

Ohel Ya'akov, *Acharei Mos*

The Morning Service

הַמֶּלֶךְ

"Ha-Melech—the Supreme King Who sits upon a high and lofty throne."

The holy *Megaleh Amukos* (Rav Nasan Nota Shapira, זצ"ל) led the morning prayers on Rosh Hashanah. *"Ha-Melech!"* he cried out, but, unable to go on, he broke down and began to sob uncontrollably.

After the prayers, the other congregants asked him what had caused him to weep so. His answer went something like this:

I remembered the *gemara* in *Gittin* (56a) about Rabban Yochanan ben Zakkai. Jerusalem was under siege by the Roman general Vespasian, and within the city, the *Biryonim* (Zealots) had burned all the supplies in order to force a confrontation with the enemy. People were starving. Rabban Yochanan's own nephew, Abba Sikra, was head of the *Biryonim*. He convinced the latter to allow him to leave Jerusalem in order to plead with the Roman general for his people...

When the Jewish leader stood in front of the Roman general, he said, "Peace to you, O king!"

The general informed him that he was now liable for the death penalty on two counts: First, for calling him a king when he was only a general, and second, he went on, "If I am really a king, why did you not come to me before this?"

The *Megaleh Amukos* explains: "Thus it is with us. Our fate and the fate of each and every one of our families hangs in the balance. The scales of life and death are in Hashem's hands. When we come before Him and call out, 'King!' He might very well answer us, 'If I am really King, why did you not come to Me before this?'"

Luchos Avanim 39

ה׳ שִׁמְעָה בְקוֹלִי, תִּהְיֶינָה אָזְנֶיךָ קַשֻּׁבוֹת לְקוֹל תַּחֲנוּנָי

"God, hear my voice; let Your ears be attentive to the call of my supplications."

The Maggid of Dubno explained this verse with the following parable:

There was once a man who uprooted himself from his home and traveled to a distant country to find success. Good fortune shone on him and he became extremely wealthy. When he returned to visit his birthplace, he was received with the honor reserved for one of their own who had succeeded in the world.

In the midst of his rejoicing, he turned to his relatives and friends and declared, "Hashem has granted me great wealth. I therefore wish to share it with you. Let each one of you voice his request and I will try to fulfill it!"

His relatives replied, "Permit us to return to our homes and discuss the matter with our wives."

He willingly agreed.

One returned and announced that he and his wife would like to move to a larger home. Another said that he would like to expand his business, and stock a larger selection of goods. Another wished to pay off his outstanding debts.

One of the relatives present was extremely poor and destitute. His house lacked even the basic necessities. There was never enough bread to go around. His children went barefoot and they had only rags to wear. His wife was sickly and his debts had long ago soared beyond his ability to pay them. What should he request? What did he need most? What didn't he need?

When he appeared at the home where his rich relative was staying, he stood at the door and began to weep. The rich man was alarmed. "What's the matter?" he inquired. "Just state your desire, and it shall be done!"

"How can I speak, and what can I say?" the poor man wept. "I can only cry. It is for you to interpret the reason for my crying. Any way you interpret it, you will be right. If you think it means I need money to pay my medical bills, you are right. If you hear me calling out for bread to feed my starving children, you are right again! If you surmise that they are naked and barefoot and need clothes and shoes, you have surmised well. If you discern that my one-room hovel is insufficient and I need a larger home to live in, you have discerned correctly. If you perceive that I have debts to pay, you have perceived correctly. If you interpret my tears as a request for a decent livelihood, I need that as well. How can I ask for any one of these? How can I choose when I need all of them? I have therefore concluded that there is nothing for me to do but cry. You then can choose whatever way you wish to help me."

This is what we mean when we say, "God, hear my voice, let Your ears be attentive to the call of my supplications!" We are telling Hashem: "How can we speak, and what can we say? There are no words to express our grief. We can only call out. We raise our voices to You, together with the shofar. Wordlessly, it expresses everything that we cannot say. It is our voice, the call of our supplications. However You interpret it, You will be right!"

Ohel Ya'akov

זָכְרֵנוּ לְחַיִּים... לְמַעַנְךָ אֱלֹקִים חַיִּים

"Remember us for life, O King Who desires life. Inscribe us in the Book of Life, for Your sake, O God of Life!"

The Chafetz Chayim related the following parable about the need to concentrate on that which is most essential and leave the rest to Hashem during the Days of Awe:

A great king once came to inspect his legions. He was

pleased with their perfect discipline and the expertise with which they performed their maneuvers. Indeed, he was so pleased that, following the inspection, he stood facing his troops and made the following announcement:

"Whoever among you has any request, let him come and request! I will be holding court in my temporary quarters."

During the next few days, the soldiers lined up and were received by the king in his private quarters. Each request was inscribed by the king's secretary in a special record book, and promised due consideration.

One of the men approached the monarch and addressed him thus: "Your majesty, the king! Behold, I am in your service, and I am dedicated to serving you with all my heart and soul. I am prepared to give my life for your sake! I therefore cast my supplication before your highness: Please provide me with my rations each and every day!"

All present began to laugh. They chided him, saying, "Silly man, don't you realize that your rations are given to you automatically as long as you are in the king's service?! You are one of his soldiers, and the king cares for all his soldiers!"

But, the Chafetz Chayim concluded, we all resemble this soldier. We come before the Almighty on the High Holidays with numerous worries, not the least among them being our desire to make a living. We forget, however, that this is not what interests our King. He wants us to rise up above our own concerns, to work to elevate His Glory and His Torah from the dust, and increase His Honor in the world. For this He is willing to provide all our needs without our even asking. If only we will pray for His Honor, that the exile be brought to an end, that mankind be spiritually uplifted, that His Sovereignty be revealed—all our needs will automatically be fulfilled...

Chafetz Chayim on the Torah, *Vayigash*

"Inscribe us in the Book of Life, for Your sake..."

It is phenomenal! the Maggid of Kaminetz exclaimed. We ask for a good year, not for ourselves but for God! Not for our physical comfort, but for our spiritual elevation. We ask that all the blessings of life that He provides us with—serenity, happiness, livelihood, and health—be utilized as means to serve Him and fulfill His will.

It is similar to a young man in the prime of life who made a good living. One day he received a call-up notice from the government, ordering him to serve in the army for two months in a very dangerous location.

He immediately began to compose a request to be excused from army duty, in which he explained that his mother was old, and that he was her only child, and she depended completely on him. He must therefore continue to work in order to support his mother and sustain her honorably in her old age.

Although the officer in charge was very impressed by the letter, nevertheless he sent a soldier to verify its contents. The soldier knocked on the young man's door and requested an audience with his mother. "She is not here presently," he was told by the servant. "She is staying somewhere else."

He obtained the address and set off for another part of town. After searching for quite a while, he found himself in the poorer part of town. Gone were the tall buildings and the clean city streets. And there, snuggled in between two dilapidated houses, he saw the old woman's quarters. She lived in a hovel, a miserable and pathetic shack.

The soldier introduced himself and asked the old woman how she supported herself.

"From charity," she replied, sighing.

"And what about your son—doesn't he support you?" the soldier asked.

"My son?" The woman looked pitifully at the soldier and smiled a bitter smile. "My son is a complete stranger to me. He has no interest in even seeing me. He threw me out of his house, and forbade me to even cross his threshold!"

Think for a moment. Is there even the slightest chance that this heartless son could ever hope to be excused from duty? And what about us? We ask for a good year, saying, "For Your sake, O God of Life," to learn Your Torah, to fulfill Your commandments, to pray to You, to serve You, with reverence and with love...

But a messenger is sent to our mother, the Torah, to verify our claim! Do we support her? Do we study her? Do we perform her commands in order to serve Hashem with all our hearts? The messenger will inquire about how we pray. Do we think of what we say? Are we awake or asleep, alive or dead? Do we realize to Whom we speak and before Whom we stand? If not, what chance do we have to deserve a positive response to our requests?

Ateres Chachamim, *Derush 22*

"...for Your sake, O God of Life!"

Rabbi Simchah Zissel, known as the *Saba* (Grandfather) of Kelm, queried: In what merit do we ask for a good and happy year? Suppose we have fulfilled many commandments; suppose we have not committed any sins; suppose, furthermore, that the reward for serving God could be paid in this world—could we still demand a good year?

"Why not?" you will ask.

To understand why the answer is not so simple, the Saba explained, let us examine the life of our forefather Avraham.

The Torah does not exaggerate. When it informs us that Avraham served Hashem with his whole heart and being, we can believe it. When it tells us that He spread God's Name throughout the ancient world by teaching his contemporaries of His great lovingkindness, and by instructing them to call out to Him directly, we can be sure that this is just what

Avraham did. The more we understand and contemplate the magnitude of the ordeals Avraham had to endure and the trials he had to overcome in order to become the progenitor of the Jewish People, we stand in awe. Together, Avraham and Sarah began correcting the sin of Adam and Chavah. They were giants who achieved the impossible. And they established the precedence and set the stage for us, their progeny, to do the same.

One of Avraham's trials was the war he fought almost singlehandedly against the four kings, Amrafel, Aryoch, Kedorlaomer, and Tidal, to save his nephew Lot. After returning from his victory over these kings and their armies, he sanctified God's Name by refusing any payment from the king of Sedom. "I lift up my hand [in an oath]," he said, "to God the Most High, Possessor of Heaven and earth! Not a thread or a shoelace [shall I take from the spoils]! Nor will I take anything that is yours [as reward], lest you mistakenly think, 'It was I who made Avram rich'" (*Bereshis* 14:22-23, according to Rashi).

There is no greater act that a human being can do than to publicly sanctify God's Name. In this case, Avraham did so by making it clear to the people of Sedom that all human power, wealth, and glory come from God alone. To have taken even a thread of clothing for himself would have lessened the impact of this important lesson.

Yet, immediately following this, God appears to Avraham in a vision and assures him, "Fear not, Avram. I am your shield. Your reward is exceedingly great" (*ibid.* 15:1). What was Avraham afraid of? What assurance did he require? He had just sanctified the Name of Heaven! What could he possibly be worried about?!

Our Sages tell us that Avraham was still pondering the great miracle God had wrought for him by allowing him to singlehandedly pursue and overcome the four mightiest kings of the ancient world. As Rashi explains, Avraham was concerned that the great miracle of emerging alive from such a battle (and victorious on top of it) might exhaust the sum total of reward for all the righteous deeds he had ever performed. Avraham was worried lest the reward he received for a single act exhaust the reward for all his other deeds put together! For this he was worried lest he lose his portion in eternity!*

Let us examine another great *tzaddik*. Can we possibly gauge or even imagine the greatness of Rabbi Eliezer ben Hurkanos, one of the greatest Sages of his generation, known as Rabbi Eliezer *Ha-Gadol*? How awesome his Torah learning and his righteousness! How great the holiness that permeated and infused everything he did! As the Mishnah states, "If all the Sages of Israel were placed on one side of a scale, and Eliezer ben Hurkanos was on the other side, he would outweigh them all" (*Pirkei Avos* 2:11).

And yet, it was only when Rabbi Eliezer fell ill towards the end of his life that his student, Rabbi Akiva, rejoiced. "My teacher," Rabbi Akiva exclaimed, "as long as your crops were successful and your wine never soured, I had reason to worry. Perhaps it was an indication that you had exhausted your eternal reward in this world! Now that you have become ill, I am reassured" (*Sanhedrin* 101a).

This is unsettling! It wasn't as if Rabbi Eliezer were that wealthy or that he had supreme power over empires and governments. His crops merely never rotted and his wine never soured. How could Rabbi Akiva even infer from this

---

* Of course, we can ask, what kind of reward could Avraham possibly have been thinking of? What did he consider his "portion in eternity"? The answer is given in the following verses in the Torah. Avraham says to God, "What will You give me, seeing that I am childless?" (*Bereshis* 15:2). The reward Avraham was concerned with was becoming father of the Jewish nation, who would complete his work and transform the world into a Temple for God. In answer to Avraham's request, God lifted him up above the heavens and showed him his progeny. "Look down at the heavens and count the stars. See if you can count them... This is how [numerous] your descendants will be" (*ibid*. 15:5).

that his teacher had exhausted his eternal reward?

What shall we say? How many free gifts have we received! How much good fortune have we been blessed with! Have we paid? Have we done anything compared to Rabbi Eliezer or Avraham *Avinu*?!

Not for naught did my teacher, Rabbi Yisrael Salanter of blessed memory, say that this world resembles a hotel, a very expensive hotel indeed. For it is possible to exhaust the reward for every good deed we ever did with just a single spoonful of sweet dessert!

Our question is therefore justified. In addition to all we have received thus far, in what merit do we ask for a good year?

Let us consider further this idea of the world as a hotel. Just as in a hotel, every enjoyment must be paid for. The service, even the pleasant atmosphere, the gardens, the air conditioning—nothing is free. We will be handed a bill for everything, even for the glass of water we just drank!

There is only one kind of person who gets away without paying a thing. He enjoys all the services of the hotel; he eats and drinks to his heart's desire; and yet, he doesn't pay a cent! Moreover, he gets paid a very generous salary!

Who is he? He is the steward! He works for the hotel. He serves the guests and is in the service of the owner of the hotel.

"The world is Mine. You are sojourners and temporary residents as far as I am concerned" (*Vayikra* 25:23), says God. This world is God's hotel. We are His guests. Is it then possible to live here without paying, and still not have the reward for our good deeds lessened in eternity?

Yes. We can work for the Owner! We can serve the other guests. We can do everything in our power to help others and elevate them. We can be kinder to others, helping them spiritually as well as materially! And then, not only will our reward not be taken off the bill, but we will actually receive a much greater reward.

This is what we should think of when praying, "Remember us for life, O King who desires life. Inscribe us in the Book of Life..." And if you will ask, in the merit of what? The answer is: "For your sake, O God of Life!" To serve You, to work in Your hotel, to serve Your guests.

Chochmah u'Musar 1:19

מֶלֹךְ עַל כָּל הָעוֹלָם כֻּלּוֹ בִּכְבוֹדֶךָ
"May Your Sovereignty over the entire world be revealed in all its Glory!"

Let us understand, the Maggid of Dubno writes, that on the Day of Judgment our lives are hanging in the balance. The Books of Life and Death are open before the *Melech Ha-Mishpat*, the King Who passes judgment. No one can escape His scrutiny. Everyone is recorded in the books.

If this is so, then why are our requests for life, health, fulfillment, and livelihood not detailed in our prayers? Why is the *Amidah* (the standing prayer which is the quintessence of all our prayers) concerned exclusively with the final redemption?

Even the four requests beginning with, "Remember us for life, O King who desires life; inscribe us in the Book of Life, for Your sake, O God of life," and concluding with, "In the Book of Life, Blessing, Peace, Prosperity, Deliverance, Consolation, and Good Decrees, may we be remembered and inscribed in Your Presence, we and Your entire people, the house of Israel, for good life and peace," were added by the *Geonim* and are not part of the original Festival prayers. Why were these basic requests never made part of the original standing prayer? Why are we to concentrate only on praying for the final redemption?

The answer should be clear. Throughout the rest of the year, we are usually occupied exclusively with our personal lives and the lives of those around us. Rosh Hashanah, on the other hand, is the Day of Judgment for the entire world. It stands to reason that if we elevate ourselves above all personal concern and pray for the *Shechinah* (the Divine Presence, also known as *Kenesses Yisrael*, the sum total of all the souls of Israel, and *Em Ha-Banim*, the Mother of Souls, who is in exile with her children as long as the world does not recognize Hashem), our personal concerns will be resolved.

A parable will help to clarify this important point.

A wealthy man once sent his four sons to the capital city to learn in the yeshivah there. From time to time, the boys would send letters to their father, inquiring if everyone at home was well, and making small requests.

One day, one of the boys fell ill, and a doctor was called. He examined the boy thoroughly and announced that his condition was serious. In order to insure his recovery, a long, drawn-out treatment with expensive medications was required. He was prepared to begin the treatment. Could the boy's brothers guarantee sufficient funds?

Yes, the boys promised, no amount was too great. They would write home and the money would be sent immediately.

They sat down to write as usual: "How are you, Father? How is everyone? Can you send a new suit for Moshe, and a watch for Yehudah. Eliezer needs a new hat, and Yitzchak requires expensive medicines. He is mortally ill."

Since Yitzchak's condition was serious, they decided to send the letter as a telegram. They went to the post office and presented it to the clerk. He read the text, looked at them, and exclaimed, "Have you lost your senses? Do you think that your father will send you a suit, a watch, and a hat when your brother is about to die?! Won't he be extremely upset with you for thinking of your own petty needs at a time like this?!"

"What do you suggest we do?" they asked with genuine sincerity. "It is true that Yitzchak needs the medicines. But it's also true that Moshe's suit is completely worn out, Eliezer's hat is impossible to wear, and without a watch, Yehudah is always late for class!"

"I suggest," the clerk concluded after carefully considering the matter, "that you ask your father for a general sum of money. Do not bother detailing what you need the money for. This sum will cover all your expenses, and each one will receive what he needs."

The moral: During these Days of Awe, every Jew stands before God with his own personal concerns and requests. Some require assistance in their learning and in refining their personalities. Some request health and livelihood. At the same time, however, there are tens of thousands of our brothers and sisters who are dying spiritually because they are almost completely cut off from their roots. Tens of thousands who have forsaken the living waters of their heritage. Tens of thousands of lost sheep grazing in foreign pastures.

There are also tens of thousands who live in abject poverty, as well as tens of thousands who are deathly ill, who suffer affliction and cry out in their agony.

How can we be so naïve as to ask for luxuries—spiritual or material—when so many are standing at the mouth of the abyss?

Let us therefore make the Ultimate Request: Redeem the *Shechinah*, redeem Israel, redeem the world: "May Your Sovereignty over the entire world be revealed in all its Glory! May Your incomparable Highness and Eminence be recognized over the entire earth in all its Splendor! Reveal Yourself in Majestic Transcendent Power over all the inhabitants of Your planet Earth!" We will then automatically sanctify ourselves to perform Your commandments wholeheartedly and receive our own unique portion in Your Torah. All together we will be satiated with Your goodness and rejoice in Your redemption. And each and every one of us will receive his personal redemption as well.

Ohel Ya'akov, *Vayelech*

"May Your Sovereignty over the entire world be revealed in all its Glory!"

The Maggid of Dubno illustrated the above with yet another parable. In doing so, he was emphasizing the importance of grasping the quintessential point of the Days of Awe. As our Sages explain, this point is twofold: First, we pray for the awesome revelation of Hashem's Oneness above and beyond the world as we know it; second, we pray that His absolute Sovereignty and constant Providence be revealed in every facet of our lives. When we pray for material goods, and even for life and health, we are missing this all-important point.

A king once became angry at his son and banished him from his palace and his capital. The son wandered far and wide, and hunger finally forced him to seek work.

He hired himself out to a businessman who recognized his capabilities, and took him on as his accountant.

Time passed. The businessman died, and his inheritance went to his son. The son was a tyrant and acted cruelly towards the king's son. He worked him to the bone, treated him tyrannically and contemptuously, insulted him, and beat him. The king's son couldn't bear it. He became embittered and wanted only to die.

By now, he had long forgotten the idyllic days of his youth, the happy moments he had spent with his father. He couldn't remember a time when he was anything but a servant... His only thought was to ease the yoke of his servitude, sleep a bit more, eat an extra morsel, receive less insults and fewer blows.

In the meantime, over the years the king had regretted sending his son away. He was prepared to forgive him, if only he would ask to be pardoned, if only he would desire to repent and return. But not only was no such request ever submitted; the king did not even know his son's whereabouts. He did not even know where to look for him. He therefore decided to travel throughout his kingdom, from city to city and from town to town. Town criers would be sent out to announce the king's arrival: "Whoever has a request of the king, let him state it before his majesty. No request shall go unfulfilled!"

Multitudes gathered around whenever the king arrived. Some requested wealth and others honor; some requested livelihood and some healing for their ills. In one city, the king suddenly recognized his son among those assembled. He was dressed like a serf. He had aged, and he looked pathetic in his suffering.

The king's mercy was roused for him and he turned to listen to his request. The young man fell at his father's feet and cried, "Great and beneficent king, hearken to my supplication. I once had a kind master for whom I worked as an accountant. He was satisfied with my work; he provided me with as much bread as I wanted, and granted me all the sleep I required. Now my master is gone, and his cruel son has taken his place. My whole world has become dark. He works me to the bone and starves me. Though I am innocent, he mercilessly torments me, insults me, and beats me. Please, I beg you, command him to treat me respectfully and not take such advantage of me!"

The king was overcome and cried out in a tear-filled voice, "My son! My son! Have you forgotten your own father? How have you ceased to remember that you are the son of the king? Do you not recall how you once lived in the palace, how servants stood ready to fulfill your every request?! And now your only request is that you find grace in the eyes of some barbaric tyrant! You want him to give you an extra slice of his moldy bread, and allow you to sleep just a few minutes longer!! Instead of asking my forgiveness and returning to your former honor..."

This is what the prophet means when he cries out, "Who are you that you fear mortal men?" (*Yeshayahu* 51:12). He means, O Israel, how have you forgotten who you are to such an extent that your only concern is to find favor in the eyes of other mortals, in the eyes of men who 'fade like the grass'? "How have you forgotten Hashem your Maker?"—that you are His precious children—"and constantly fear the fury of the oppressor as he prepares to destroy?—Where is the oppressor's fury? He who is bent down will speedily be released. He will not go down dying into the pit, nor will he lack bread..." (*ibid.* 51:13-14).

If Hashem will return us to our former greatness, our oppressors will disappear like grass. Why pray for them to treat us kindly? Rather, pray that our King take us back!

Kochav Mi-Ya'akov, *Haftarah* of *Shoftim*

Requesting the Ultimate Redemption Includes Everything

The Maggid of Dubno illustrated this same all-important lesson with another parable.

A man was traveling, and hunger gnawed at him. With nothing to satisfy his hunger, he continued to walk along. The sun beat down on his head, and he suffered from thirst. His tongue stuck to his palate. He felt that he was on the verge of fainting.

Suddenly, he saw a small hut by the side of the road. He turned in, and looked through the tiny window. To his disbelief and delight, he saw a full table set with food! He knocked on the door. The owner of the house answered and invited him in.

He thought to himself: What should I ask for? If I ask for a drink, I will remain hungry. If I ask for food, I will remain thirsty. What to do?

He requested that the owner invite him to partake of the meal on his table. This way, he had enough to eat and drink.

The moral: We are in exile. We lack everything. Our souls

are thirsty for God and our bodies are hungry for material needs. What should we ask for? What should we emphasize first?

The only complete solution is to ask Hashem to invite us to His table, namely, to redeem our outcast nation, to gather us from the Diaspora to His Land, and to build His Temple!

Ohel Ya'akov, *Ki Sissa*

Petty Requests are Fulfilled in Lieu of the Redemption

The Maggid of Dubno illustrated this lesson with yet another parable.

A certain poor man was blessed with many children. He had a very wealthy father who lived in a distant city, however, and when his daughter reached marriageable age, he decided to travel to his father and request his assistance in paying for the wedding.

He set off on his journey, but when he arrived at the outskirts of his father's town, he suddenly fell ill. He was taken to his father's house, where the best doctors were called to treat him at great expense. Finally, he recovered and was back on his feet.

"You are fortunate!" people told him. "You should be very thankful to Hashem for falling ill so near your father's house. If you had gotten sick in your own home, where would you have obtained the money to cover the medical expenses?"

"On the contrary," he replied. "It is my bad luck, the result of my sins! If I hadn't fallen ill here, my father would have granted all the money he spent on medical bills for my daughter's wedding."

The moral: In the *Musaf* service of our Festival prayers, we acknowledge, "As a result of our sins, we were exiled from our Land." Exile from our God and our Land was supposed

to bring us to our senses, to wake us up and make us appreciate the closeness we once enjoyed. And this is what it did. To
a great extent, the longing we felt to return and repent served
to atone for our sins.

But then, the prayer goes on, "We distanced ourselves
even further away from our soil." What had begun as a punishment, continued as a self-imposed curse. Oh, how we
should have prayed to be redeemed! Oh, how we should have
pleaded to be restored to our ancient, Holy Land. But no, we
fell into a deeper, sounder sleep! We spent all of our time
crying out to be saved from our particular problems, and
forgot—forgot to yearn for *Eretz Yisrael* and the *Beis Ha-Mikdash*. Some of us prayed for health and some for livelihood;
some for glory and some for children. But none of us put
much effort into asking for what was far more important. And
God... He saw that His children had forgotten to ask for the
main thing, the essence, the ultimate thing which would solve
all our particular problems!...

David *Ha-Melech* foresaw this. He pleaded, "O that Israel's
salvation would come from Zion! When God restores the
captivity of His people, Ya'akov will exult, Israel will rejoice"
(*Tehillim* 14:7). O that the salvation Israel would request would
be from Zion, that is, that salvation that will come automatically when God restores His *Shechinah* to Zion. Then—when
God restores the captivity of His people—Ya'akov will exult
and Israel will rejoice, for all their requests will automatically
be fulfilled.

This is the meaning of the Midrash: "If you had been
worthy (*zochim*), you would have read the Song of the Sea in
which it is written, 'O bring them and plant them on the
mountain of Your Inheritance' (*Shemos* 15:17). Now that you
have not been found worthy (*zochim*), you read (*Eichah* 1:22),
'Let all their wickedness come before You'" (*Eichah Rabati* 1).
The word *zochim* also means "refined" and "purified." The
Midrash is teaching us: If our minds had been purified and we
had perceived clearly, we would have yearned for the redemp-

tion and been worthy of being eternally redeemed. Now that we did not become purified in the Exile, we detail our petty sins before God, and new ones are always in sufficient supply to take the place of the old...

Kol Bochim 74

Do Not Make Your Request for Redemption an Afterthought

But the question persists. We do ask for redemption in every single one of our prayers! We ask, "Return to Yerushalayim Your City with mercy. Dwell in its midst as You promised. Rebuild it soon, in our days, as an eternal edifice. Reestablish the throne of David quickly in its midst"..."Make the shoot of David, Your servant, spring forth soon. Raise his horn up [from the dust] with [the open miracles of] Your salvation. O how we yearn throughout the day for [Your] salvation"..."Let our eyes behold Your return to Zion with mercy!"

Each time we recite *Birkas Ha-Mazon* after a meal, we ask, "Please have compassion, O God our God, on Israel Your people, on Jerusalem Your City, on Zion, Abode of Your Glory, on the Kingdom of the Family of David, Your anointed *Mashiach*, and on the Great and Holy House that bears Your Name... Rebuild the Holy City of Jerusalem soon, in our days!"

If so, then everything is fine: We ask for the details—life and health, livelihood and honor—but we also ask for redemption, the main thing that includes everything.

No! the Maggid of Dubno answered. There is still something missing. And he explained with a parable.

There was once a wealthy man, a businessman with extensive assets. He had a son who was rambunctious and never listened to him. The boy caused his father endless grief, and he embittered his life by refusing to do anything he requested. Finally, the father's patience came to an end, and he banished his son from his house.

At first, the boy was very sure of himself, thinking that he could get along just fine on his own. He went out into the big world and tried his hand at all kinds of professions. Before long, however, he was wandering from place to place, living from hand to mouth, and hardly eking out a living. Wherever he went, he would work like a slave, but never see blessing from any of his endeavors.

A father, of course, even when he becomes angry at his son and punishes him, still loves him. This father was no exception, and he made every effort to keep tabs on the boy... He inquired about him at every opportunity and was pained to hear how difficult the boy's life had become. After a while, his heart softened, and he wanted the boy to come back. Still, he bided his time, hoping that with each passing day the boy would learn his lesson, that his heart would become less coarse, that he would learn to appreciate his father's house, and desire to return to him. Ah, if only the boy would return and ask his father's forgiveness! If only he would express his desire to return to his father's house! If only he would declare his regret for his past sins, and promise never to repeat them in the future! If...

One day, one of the father's acquaintances, who lived in the same city as his son, came to speak to the father about a business matter. After striking a deal together, their conversation turned to news about the boy. The associate asked, almost as an afterthought, "And when will you finally decide to take your son back?"

"The moment he asks my forgiveness," the father replied, "and declares his desire to return to my house!"

"How wonderful!" the man exclaimed. "It seems that I have been given the chance to do a mitzvah. Our Sages teach that a good deal can be struck for someone in proxy, and that another man's agent can act in his stead. Let me then act as your son's agent. In his name, I hereby declare sincere regret before you and request, in his name, as it were, that you restore him to your house! It's a deal, isn't it? I will return to my city with the good news!"

"No." A sad smile formed on the father's lips. "It can't work that way, my friend. You cannot be the one to bear good tidings, not for me and not for him."

"But why?" the associate asked in surprise. "If an agent from your son were to come in here right now, you would receive him and acquiesce. Aren't I better than ten agents?!"

"You are better than a hundred, and a thousand. It is not you who are inadequate, but my son. Listen and I will explain. You see, there is nothing I would like more than to be certain of my son's true and sincere remorse. I yearn to be sure that he will not revert to his former ways. If he would come himself and fall at my feet—or even send an agent in his stead if he is too ashamed to appear before me himself—I would gladly receive him. I would forgive him with all my heart.

"But he didn't send you. You happened to come here because of our mutual business concerns. As an afterthought, you asked about my relationship with my son, and you decided to ask my forgiveness in his name. Do you understand why it isn't enough for you to ask me? He must be the one who asks."

The lesson is: If we stand before our Creator to plead for redemption, if we arouse ourselves to gather in our synagogues and houses of study, to break down the walls between us, to pierce the Heavens, to place this at the summit of our lives—there is no doubt that we will be redeemed.

We come to pray, however, with other requests. We ask for life and health, for children and livelihood, for wealth and honor, and we leave praying for the rebuilding of the *Beis Ha-Mikdash* and the restoration of the Temple service for an afterthought. As long as we continue to emphasize auxiliary needs and downplay what is primary, to transpose minor and major concerns, we will not be answered...

This is the meaning of God's charge through His prophet: "They have not cried to Me with their heart. When they wail upon their [idolatrous] beds, they rouse themselves [to pray] for corn and wine, [all the while] continuing to rebel against Me" (*Hoshea* 7:14). We cry out, but not because we are ready to return to God. We supplicate, but only that our needs be satisfied.

Yirmeyahu the prophet was therefore told to declare, "Thus says the God of Hosts, the God of Israel... 'When you call upon Me, *you must go* and pray *to Me*. Then I will hearken to you'" (*Yirmeyahu* 29:12). That is, if we truly desire the redemption, if we truly wish to renew our connection with God, we must not mention it as an afterthought, at the conclusion of all our detailed requests. We must rouse ourselves to make the first move, to go and to pray for it with all our hearts. Only then can we know with certainty that our prayer has been accepted. Only then will we be worthy to actually see the redemption coming. This is exactly how Yirmeyahu himself concluded God's message to us. "If you seek Me, you will surely find. If you inquire after Me with all your hearts, I will make Myself available to you... I will restore your captivity, I will gather you from among all the nations... and I will restore you to the [sacred] place from which I exiled you" (*ibid.* 29:13-14).

Ohel Ya'akov, *Vayetze*

The Purpose of Troubles— Arousal to Pray for Redemption

We must seriously consider the troubles that are presently coming upon us and which seem to grow greater as the days go by. Our Sages bemoaned the fact that, since the Temple was destroyed, hardly a day goes by that does not bring with it more suffering and affliction for our people.

They foresaw, moreover, that this historical process would

grow and gather momentum as the final "footsteps" of the Messiah approached. At that time, they warned—and all signs indicate that we are living in that time—we would be inundated by troubles coming in rapid succession. Our only island of sanity would be the knowledge that God was sending these troubles for one all-inclusive purpose: to arouse us from our slumber, the slumber of this world, to raise our eyes Heavenward and to implore, "O God, return us to You. Then we shall surely return. You initiate [the redemption] as You did long ago" (*Eichah* 5:21). The prophet Hoshea likewise foretold that we would admit our mistake and seek to return to God after having gone astray: "I will go and return to my first husband. It was better for me then [when I took refuge under His wings] than now [when I am overwhelmed by grief]" (*Hoshea* 2:9). This change of heart on the part of our nation would only occur, however, after, "She shall run after her lovers, but she shall not overtake them. She shall seek them, but not find them..." (*ibid.* 2:9).

The Maggid of Dubno explained this with a parable.

There was once an extremely wealthy man who had an only son. He loved the son more than anything in the world. He therefore desired that the boy sit in the *Beis Midrash* and elevate himself in Torah. He wanted him to devote himself exclusively to Torah study, without the slightest worry, and he therefore decided to provide him with all his needs.

The son, on the other hand, desired to prove to his father that he could earn a livelihood through his own efforts.

He began with a small business, but met with little success. The son considered this and thought to himself: Perhaps a change of location will change my luck. He picked himself up and moved far away, to the city where the fair was held.

The father, in the meantime, was pained by his son's absence. What pleasure does a father have if not to enjoy his children and grandchildren! The father constantly inquired about his son from the merchants with whom he did business. They informed him that the young man was not having such an easy time—he was barely making ends meet, and his children had little more than bread to eat.

The father's heart went out to his son. He sent gift packages to him and his family, and these were always received in a spirit of gratitude. He sent clothing to the grandchildren, as well as birthday gifts...

One day, the father sat down and asked himself: How long is it going to go on like this? What is life all about? I love my son, and I want him to be closer to me. I am more than happy to provide all of his needs. He wanted to prove his self-sufficiency, to show that he could get along without me, but still, he is grateful to receive anything I send him.... I know him. He is stubborn, and as long as he has a morsel of bread left to eat, he will harden his heart and stay where he is, to prove, as it were, that he can get along on his own, without my help...

So what did the father do? Since he was so wealthy, and had numerous connections with various merchants, he requested that a certain merchant who did business with his son withhold credit from him. This bitter turn of events overwhelmed the young man. Without credit, he would not even be able to obtain the bare minimum he had gotten up until now.

He hurriedly sent off a letter to his father. "Good and loving father, can you please send me money to buy merchandise? Without your help, I am in danger of starving!"

The father's reply was already prepared: "My dear son, delight of my eyes, if you desire to be saved from starvation, return to me and eat at my table..."

The moral is clear. God tells through His prophet Yirmeyahu, "My people have committed two evils: they have forsaken Me, the fountain of living waters, and they have hewn out cisterns for themselves, broken cisterns which cannot hold water" (*Yirmeyahu* 2:13). Once, we ate at our Father's table. We were sustained by His goodness. We decided, however, to try to live on our own, without His sustenance. We thought we could prove our strength and our power... In the meantime, God is grieved. He pines for us as a father pines for his son. The Sages thus declared, "Each day the Holy One roars and says, 'Woe to the Father who has exiled His own children! Woe to the children who have been exiled from their Father's table!'" (*Berachos* 3a).

Why does He wait to redeem us? The Midrash provides us with the answer:

> R. Pinchas said in the name of R. Reuven: "Five times in *Sefer Tehillim* did David *Ha-Melech* attempt to arouse the Holy One to redeem Israel: 'Rise up, O God, save me!' (*Tehillim* 3:8); 'Rise up, O God, in Your anger, lift Yourself up in indignation against my tormentors' (7:7); 'Rise up, O God, let not [the evil] man prevail' (9:20); 'Rise up, Almighty God, lift up Your hand, do not forget the humble' (10:12); 'Rise up, O God, defy [the wicked one] to his face, bring him to his knees' (17:13). The Holy One said to David, 'Though you arouse Me a thousand times, I will not arise! When shall I arise? When I see the poor oppressed and the persecuted crying out, as it is written (12:6), "On account of the oppression of the poor, on account of the crying of the persecuted, now I will arise"'" (**Yalkut Shimoni** II:626).

Is it not clear that God brings all this about so that we should return to Him wholeheartedly? Will He not then return us to Him with joy?

Ohel Ya'akov, *Va-es'chanan*

The Purpose of Troubles

The Maggid of Lublin told a parable about the same thing.

There were once two men, who both had trouble eking out a livelihood and supporting their families. One was a wagon driver and the other a schoolteacher. Thinking to change their fortune, they both decided to move to another city. Perhaps a change of location, they thought to themselves, will bring about a change in luck. They set off without their families in search of their fortunes.

They arrived at their destination and immediately set out inquiring about work. Success shone its face upon them. The teacher gathered together a group of pupils, children of well-to-do parents, and supported himself quite comfortably, while the wagon driver hired himself out to a number of merchants, who used his services extensively. The two lived off a small part of their earnings, and regularly sent the rest home to their families.

A number of years passed. The teacher's pupils grew up and left town to learn in the large yeshivos, and he was unable to gather together a new group of students. He began to ponder his situation. As long as I am out of work, he thought to himself, why should I remain here, a stranger in a strange land? It would be better to return home and enjoy the company of my family. He began yearning to return, but he was unable to carry out his desires, for he didn't even have enough money for the long trip.

He thought, and hoped: Wouldn't it be wonderful if the wagon driver lost his clients and found himself without a job! He too would then want to pick up and return home, and I could get a free ride!

The lesson: We are languishing in exile. Even the *Shechinah*, God's own Presence, is in exile with us. Like our mother, She feels our anguish. The *Shechinah* wishes to return to Her place in the *Beis Ha-Mikdash*, to Zion, the source of all holiness, as it is written, "Torah shall go forth from Zion, the Word of God from Jerusalem" (*Yeshayahu* 2:4, *Michah* 4:2). The *Shechinah* is unable to return to Zion, however, until we repent and are worthy of redemption. In the meantime, the redemption is not first on our list of priorities. We are sunk up to our necks in the vanities of this world, overwhelmed by the irritating business of earning a living. God therefore says: Perhaps it is the only way to wake them up... I will cut off their source of sustenance. Then they will be forced to lift up their eyes to Me and beseech salvation. I will then return to My place...

Ohel Ya'akov

בְּסֵפֶר חַיִּים בְּרָכָה וְשָׁלוֹם וּפַרְנָסָה טוֹבָה
"In the Book of Life, Blessing, Peace, Prosperity..."

The Maggid of Horodna said:

Pay careful attention to the order of the words in this prayer. First we ask for life, then for blessing and peace, and only then, for prosperity... There are those among us who would break down the doors of Heaven in their quest to make a livelihood. They do not consider, however, that their very lives may be endangered by this quest. Is it not written, "On this day, all creatures are recalled, recollected for life and for death"? Who can escape being called upon?

To what can these people be likened? To a man who went down to the river to bathe. He took off his clothes and placed them in the bushes on the bank. With his bathing suit on, he entered the water... Suddenly he was caught in a whirlpool and dragged down to the depths. With his last ounce of strength, he struggled against the current and cried out to those standing on the bank, "Watch out for my clothes! Make sure they aren't stolen!"

"Watch out for yourself!" they yelled back. "Rescue yourself from the raging waters. Struggle against the current and extricate yourself from the whirlpool. Concentrate on the main thing, not on what is unimportant. If you drown, you won't have any use for your clothes..."

Divrei Haskel 13b

נִזָּכֵר וְנִכָּתֵב לְפָנֶיךָ אֲנַחְנוּ וְכָל עַמְּךָ בֵּית יִשְׂרָאֵל,
לְחַיִּים טוֹבִים וּלְשָׁלוֹם

"May we be remembered and inscribed in Your Presence, we and Your entire People, the House of Israel, for good life and peace!"

The Maggid of Dubno told a similar, chilling parable.

A group of men were traveling together. They climbed mountains, descended into valleys, and passed through forests. When they came to a treacherous swamp, they found a winding path that led through the swamp, with quicksand pits on both sides. They slowed down to a snail's pace. Every step was potentially fatal and had to be checked thoroughly to determine whether it was solid ground or treacherous quicksand.

Suddenly, one of them began to sink. He cried out for help and his friends hurried to his rescue. They grabbed him, but before they knew it, had lost their own balance. There was sudden panic. Others ran to the scene and threw ropes to their sinking friends. They tied the ropes under their arms, and the rescuers pulled with all their might—but for naught. The quicksand took hold of one like a pair of clamps.

"Save us!" they cried. "The swamp is engulfing us."

They continued to sink while their friends stood by and watched helplessly.

"I have an idea!" the leader of the group cried out. "We'll run to the nearest village and return with a rescue squad. They must be experts at this type of operation, and will surely be able to get you out."

He began to run, and his friends followed on his heels. They ran with every ounce of their strength and arrived completely exhausted, hungry and thirsty.

They saw lights shining in the distance and heard a band playing cheerful music. As they approached, they saw that the townsfolk were celebrating a wedding.

They immediately sat down at one of the tables and rested from their run. They ate some of the delicacies and drank some of the wine. "What!" their leader reprimanded them. "Have you forgotten that our brothers are drowning in the swamp? Who knows if they are still alive! How can you sit here and rest, and enjoy the meal?!"

The lesson: We are privileged to realize our connection to the Holy One. We observe His commandments and His statutes. We approach Him with fear and trembling, and we lay our souls down before Him in requesting a good year. We come to Him filled with thanks and praise. We thank and acknowledge Him, and bless Him for all we have. How fortunate we are!

But can we concentrate on our own private requests and forget that so many of our brothers are drowning? Can we forget how many are groping in the dark, estranged and alienated from the source of light and joy, suffocating in quicksand without anyone to rescue them, drowning slowly in the swamps?

Let us also pray for them. Let us plead that all of us be remembered and inscribed in Your Presence—we and Your entire people, the house of Israel, for good life and peace!

Ohel Ya'akov, *Acharei Mos*

Our Father, Our King!

אָבִינוּ מַלְכֵּנוּ, חָטָאנוּ לְפָנֶיךָ

"Our Father, our King, we have erred before You."

The Maggid of Dubno spoke: When a man's life is in danger and he needs a doctor to perform a difficult operation, which doctor does he choose? He will certainly choose the greatest expert in his field. If there are two, and both are top specialists, but one of them is weak and sickly while the other is hale and hearty, which will he choose? It is preferable to choose the sickly doctor who has suffered plenty on his own.

It might sound strange, but it is true nevertheless. The healthy doctor who has never experienced pain and privation in his life does not identify very much with the suffering of his patients. He doesn't empathize with their pain. On the contrary, they irritate him. He would like to concentrate on the sickness, and ignore the patient. He is businesslike, cold and calculating.

The weak doctor, on the other hand, has suffered, and therefore understands very well what his patient feels. This is all the more so if the doctor has undergone a painful operation himself. He identifies with what his patient is going through. He will think twice before intensifying that pain. He may choose another kind of treatment, an easier one, even if he knows it is longer and more drawn-out, if only to lessen the pain.

The prophet Yeshayahu said, prophesying about the wicked Babylonian king, Nevuchadnezzar, who destroyed the First Temple and exiled our Nation, "Woe, plunderer, you who were never plundered" (*Yeshayahu* 33:1). Yeshayahu was not bemoaning the plunderer, but the one who would fall into his clutches. Because Nevuchadnezzar had never fallen in battle, he was perhaps the most ruthless and wicked king ever to have lived. He had never tasted the bitter sting of defeat, plunder, torture, and captivity. Yeshayahu was bemoaning the fate of his people who, as a result of their sins, were creating a situation in which they would be plundered...

Notwithstanding everything we have said, even if our patient were to choose a doctor who had experienced a painful operation and had even suffered the same ailment, and this doctor empathized with his predicament and took his pains into consideration, he would nevertheless have to fulfill his charge as a doctor and treat the specific ailment. Even if he knew the treatment to be painful, he might decide to apply it nevertheless. He would thus ignore the pain involved and go ahead with the operation rather than choosing a long and drawn-out, round-about and more expensive treatment which might not promise complete recovery. After all, a doctor's first priority as a doctor is to cure the patient. Only after he can ensure this may he also take his pain and suffering into consideration.

The matter is completely different, however, when the doctor is one's father. When one's child falls ill, God forbid, and the father must choose the best treatment, the father's first priority is to treat his son with compassion. Only after this does he make his decisions as a doctor. Therefore, not only does he take his son's suffering into consideration—he even feels them himself.

When treating his son, he will spare no effort to heal him in the most natural and comfortable method. Even if this is more costly, and lasts longer; even if recovery is not guaranteed, he will apply this method before resorting to the more painful one.

This is what Rabbi Akiva meant: "Happy are you, Israel! Before Whom do you purify yourselves [on Yom Kippur], and Who purifies you? Your Father in Heaven!" He is the Father who loves you and who feels your pain. When a Jew is in pain, the *Shechinah* says, "My head hurts, My arms hurt...." (*Sanhedrin* 37a). If it can be said, the *Shechinah* feels his pain and suffers with him, as David *Ha-Melech* wrote, "I [God] am with him in affliction" (*Tehillim* 91:15). How fortunate we are that our King, our Judge and our Physician is also our Father!*

Ohel Ya'akov, *Acharei Mos*

"...we have erred before You."

The Maggid of Rotzky explained why we say "before You."

There was once a man who ran a gambling parlor. His customers would gather around the fancy green roulette table, place their money on one of the numbers, and spin the wheel. When it came to a stop on one of the numbers, whoever had placed a sum on that number automatically doubled his money. Everyone else lost their investments.

The ruler of the little township knew of the gambling parlor. As long as it was kept private and quiet, he was willing to ignore the fact that the law prohibited operating a gambling establishment. When the neighboring township was preparing to host its great annual fair, however, and all the merchants would stream there to set up their stalls—and, as was the custom at such fairs, brightly colored amusement stalls would also be set up—the ruler called on the owner of the roulette table and warned him, "Don't let me see you at the fair. You may not set up your roulette wheel there."

"But why should I be discriminated against?" the man protested. "All the other game tables and amusement stalls will be permitted."

---

* This same lesson is contained in the eighth blessing of the *Amidah* prayer, in which we say, "For You, God, are a compassionate and trustworthy healer. Blessed are You, O God, Healer of the sick of His people, Israel." Generally speaking, a good doctor must be trustworthy and fulfill his charge without compassion. Indeed, if a doctor does not control or withhold his compassion, he might be prevented from being trustworthy. Only Hashem, the ultimate Healer, is both compassionate and trustworthy.

The ruler replied, "There is nothing wrong with someone paying a penny for an innocent game, or a merchant spending a few pennies on toys for his children. These stalls simply add color to the fair and are part of the fair's atmosphere. But games which attract and entice a person to gamble away all his money, which impoverish people and leave families penniless—these I cannot allow. I cannot allow a merchant who made a nice profit at the fair to lose his entire fortune just because you happen to be lucky on that day!"

But this only made our gambling friend more eager to set his table up. He knew very well that merchants made their fortune selling at the fair. And so why shouldn't he direct some of it his way?

He defied the ruler's orders, despite the fact that he knew what was in store for him if he were caught: his equipment would be confiscated, he would be fined heavily, thrown in jail, and his gambling hall might be closed for good. But the lure of making so much money was too strong, and he traveled to the fair.

The great fair opened with excitement, and after it was well under way, the ruler came to inspect the stalls. Suddenly, he stopped in his tracks: great crowds of people were gathered around a gambling table—and the gambler was raking in the money faster than they could put it down.

With great difficulty, the ruler overcame his rising anger. He strode through the crowd, went up to the man, and said very quietly, "Didn't I warn you not to show up here with your wares?"

The gambler lifted up his eyes and trembled. In a contrite and remorseful voice he said, "Yes, but I didn't know you would carry out an inspection! Had I known, I wouldn't have come."

The gambler noticed that the crowd was growing and more and more people gathered to see what was going on. Suddenly he raised his voice and called out to the throng, "Step right up and place your bets. Put your money on any number you wish. The wheel turns round and round, and where it stops, nobody knows! Maybe *you* will win!"

The ruler ordered the police to wreck the table and to drag its owner away to the local jailhouse.

Do we not resemble the gambler? Not only do we defy God's commandments, but we also know that He is watching us, as David *Ha-Melech* said: "Where shall I go [to escape] from Your Spirit, and where shall I turn to flee from Your Presence? If I ascend to Heaven, You are there. If I descend to the deepest hell, behold, You are here!" (*Tehillim* 139:7-8). Yirmeyahu also asked, "Can a man hide himself in secret places so that I will not see him?... Do I not fill Heaven and earth?" (*Yirmeyahu* 23:24).

Knowing this, our wrongdoings are ten times worse. It is for this reason that we admit, "We have erred before You!"

Akleda d'Rachamei

אָבִינוּ מַלְכֵּנוּ, אֵין לָנוּ מֶלֶךְ אֶלָּא אַתָּה
"Our Father, our King, we have no king but You."

The Maggid of Rotzky told a parable about a regiment of soldiers who served under a tyrannical commanding officer. He ruled over them with an iron hand and made their lives miserable.

One day, an order arrived from the high command: the regiment was to march eastward toward a particular city. Sites had been designated and encampments prepared for them, where food and supplies awaited them.

The commanding officer was overcome with a spirit of rebellion and decided to march his regiment in the opposite direction, to the west! The soldiers tried half-heartedly to protest, but the officer's decision was final, and he made sure there were no dissenting opinions. They set off towards the west, but, as could be expected, before long everything began to go wrong. They found nowhere to set up their encampments; no food supplies were available to nourish their bodies and souls. No transportation facilities were made available to them, and they began fainting from hunger and thirst. As if this weren't enough, an envoy arrived from high command with a warning: "If you don't turn around in your tracks immediately, you will be declared AWOL (absent without leave), and courtmartialed!"

The soldiers could no longer keep their peace. They denounced the commanding officer, surrounded him, and placed him in custody. They turned around, started marching eastward, and asked the envoy to deliver a message to the commander-in-chief: "We are loyal to you. We were misled and forced to disobey your orders. We have now overcome the former commanding officer and have no other commander but you."

The moral: God instructed us to follow His ways and observe His commandments. He promised that if we walk a straight path He will provide us with all that is good and satisfy all our needs. We, however, have followed after our Evil Inclination, about which we were warned, "Do not stray after [the base desires of] your hearts and your eyes, which have led you to immorality" (*Bemidbar* 15:39), and "Let no alien power reside with you, and do not bow down before any external force" (*Tehillim* 81:10). We have gone astray. We have therefore been cut off from all that is good, beaten down at every turn. Before we are declared "AWOL," traitors to Hashem's Sovereignty, God forbid, and before we are judged guilty in the highest court, let us mount an insurrection against our little commander, the Evil Inclination, and place him behind bars! Let us return to our Father in Heaven and declare: "We have no king but You!"

Akleda d'Rachamei

אָבִינוּ מַלְכֵּנוּ, עֲשֵׂה עִמָּנוּ לְמַעַן שְׁמֶךָ

"Our Father, our King,
act [kindly] towards us for Your Name's sake."

The Maggid of Rotzky told a parable about a master clock-maker. His clocks were unique. There were none to compare with them in all the world for precision and exquisite beauty. Nevertheless, the clock-maker was not famous, and his clocks were not the talk of the town—people simply did not know about him!

A connoisseur of clocks once happened to walk into his workshop. He was amazed at the quality craftsmanship, and even more astonished by the fact that the clock-maker was not well-known. How could it be that people were not aware of his distinctive and exceptional work? Everywhere the connoisseur went he spoke about the remarkable clock-maker and praised his creations. As a result of this acclaim, the clock-maker eventually became a famous man. His clocks were purchased by kings and aristocrats. Their chimes were heard in palaces and mansions. The clock-maker became exceedingly wealthy.

The same connoisseur once happened to return to the city where the clock-maker lived. Since his wristwatch had received a knock and stopped running, he decided to go to the clock-maker's workshop and ask him to repair it.

When the clock-maker heard his request, he looked surprised. "How dare you make such a request of me! You must know that my workmanship is costly and of the highest quality. My time is more expensive than gold. I make the best clocks in the world. Do you really think I would stop my work, which is so much in demand, to take the time to fix your simple watch?!"

The connoisseur answered, "I will tell you why I have the right to ask you to fix my simple watch. Do you remember, a long time ago, when you sat hoping for a single customer? Well, it is I who made your name known in the world. It is on my account that your work is celebrated and appreciated today by the many people who inundate you with orders and purchase your clocks at the highest prices. Shouldn't you be willing to fulfill my simple request, as a payment for all I did for you?"

The moral: Our father Avraham made God's Name known throughout the ancient world. Later, mankind degenerated and His Name was forgotten. Before being struck by the ten plagues, Pharaoh defiantly declared to Moshe, "Who is God that I should obey His command to let Israel go?" (*Shemos* 5:2). Through the plagues, however, God's Name was greatly magnified.

In warning Pharaoh about the impending plague of hail, God thus spoke through Moshe, saying, "Now you will know that there is none like me in all the world. I could have unleashed My power, killing you and your people with the epidemic [sent against the animals], and you would have been obliterated from the world. The only reason I let you survive was to show you My strength, so that My Name would be spoken of all over the world" (*Shemos* 9:14-16).

And so it was. In the Song of the Red Sea, we sang, "Many peoples heard and shuddered. Terror gripped the inhabitants of Peleshes. The chieftains of Edom were terrified. The power-gods of Moav were seized with trembling. All the inhabitants of Canaan melted [in fear]" (*ibid.* 15:14-15).

The Canaanite Rachav echoed this when she told the spies, "Your terror has fallen upon us, and all the inhabitants of the land melt [from fear] because of you. For we have heard how God dried up the waters of the Red Sea before you when you came out of Egypt... We heard and our hearts melted... for God your Lord is the Supreme Power in Heaven above and on the earth below" (*Yehoshua* 2:9-11).

Since then, the Nation of Israel has been God's instrument for making His Name known from one end of the world to the other. At the inauguration of the First Temple, Shelomo *Ha-*

Melech said, "There may also be strangers, not from Your people Israel, who come from faraway lands for the sake of Your Name. For they hear of Your great Name, Your mighty hand and outstretched arm, and they come and pray towards this Temple" (I *Melachim* 8:41-42).

After being healed of leprosy by Elisha the prophet, Na'aman, the commander of the Syrian forces, proclaimed, "Now I know that there is no God in all the earth but in Israel" (II *Melachim* 5:15).

An Arab farmer was unaware that the donkey he had sold to Rabbi Shimon ben Shetach had a pearl hidden in its ear. When the rabbi returned the pearl to him with the specific purpose in mind of sanctifying God's Name, the Arab proclaimed, "Blessed is God, the God of Shimon ben Shetach!" (*Yerushalmi, Bava Metzia* 2:5).

Antoninus exclaimed to Rabbi Yehudah *Ha-Nasi*, "I know now who you are. The most insignificant among you can raise the dead" (*Avodah Zarah* 10b). [At the end of his life, Antoninus converted to Judaism.]

The Talmud teaches that, "The people of Israel were exiled and dispersed among the nations only in order to draw converts" (*Pesachim* 87b). Who were these converts? Based on the verse, "It is not with you alone that I am making this covenant... I am making it both with those who are standing here with us [physically] today... and with those who are not here with us [physically] today" (*Devarim* 29:13-14), the Talmud teaches that they were the souls of future converts who joined Israel at Mount Sinai to receive the Torah (*Shabbos* 145a). That is, the exile—in addition to being a punishment for the Jewish people for not having fulfilled their mission of being a light to the nations in their land—has a deeper reason.

One way or the other, Israel must illuminate the world with the light of Torah, to make God's Name known throughout the world, and draw back these kindred souls. Ideally, this light would shine forth from the Temple, as it is written, "Torah will go forth from Zion and the Word of God from

Jerusalem" (*Yeshayahu* 2:3, *Michah* 4:2). When we failed to illuminate the darkness of the world from the Temple, God's light was splintered into millions of tiny sparks (the Jewish people in exile), and dispersed to almost every corner of the world. To a certain extent, we have been successful. Select souls were drawn to this light, among them that of Antoninus. They became righteous converts who sanctified the Name of God by attaching themselves to the Jewish people.

Now the Days of Judgment have arrived. Our watches have stopped running. We are in need of our Father's mercy. We therefore turn to Him and ask: Please, act kindly towards us and redeem us. And if You will ask, in what merit? Act [kindly] towards us for Your Name's sake! The very Name we proclaim throughout Your world!

Akleda d'Rachamei

אָבִינוּ מַלְכֵּנוּ, בַּטֵּל מֵעָלֵינוּ כָּל גְּזֵרוֹת קָשׁוֹת
"Our Father, our King, nullify all harsh decrees [that hang] over us."

In our *Avinu Malkenu* prayers, we pray, "Our Father, our King, nullify all harsh decrees that hang over us," and then "Our Father, our King, tear up the evil decree of our judgment." What is the difference between nullifying a harsh decree and tearing up an evil decree?

The Maggid of Rotzky answered with a parable.

A man was once walking down the street when a band of robbers assaulted him and tried to steal his wallet. The man tried to resist, and the robbers began to beat him. He called for help, and a policeman heard him and hurried to the scene. The robbers were apprehended and taken into custody. They were brought to trial, found guilty, and forced to pay heavy compensation for the assault and battery, and for the attempted robbery. As a result of receiving this compensation, the man was able to make an old dream of his come true, which his financial position had never allowed him to realize before. The man then raised his hands to Heaven and thanked God for putting him through this ordeal.

Of course, if we had asked him about this at the very moment he was being assaulted—even if we had divulged to him that he stood to gain considerably after the ordeal was over—he might have answered with the Hebrew proverb, "I don't want either the stings of these bees, or their honey!"

We can now answer our original question about the difference between a harsh decree and an evil decree. Since the man in our case was able to receive compensation, the assault was no more than a harsh decree (for he certainly suffered terribly at the time). But if no monetary or other advantage had resulted from the assault, it would be considered an evil decree.

We can now extend this definition and apply it to our general situation. There are evil decrees—and among these are all those decrees which cause us to deteriorate and decline spiritually. And there are harsh decrees which, though they appear evil and involve suffering, are for our good because they end up averting a greater evil, bringing about a much greater good, or boosting a person to the loftiest spiritual heights. Our Sages thus distinguish between suffering or punishment which interferes with a person's studies or prayers, and "sufferings of love" which do not interfere (*Berachos* 5a). Regarding the latter, it is written, "God corrects those whom He loves, just as a father [corrects] a child whom he cherishes" (*Mishlei* 3:12).

In truth, all suffering can be seen as "suffering of love" if we accept it with love, that is, if we know that "everything God does is for the good" (*Berachos*; see *Ta'anis* 8a). Nachum Ish Gamzo was a man who suffered greatly in his life; nevertheless, he always was able to say, "This also (*gam zo*) is for the good." This is clearly illustrated in the story of the farmer who was once plowing his field with his ox. The ox fell into

a ditch and broke its leg. When the farmer found a treasure
buried in that very spot, he rejoiced, saying, "It was for my
own good that my ox broke its leg!" (*Niddah* 31a). Another
man who was about to embark on an ocean voyage was
prevented from doing so when he got a large splinter in his
foot and he became incapacitated. He was upset by this until
he learned that the ship had sunk at sea. He was then able to
thank God that, as a result of this slight inconvenience, his life
was saved (*ibid.*).

From all of these examples, we learn that harsh decrees—
apparent injustices—may very well be for our good. Still, like
David *Ha-Melech*, we ask, "May only goodness and kindness
pursue me all the days of my life" (*Tehillim* 23:6), that is, if we
must be pursued, may it be by good decrees! Even if we must
suffer so that some good will result in the end, our prayer is
that the means used should not be harsh. We therefore ask,
"Our Father, our King, nullify all harsh decrees from us"—
harsh decrees, even if they are for our good!

Akleda d'Rachamei

אָבִינוּ מַלְכֵּנוּ, בַּטֵּל מַחְשְׁבוֹת שׂוֹנְאֵינוּ
"Our Father, our King,
nullify the schemes of our enemies."

The Maggid of Rotzky asked: What difference does it make to
us if our enemies continue to concoct evil schemes? As long as
God doesn't allow them to carry out their schemes (as we
continue: "Our Father, our King, blot out the plans of our
foes. Our Father, our King, eliminate all our oppressors and
accusers") let them think as they wish!

He answered with a parable.

There was once a minister of finance who faced the proverbial problem: the government was paying out huge sums of
money for various undertakings, all for the good of its citi-

zens, but the tax money entering the treasury was insufficient to balance the budget. How could the budget be balanced? How could the national deficit be reduced?

The king's financial advisers convened a meeting. They sat down to devise an effective, comprehensive plan for cutting back on expenses. Their proposal struck hard at the taxpayers. They presented it to the monarch for his authorization, and the king, who was an extremely benevolent ruler, vetoed the plan immediately. He ordered them to present an alternate plan. The advisers honored the king's decision, filed the plan away in the national archives, and sat down to devise a new one.

The king thought: My subjects have been saved from a very difficult decree. But what if the new plan fails? Tax payments will continue to dwindle, expenses will continue to grow, and I will be under more pressure to remedy the situation. Instead of drawing up yet another plan, surely my advisers will pressure me to implement the harsher plan which is already prepared. I will be forced to submit and sign...

What did the king do? He ordered that the original plan be removed from the archives and destroyed!

What is the moral of this parable? Certainly, we ask God to prevent our enemies from executing the evil schemes they have devised. As long as those very evil schemes exist, even as thoughts, however, the danger exists that a time will come when we are found lacking even the slightest merit, God forbid. At such a time, these enemies may attempt to use these very accusations against us and thereby bring their evil schemes to fruition. We therefore plead, "Nullify the schemes of our enemies"—obliterate them, let it be as if they never existed, let them boomerang against those who wished to perpetrate them!

Akleda d'Rachamei

אָבִינוּ מַלְכֵּנוּ, כַּלֵּה כָּל צַר וּמַשְׂטִין מֵעָלֵינוּ
"Our Father, our King, eliminate all our oppressors and accusers."

The Maggid of Rotzky continued with another parable.

When the father of a family travels and must be away from home for long periods of time, he trusts that his wife will take care of the children, and manage the house and all his affairs in his absence. He trusts that she will make sure the children eat and dress properly and that she will oversee their education. He trusts that the children will listen to their mother and honor her as is befitting.

If, on the other hand, the mother is undependable, if she abuses and neglects the children, it is certain that they will become street children. Their education will have been for naught. They will regress and their behavior will degenerate.

When the father then returns from his travels, he will immediately sense that the children's conduct is wanting. In addition, he will hear their mother denounce them. He will wonder, as she details all their escapades and wrongdoing, and have difficulty believing his own eyes and ears. "How can this be?" he will ask. "When I left, the children were well-behaved and lovely. How did they become like this?"

But as he continues to listen to his wife's accusations, he begins to discern the answer. It is because of her! When their mother neglected them, the children found themselves in the street. Because she hated them, they had no choice...

Instead of becoming angry at his children, he will be infuriated at their mother. He will chastise her...

Our Sages alluded to such a situation when they stated, "Master of the universe, it is revealed before You that we desire only to do Your will. What prevents us? The leaven in the dough [the Evil Inclination within us] and [the princes of] the nations of the world who subjugate us" (*Berachos* 17a).

Now, on the Day of Judgment, these two types of enemies wish to accuse us. First comes the Evil Inclination, which, as our Sages explain (*Bava Basra* 16a), is none other than the Accuser, the Satan himself. Second come the princes of the nations. These are the enemies who wish to see our downfall. These are our oppressors and our accusers.

We therefore pray to God: Please listen well to what these accusers say. From their own gleeful accusations, understand that they are the cause of our downfall! They drove us to fall. By abusing and tormenting us, they made us regress. Therefore, "Eliminate all our oppressors and accusers!" Let them suffer the annihilation they thought to bring upon us. Let their hatred fall upon their own heads, to destroy them! As for us, judge us favorably, and may our desire to serve You weigh down the scales to the side of merit for all Israel!

Akleda d'Rachamei

אָבִינוּ מַלְכֵּנוּ, סְתוֹם פִּיוֹת מַשְׂטִינֵנוּ וּמְקַטְרִיגֵנוּ
"Our Father, our King, silence our accusers and denouncers."

The Maggid of Rotzky explained this supplication as well.

A stranger once convinced a group of youths to organize a revolt against the government. Just as the group was prepared to commit their first terrorist act, the stranger slipped away and denounced them to the security forces.

The latter immediately set a trap around the house which was the group's stronghold. They fired into the house, and ordered them to surrender. In the end, the entire group was thrown into jail. At their trial, the stranger stood up for the prosecution and denounced them. The youths' attorney protested and was able to prove that the stranger was an undercover agent. He had deluded them. He had lured them with his smooth talk, capitalizing on their youthfulness, until they fell prey to everything he said. The stranger was immediately found guilty, imprisoned, and punished to the full extent of the law. The youths were let off with a warning.

The moral: "The Evil Inclination [in a man's heart] is none other than the Prosecutor [on high]. And the Prosecutor [on high] is none other than the Angel of Death. [As the Evil Inclination,] he comes down [into a person's thoughts] and tempts him to sin. He then [dresses up as the Prosecutor,] goes up to Heaven, and accuses. [Finally, taking off all his disguises,] he comes down and takes a man's soul" (*Bava Basra* 17a).

We therefore pray: "Expel the Evil Accuser from before us and from behind us." Expel him "from before us"—before he has a chance to deceive and delude us into doing wrong. Expel him "from behind us"—prevent him from accusing us after we have done wrong, so that we can return to You.

When the Prosecutor stands in the heavenly court on the awesome Day of Judgment and accuses, we point to him and say, "This is the one! This is the Satan who deluded us until we fell into his trap. And now when he dresses up in a mantle of righteousness, he is our denouncer?! It cannot be! 'Our Father, our King, silence our accusers and denouncers!' Let him be tried, as our Sages promised, 'In the ultimate future, the Holy One will slaughter the Evil Inclination!' (*Sukkah* 52a) Let him be slaughtered, and let us be inscribed in the Books of Life and Peace!"

Akleda d'Rachamei

אָבִינוּ מַלְכֵּנוּ, סְלַח וּמְחַל לְכָל עֲווֹנוֹתֵינוּ

"Our Father, our King, forgive and pardon [us] for all our sins."

The Maggid of Rotzky posed a problem. First we pray to be spared all kinds of punishments: "Our Father, our King, eliminate epidemics, war, famine, captivity, destruction, forced sin, and forced conversion from Your covenant... prevent any plague from [harming] Your inheritance." Then we beseech: "Our Father, our King, forgive and pardon [us] for all our sins!" Shouldn't the order be reversed? Shouldn't we beseech pardon and forgiveness before we pray to be spared punishment?

He presented his answer in the form of a parable.

A father once warned his son not to walk out on the frozen lake lest he slip on the ice and hurt himself. The child disregarded his father's warning, went out on the ice, slipped and injured his leg. How can he now come before his father and ask him to bandage his wound? He is too embarrassed. First he must ask forgiveness for having disregarded his father's instructions, and only then can he show him the wound and ask him to bandage it.

If, however, the child has fallen on the ice and broken his leg, if he is lying there helpless, unable to move—then he will not begin with a request for forgiveness. He will cry out. He will call his father to come and rescue him. Only after he is out of danger and his pain has subsided will he ask for forgiveness for having transgressed his father's command!

Akleda d'Rachamei

אָבִינוּ מַלְכֵּנוּ, הַחֲזִירֵנוּ בִּתְשׁוּבָה שְׁלֵמָה לְפָנֶיךָ !
"Our Father, our King, bring us back before You in wholehearted repentance."

What is wholehearted repentance? Repentance out of fear cannot be wholehearted; repentance out of love is wholehearted repentance. The Chasam Sofer explained with a parable.

A group of villagers decided to travel to the royal capital together. Shortly after they arrived, they stood at the side of the palace and began throwing stones into the courtyard! In an instant the royal guards surrounded them, took them into custody and imprisoned them in the royal dungeon deep underground.

"We don't belong in a dungeon!" the prisoners cried out.

"Bring us to the king and we will explain why we threw stones!"

They were brought before the king, where they prostrated themselves before him and cried, "Although we have done wrong to throw stones into the courtyard, this is only true from the point of view of outward appearance. Those 'stones' were raw diamonds, your majesty. You see, we are diamond cutters, and we can make those stones shine like the noonday sun!"

The king replied, "Do as you say you can do!"

The villagers set about cutting and polishing the diamonds until they shone and sparkled. They were the most beautiful gems in the kingdom, and the king set them in his crown. He drew the villagers close to his throne and gave them great honor.

The Psalmist says, "One day You will arise [and reveal Your] compassion on Zion, when the time to favor her will have arrived, when the appointed time will have come!" (*Tehillim* 102:14). When? "When Your servants will take pleasure in her stones and cherish her dust!" (*ibid.* 102:15). Even the stones and mud (vices) with which Israel "dirties" the King's courtyard are transmuted into diamonds (virtues) when they repent out of love!

Chasam Sofer on the Torah, *Devarim*

אָבִינוּ מַלְכֵּנוּ, הַחֲזִירֵנוּ בִּתְשׁוּבָה שְׁלֵמָה לְפָנֶיךָ

"...bring us back before You in wholehearted repentance."

What is repentance "before You"? Is there such a thing as repentance not "before God?" The Maggid of Mezrich explained this with a parable.

There was once a king whose two sons were taken captive.

After a while, both sons resolved to escape and return to their father. One of them thought to himself: "When I return, I will be able to enjoy the comforts of being at home again." But whenever the conditions of his captivity improved slightly, he would actually forget about his resolve to return to his father.

The other son thought to himself: "What does my father lack in his house? He lacks me, his son! I want to go home so that he can rejoice in me, so that his joy will be complete." This son's resolve was not influenced by changes in the condition of his captivity. Nothing took away his constant desire to return, to delight and please his father.

We should resolve to be like the second son. Repentance for one's own benefit is not considered repentance "before God." A person could repent in order to improve his material standing in life, or in order to be inscribed for a comfortable life. But this is not wholehearted repentance. Even if a person wishes to reach the highest spiritual rungs, his intention is still considered selfish.

Rather, one should desire to become spiritually elevated in order to please and delight God. This is the meaning of our plea: "Our Father, our King, bring us back before You in wholehearted repentance!"

Likutim Yekarim 293

אָבִינוּ מַלְכֵּנוּ, שְׁלַח רְפוּאָה שְׁלֵמָה לְחוֹלֵי עַמֶּךְ !

"Our Father, our King, send a complete recovery to all the sick among Your people."

Our request here is not just for ourselves but for every Jew. The Maggid of Rotzky explained why this is necessary.

A sick man from a small village traveled to the city to be treated by the doctor there. But the doctor refused to treat him, explaining, "This disease is contagious, and it is likely that all the inhabitants of your village are carrying the infection. What good will it do if I cure you? When you return home, you will get it again. The only solution is to go to the government health authorities and request that they send a doctor to your village to heal all the inhabitants and pinpoint the source of the disease."

Rambam (Maimonides) wrote that a person's soul is just as susceptible to illness as is his body (*Shemonah Perakim*). For example, one type of infectious soul disease is called, "Everybody else does it—why can't I?" As our Healer, God wishes to help us overcome the source of this disease. The Talmud thus states, "A man's Evil Inclination tries to overwhelm him each and every day. If the Holy One did not come to his assistance, he would be unable to survive" (*Sukkah* 52a). He provides us with the most powerful medication known to heal its infectious influence. In the Talmud, Hashem is said to say, "I have created the Evil Inclination [to test a man], but I have created Torah as its antidote" (*Kiddushin* 30a).

We ask for a complete recovery for *all* of us who are sick with this contagious disease. Only then can we be assured that we will have been healed and will never have to suffer its infection again.

Akleda d'Rachamei

אָבִינוּ מַלְכֵּנוּ, זָכְרֵנוּ בְּזִכָּרוֹן טוֹב לְפָנֶיךָ

"Our Father, our King, remember us favorably before You"

The Talmud (*Berachos* 32b) explains how God "remembers" those who find favor in His eyes. The problem is, if God remembers everything, perhaps He also remembers our sins. This would not be a favorable remembering...

The prophet Yeshayahu expressed Israel's sense of forlorn-
ness in the exile, as well as God's promise of redemption,
when he wrote, "Zion said: 'God has forsaken me; my God
has forgotten me.' [God replied:] 'Can a woman forget her
nursing child, not have compassion on the son of her womb?
Even these (*eleh*) may be forgotten, yet I (*Anochi*) will never
forget you'" (*Yeshayahu* 49:14-15).

Based on these verses, the Talmud deals with the problem
of whether God forgets our sins. The key verse is, "Even these
may be forgotten, yet I will never forget." The first half of this
verse, "Even these (*eleh*) may be forgotten," alludes to the sin
of worshiping the golden calf, at which time the mixed multitude called out, "O Israel, these (*eleh*) are your gods who
brought you out of Egypt!" (*Shemos* 32:4). The second half of
this verse, "Yet I (*Anochi*) will never forget," alludes to our
receiving the Torah at Sinai, at which time God said, "I (*Anochi*) am God your Lord who brought you out of the land of
Egypt" (*Shemos* 20:2).

The Talmud states: "The Congregation of Israel said before
the Blessed Holy One, 'Master of the world, since there is no
forgetfulness before Your Throne of Glory, perhaps You will
never forget that I once worshiped the Golden Calf?'" God
replies, "'Even these (*eleh*) may be forgotten,' i.e., even the sin
of calling out 'These (*eleh*) are your gods who brought you out
of Egypt' may be forgotten."

The Talmud continues: "The Congregation of Israel spoke
again before the Blessed Holy One, 'Master of the world, since
there is forgetfulness before Your Throne of Glory, perhaps
You will forget my receiving the Torah on Sinai?' God replies,
'Yet I (*Anochi*) will never forget,' i.e., God will never forget
how Israel received the Ten Commandments which begin, 'I
(*Anochi*) am God your Lord who brought you out of the land
of Egypt.'"

God remembers the good deeds of those who find favor in
His eyes, and forgets their wrongdoing. This is the meaning
of our plea: "Our Father, our King, remember us favorably

before You!"

The question is, how can we make ourselves worthy of this? The Maggid of Rotzky answered with a parable.

A king had two officers who were caught for disobeying his command. They were incarcerated and brought for trial before a military tribunal. When they heard the judges' decision that they should be punished to the full extent of the law, the officers fell at the king's feet. They pleaded for grace and amnesty, attempting to arouse the king's mercy by reviewing before him their steady and faithful service, the commands they had carried out, and the victories they had won for the crown.

The king considered their plea and replied thus: "I cannot decide on the spot. I need time to weigh the matter. In the meantime, you will not be confined, nor will you be returned to your posts. What shall I do with you?"

He thought for a few moments until he came up with a suitable post for the officers. They would act as judges in the king's military tribunals! A third judge was appointed to preside as chief justice.

A soldier who was guilty of deserting his post was brought before them. The soldier admitted he had done wrong and pleaded guilty. He explained that he missed his family so much that he was overcome by his desire to see them. He asked to be pardoned and granted amnesty. "I admit that I made a mistake, but I promise never to repeat the offense again. I will be a good soldier, loyally discharge all my duties, and follow all orders!"

"What do you mean you made a mistake?!" the first officer thundered. "Absence without leave is tantamount to defection! This is an inexcusable crime!"

"And you, what is your opinion?" the chief justice asked the second officer.

"What can I say?" he sighed. "It is a serious offense, but he is only human. We too were once soldiers. We know what it is like to yearn for home..."

"True, but we didn't desert," the first officer replied. "If we are lenient with him, we will be setting a precedent, and discipline will suffer. We must not be soft-hearted."

"We are divided in our opinions," the second officer summed up. "It can only be decided by the chief justice."

"True, but it is not my intention to decide this case right now," the chief justice replied. "After all, this soldier has a right to be judged by competent judges."

"But if we are not considered competent judges, why were we called upon to judge this case in the first place?" the officers asked.

"Obviously, at the king's behest," the chief justice replied. "Come with me—we are now going to the king."

They got up and returned to the king. The chief justice gave him a brief summary, and immediately the king pronounced his verdict on their own cases: "The first officer is pronounced guilty and will be punished to the full extent of the law. The second officer receives complete amnesty!"

The first officer was stupefied. This was outright discrimination! They had both done wrong. Both had the same rights. Why were their sentences so different?!

The king discerned the first officer's astonishment. "Why are you surprised?" he asked. "You yourselves pronounced your own sentences. *You* maintained that it is absolutely forbidden to be soft-hearted, that one lenient decision draws another one in its wake and undermines discipline. Your friend, however, judged leniently, took account of the man's good record, and of the fact that we are only human..."

Our Sages teach us that a person is always judged "measure for measure," according to the way he judges others. When we have compassion on another human being, we are judged favorably in Heaven. The Talmud thus records the following teaching:

> Rabba says: Anyone who "passes over" (overcomes) his own tendencies (to hold a grudge against those who wrong him,

to act out of spite, to be angry, to lie, etc.) will merit having even his intentional sins "passed over" (removed), as the verse says, God "pardons sin and passes over transgression" (*Michah* 7:18), that is, God "pardons the sin" of he who "passes over the transgression" (which others committed against him) (*Megillah* 28a).

If we want our Father in Heaven to forget and overlook our own backsliding, and remember us favorably before Him, let us act kindly towards our fellowman and judge him favorably. God will then do the same!

Akleda d'Rachamei

אָבִינוּ מַלְכֵּנוּ, כָּתְבֵנוּ בְּסֵפֶר פַּרְנָסָה וְכַלְכָּלָה
"Our Father, our King, inscribe us in the book of livelihood and sustenance."

The Maggid of Rotzky told a parable to explain this heartrending supplication.

A young man once came to a manufacturer and offered his services as a salesman for his products. The manufacturer hired him, provided him with merchandise on credit, and suggested he try selling his wares in a certain country. The salesman traveled to that country, discovered that his products were in great demand there, and managed to sell them at a decent profit. The problem was the living conditions—the food was poor and the water acrid. The salesman decided to stay, however, in order to sell his entire inventory and exploit the situation. In the meantime, though, he suffered. In time, he returned to the manufacturer, paid him what he owed him, and requested to be sent to another, more pleasant location. The manufacturer suggested a certain country, and said, "I am sure you will be extremely satisfied there!"

The salesman went there, and when he arrived, his eyes lit up. Living accommodations were spacious, food was in abundance, and the water was refreshing and healthy. He soon discovered, however, that the product he was selling was also found there in abundance. There would be no way to sell it except at such low prices that he would be left with no profit whatsoever.

He hurried back to the manufacturer, and requested of him with all his heart, "Find a place for me in which I will have both livelihood and sustenance!"

The moral: There are people whose whole lives are dedicated to making a living. Day and night, their minds are occupied with business. They never have a moment to rest, a moment to themselves. Chances are that they become extremely wealthy. Chances are that they have enough to live on and more. They only lack one thing—sustenance—something to sustain their souls.

Akleda d'Rachamei

אָבִינוּ מַלְכֵּנוּ הָרֵם קֶרֶן יִשְׂרָאֵל עַמֶּךְ
"Our Father, our King, raise up the honor of Your people Israel."

The Koznitzer Maggid explained this supplication with a parable.

A young scholar once married and received a sizable dowry for the wedding. Since his intention was to continue devoting his days and nights to studying Torah, he greatly appreciated the opportunity to do so without having to think about how to make a living. He deposited his fortune with one of the merchants in the city. They agreed that the merchant would invest the money, and they would share the profits.

In the meantime, the merchant got involved in several unsuccessful business ventures. Not only did profits not accumulate, but losses soared. His predicament worsened by the day.

Friends came to the young scholar and advised him to get out. "For sure you won't see profits. You'd better pull out before it's too late, so that you can at least save the principal."

The Talmud teaches us: "The people of Israel were exiled and dispersed among the nations only in order to draw converts" (*Pesachim* 87b). [Who were these converts? The Talmud teaches that they were the souls of future converts who joined Israel at Mount Sinai to receive the Torah (*Shabbos* 145a). The Jewish people were ideally supposed to magnify the honor of Heaven by attracting and drawing these kindred souls back to Judaism with the powerful magnetic light of Godliness that shone from the Temple in Jerusalem. When we failed to illuminate the darkness of the world from the Temple, God's light was splintered into millions of tiny sparks (the Jewish people in exile).] In order to draw back these kindred souls as righteous converts, Israel was dispersed to almost every corner of the world... Instead of magnifying God's Name, however, the opposite occurred. We fell deeper and deeper into our exiled state. God's Name became profaned.

We therefore turn to our Father in Heaven and plead: "Our Father, our King, raise up the honor of Your People Israel." Acquiesce regarding the honor You wished to have through the nations of the world through their conversion. Save the principal! Redeem us quickly for Your Name's sake!

Avodas Yisrael

אָבִינוּ מַלְכֵּנוּ מַלֵּא יָדֵינוּ מִבִּרְכוֹתֶיךָ
"Our Father, our King, fill our hands with Your blessings."

What does it mean to "fill our hands with blessings"? The Maggid of Rotzky explained with a parable.

A villager who wished to purchase some wine loaded an empty barrel onto his wagon and traveled to the large winery in town. He lowered the barrel from the wagon, rolled it into the winery, and chose from among all the wines. The workers filled the barrel and helped him load it back onto the wagon. The villager happily drove off towards home.

When he arrived, he called his sons to assist him in unloading the barrel of wine. To his surprise, however, the barrel was empty!

Hardly able to contain his anger, he reloaded the barrel onto the wagon and returned to the winery. "Why did you cheat me?" he shouted. "I paid for a full barrel and received an empty one. This is robbery!"

The winery's owners were shocked, for they knew very well that the barrel was full to overflowing when it left their premises. On the other hand, they could see that the barrel was indeed empty now. As they examined it closely, the mystery was soon solved. There was a small crack between the slats in one place. All the wine had trickled out through the crack on the way home.

"Don't complain to us," they told the villager. "You're the one to blame. Somebody who wants to buy wine has to come with a barrel in good condition."

The same goes for someone who comes with outstretched hands and expects to have them filled with all kinds of sweets. He must make sure to hold his fingers tightly together. If not, the sweets will trickle away...

We are like this villager. We ask God for goodness and blessing and He is even ready to give, but we must first prepare the vessel with which to receive. And what is the vessel? Our Sages gave us the hint when they said, "There is no vessel that holds blessing better than *shalom*" (*Yerushalmi Berachos* 17b). The reason for this is that the Jewish people constitute one single vessel (barrel) made of many slats. When the slats are all joined together, the barrel is complete and can contain blessing.

When we ask, "Our Father, our King, fill our hands with Your blessings," we should see ourselves as the fingers of a single person stretching forth his hands... The only condition is that we all join together as one in peace and brotherhood.

Akleda d'Rachamei

אָבִינוּ מַלְכֵּנוּ, שְׁמַע קוֹלֵנוּ, חוּס וְרַחֵם עָלֵינוּ

"Our Father, our King, hear our voice, care for us and have mercy on us."

The Maggid of Rotzky asked: What is the difference between *chus* and *rachem?* In Hebrew these two words can be very similar. *Chus* means to "to care for," "to have concern for," "to shield," etc. *Rachem* means "to have mercy or compassion," "to feel sympathy," "to take pity," etc.

We generally have mercy on anything sentient that suffers pain, even if it has no value to us and we expect no benefit from it. Consider a stray cat, for example, which has been injured and is suffering. Our compassion is aroused for such a creature, and we have mercy on it.

We do not, on the other hand, have mercy or take pity on an expensive glass cup. We are concerned lest it fall and break, and because of our concern we take precautions against its breaking. If we safeguard it, that is only because it has value for us.

By way of analogy, imagine soldiers on the battlefield. Those wounded in action are immediately taken to the hospital even while the battle continues. There they are immediately separated into two groups: those superficially wounded and those seriously wounded. Those in the first group are bandaged and returned to the battlefield to continue fighting. The second group of soldiers, however, are in far more serious trouble and pain; their lives are endangered. It is no longer a question of getting them back out on the battlefield, but of keeping them alive. Clearly, we care for (*chus*) the first group while we have mercy (*rachem*) on the second.

As for us, we hardly know our condition. We have stumbled, fallen, and declined. We ask to be treated, to be healed. We ask for assistance in getting back on the right track. In the merit of what? We have a staunch and unyielding trust that we can make a comeback and return to the field of battle. We wish to prove ourselves worthy of serving our King, so we ask that He care for us (*chus*). When our wounds are mortal, on the other hand, and we cannot serve Him, we ask that He have mercy on us (*rachem*)...

Akleda d'Rachamei

אָבִינוּ מַלְכֵּנוּ קַבֵּל בְּרַחֲמִים וּבְרָצוֹן אֶת תְּפִלָּתֵנוּ

"Our Father, our King, accept our prayers mercifully and willingly."

The Maggid of Rotzky asked further: What is the difference between *rachamim* and *ratzon*? He clarified with a parable.

A man once found an abandoned infant in the street. He took the hungry, crying baby home, adopted him, and raised him as his own child. As the boy grew older, the man hired teachers for him, and soon it was discovered that the child was blessed with unusual wit and brilliance. Moreover, he was of excellent character and everyone loved him. No doubt, his adopted parent was very pleased and happy with him. At first, he had taken him in and raised him out of mercy, *rachamim*. Now he did so willingly, with *ratzon*.

We too have all gathered in God's House with fear and trembling regarding our future. We are painfully aware of our shortcomings. We are hardly worthy of the blessings for which we so fervently pray. Our only chance is to arouse His mercy.

Mercy is the only response to such an "empty-handed" prayer, one without merit and motivated by our concern over our fate. Still, we have a staunch and unyielding trust that this very unworthiness will motivate us to take stock of ourselves and resolve to better our ways. God will be pleased with us, for the fear of His judgment will have borne fruit. He will then accept our prayers not only mercifully (with *rachamim*) but willingly (with *ratzon*) as well.

Akleda d'Rachamei

אָבִינוּ מַלְכֵּנוּ, פְּתַח שַׁעֲרֵי שָׁמַיִם לִתְפִלָּתֵנוּ
"Our Father, our King, open the gates of Heaven for our prayers."

What do we resemble when we ask God to open the Heavenly gates for our prayers to enter? We resemble, answered the Maggid of Rotzky, a house which has just caught fire, God forbid. Passersby hurry to break down the front door and rescue those who are trapped inside. They are prevented from doing so, however, because the door is locked. In the meantime, the fire is spreading, the smoke is thickening, and cries are heard from within the house: "Open the door for us! Let us out! Save us from death!"

People outside call back: "The door is locked from inside! Turn the key and we will rescue you!"

Both sides shout, but the key remains unmoved...

We cry, "Our Father, our King, open the gates of Heaven for our prayers." God replies, "The key is on your side! My children, open your doors (hearts) the width of a pinhole and I will open up doors as wide as the gates of a palace!" Instead of opening our hearts, even a crack, along with our locked-up feelings and stopped-up fountains of tears, we wait for God to do the work for us. His answer to us is: Turn the key—and I will do the rest.

Akleda d'Rachamei

אָבִינוּ מַלְכֵּנוּ, זְכוֹר כִּי עָפָר אֲנַחְנוּ
"Our Father, our King, remember that we are but dust."

The Maggid of Rotzky told the following parable: At an exhibition of art objects, two pieces won prizes: first prize was awarded to a breathtaking golden pitcher, and second prize went to another golden pitcher that was delicately engraved, and was seven times more beautiful than the first.

The visitors all expressed their surprise: Surely the second pitcher should have been awarded first prize!

But the directors of the exhibition explained: The second pitcher is certainly far more beautiful than its contender, but this is no wonder, for it is made of pure gold. The first pitcher, on the other hand, is actually made of clay, and is only gold-plated. Making such a beautiful vessel from clay is seven times more difficult!

The moral: Angels are far more refined and exalted than we are, but they are made of pure spirituality (gold). We, on the other hand, are mortal dust. We are likened to broken pottery. If, nevertheless, we have striven and attained what we have attained—we deserve first prize.

Our Sages thus taught: The ministering angels do not sing God's praises in Heaven until Israel sings below (*Chullin* 92a). Although angels are more exalted, we are more important. For although we are mere vessels of mortal clay, we have mitzvos and good deeds to our credit.

Akleda d'Rachamei

אָבִינוּ מַלְכֵּנוּ, חֲמוֹל עָלֵינוּ וְעַל עוֹלָלֵינוּ וְטַפֵּנוּ

"Our Father, our King, have compassion on us, on our children and our infants."

The Maggid of Rotzky explained this supplication thus:

An ocean liner once set out to sea with hundreds of passengers—men, women, and children. Suddenly, the ship hit a reef and began to sink, and life rafts were quickly lowered into the sea. When it was discovered that there were not enough rafts, however, the captain had to make a decision. He ordered that the women and children would be saved.

One father approached the captain with an infant in his arms. The captain said, "Hand me your child. You will have to stay on the sinking vessel with the other men."

"I accept my lot. I don't claim to be better than any other passenger on this ship," the father answered. "But you wish to save the child, don't you? And if so, what will become of him when the raft is rescued? If I drown, who will care for him, give him food and drink, dress him, and find shelter for him? Who will guide him? Is this called rescue? On the contrary, you are sentencing him to a life of darkness and affliction! Poor little orphan, he will wander alone here and there in the world. If you are really concerned for his welfare, for his rescue, then you must consider saving me with him!"

This is why we plead: "Our Father, our King, have compassion on us, on our children and our infants."

Akleda d'Rachamei

אָבִינוּ מַלְכֵּנוּ, עֲשֵׂה לְמַעַן הֲרוּגִים עַל שֵׁם קָדְשֶׁךָ

"Our Father, our King, act for the sake of those who died to sanctify Your Name."

Said the Maggid of Rotzky: This is as it should be. If a loyal soldier falls while performing his duty of guarding the frontiers of the kingdom, as a sign of recognition and appreciation his family receives a monthly stipend and fixed pension from the king's treasury.

If our ancestors gave their lives to sanctify God's Name, we, their families, should benefit...

Akleda d'Rachamei

אָבִינוּ מַלְכֵּנוּ, עֲשֵׂה לְמַעַנְךָ אִם לֹא לְמַעֲנֵנוּ
"Our Father, our King, act for Your sake if not for ours."

The Maggid of Rotzky told a parable: A certain king was known for his benevolence and compassion. Every request for clemency that was brought before him was answered in the affirmative.

Once, one of the king's subjects committed a very grave crime against the king. What made the situation worse was that this particular man was beholden to the king for a tremendous kindness, and now, instead of being grateful, he had repaid good with evil. The judges found him guilty and pronounced a very harsh sentence.

When the man realized the gravity of the situation, he requested clemency from the king. His crime was so grave, however, and his ingratitude so glaring, that the king refused to grant it.

Then the man turned to the king and spoke the following words: "Your majesty! It is true that my crime is very grave, to the extent that I am completely undeserving of the clemency you have always granted offenders. Still, those clemencies have made you famous for being kindhearted, compassionate, and good. From this point of view, then, the gravity of my crime requires all the more so that you display your great kindness! Then everyone will know and recognize how truly great is your compassion!"

With this, the king changed his mind and granted him

clemency. This is what we mean when we ask God to "act for Your sake if not for ours."

Akleda d'Rachamei

אָבִינוּ מַלְכֵּנוּ, חָנֵּנוּ וַעֲנֵנוּ כִּי אֵין בָּנוּ מַעֲשִׂים

"Our Father, our King, be gracious with us and answer us, though we have no [good] deeds. Be charitable and kind with us, and save us."

It is the custom to say this last *Avinu Malkenu* supplication very quietly. Why do we do this? The Maggid of Lublin answered with a parable.

A man once came to a store to buy provisions. He asked about the price of a particular item and then began to bargain. First, he offered to pay one third of the asked-for price, but the seller would not consider it. The buyer went up a little bit, and the seller came down. They continued back and forth like this for quite a while until they finally agreed upon a price that was half the original asking price.

The buyer asked to have the item packed up and immediately inquired about another item. They then proceeded to engage in the same behavior as before. The buyer proposed an absurdly low figure, and the seller was annoyed and refused. The buyer raised his offer a notch, and the seller was forced to lower his by the same amount. After a long, drawn-out negotiation, they again agreed at half the original selling price. The buyer then turned to a third item...

To make a long story short, after numerous and exhausting rounds of haggling and bargaining, the seller ended up boxing a great deal of merchandise for his customer.

Then, suddenly everything changed. Unlike the previous exchanges, which were accompanied by shouts and arguments, demands and promises, the buyer leaned over and whispered confidentially into the seller's ear: "It's a deal... but

I don't have any money! So I'll just take the whole lot on credit."

The moral: We raise our voices and cry out all the *Avinu Malkenus*, ordering a mountain of blessings and goods, but when the time arrives to pay, we whisper, "Our Father, our King, be gracious with us and answer us, though we have no [good] deeds." We want to buy on credit. "Be charitable and kind with us. Save us."

Ohel Ya'akov

Sounding the Shofar

Praying for *Mashiach*

On the first day of Rosh Hashanah, the holy Rabbi Shmelke of Nickolsburg came to the synagogue before the blowing of the shofar and spoke the following words:

Woe to us! "Her people are all moaning" (*Eichah* 1:11). They are crying and pouring forth their supplications before the Holy One. But what are they moaning for? "They seek bread. They have given up their precious possessions for food..." (ibid.). They cry out for physical comfort. They do not consider the exile of their Mother, the *Shechinah*, the one who raised them. Instead they resemble a bunch of barking dogs: "Give, give... Give us life, give us food!" (*Tikunei Zohar* 6).

On the second day, he came again, and cried out with tears in his eyes: "Why has [David] the son of Yishai not come, neither yesterday nor today, for the bread?!" (*Shemuel* I 20:27). "Why has the son of Yishai not come?" That is, Why has *Mashiach* ben David from the stock of Yishai not come? "Neither yesterday nor today"—that is, neither yesterday, the first day of Rosh Hashanah—nor today, the second day. For on both these days we have prayed "for the bread"—for material blessings. We have not cried our hearts out over the profanation of God's Name, the exile of the *Shechinah*! We have not prayed for the Redemption...

Shemen Ha-Tov 159

Wake Up!

To what can the blowing of the shofar on Rosh Hashanah be likened? The Maggid of Dubno answered with a parable.

When government authorities made a surprise inspection of a warehouse owned by a wealthy businessman, it was discovered that he had smuggled goods. Not only was the unfortunate man guilty of tax evasion, but the contraband was brought in from an enemy country! The business was immediately shut down, and the owner was put in jail.

In the wealthy man's home, there was great sorrow. His wife and children tearfully requested permission to visit him in jail, but they were refused. He was in solitary confinement, they were told, because the charges leveled against him were extremely serious. The fact that he had smuggled goods from an enemy country indicated the possibility of secret contacts with the enemy. Perhaps he was a spy. The investigation had been turned over to the secret service. He would be tried before a military tribunal. It was likely that he would be found guilty of treason, in which case his sentence would be death by hanging...

We can imagine how the family received this distressing and bitter news. But somehow, a day passed, and another day. A week passed, and a month. Life went on in its customary manner. They had plenty of money, for the head of the family was an extremely wealthy man. Eventually, things almost returned to normal. As the months passed, the man was almost completely forgotten—as the saying goes, "Out of sight, out of mind."

One day the members of the family sat down to a lavish meal. As they ate, drank, and enjoyed themselves, they suddenly heard the sound of an alarm, the wail of a siren. One of the children ran to the window, and called out, "A military vehicle with barred windows is driving by. It is taking the prisoner to be tried!"

The atmosphere immediately changed. All the high spirits, gaiety and good appetite disappeared, as the bitter reality hit them. They had forgotten: their father was going to be tried. His life was hanging in the balance. One by one, they all began to moan. Their eyes filled with tears. They were gripped by dread...

Ohel Ya'akov, *Emor*

The Shofar of Rosh Hashanah

Rabbi David Abudraham quotes Rabbi Sa'adyah Gaon, who listed ten reasons why we blow the shofar on Rosh Hashanah. The first reason is that Rosh Hashanah marks the day on which God created man and revealed His absolute sovereignty over His world. Kings sound trumpets and horns to let it be known and heard everywhere when the anniversary of the beginning of their reign falls. In the same way, we accept the sovereignty of the Blessed Creator on Rosh Hashanah. David *Ha-Melech* thus wrote: "Call out before God with silver trumpets, [accept His absolute] sovereignty with the sound of the shofar" (*Tehillim* 98:6).

The second reason is that Rosh Hashanah is the first day of the Ten Days of *Teshuvah*. The shofar is blown to announce this. Like an early-warning system that goes off to warn of imminent danger, the shofar says: Let all who desire to return in *teshuvah*, return now. If you do not, you will have no reason to claim injustice. Kings do the same: First they warn their subjects with a proclamation, and whoever then violates the proclamation bears full liability.

The third reason is to remind us of when we stood at the foot of Mount Sinai, when "The sound of the shofar waxed louder and louder" (*Shemos* 19:19). We will then recall how our ancestors accepted the Torah upon themselves and affirmed for all generations to come, "We will do and we will obey all that God has declared!" (ibid. 24:7).

The fourth reason is to remind us of the exhortations of the prophets, which are likened to a shofar. God thus told the prophet Yechezkel, "Son of man, speak to the children of your people, and say to them: When I bring a sword upon a land, the people take one of their number and appoint him as a sentry. His task is to see when the sword comes upon the land, and sound the shofar to warn the people. If someone hears the sound of the shofar, and does not heed the warning, then if the sword comes and takes his life, his blood shall be upon his own head. He heard the sound of the shofar and did not heed its warning. His blood shall be upon him. If he had heeded the warning, he would have saved his own life... You, son of man, I have appointed you as a sentry for the house of Israel. When you hear a word from Me, warn them in My Name" (*Yechezkel* 33:2-7).

The fifth reason is to remind us of the destruction of the Temple and the bloodcurdling battle cries of the enemy. Yirmeyahu thus cried out, "I tremble [like a woman suffering birth pangs]. My heart wells up within me. I cannot be silent, for my soul has heard the sound of the shofar, the blast of war" (*Yirmeyahu* 4:19). When hearing the sound of the shofar, we ask God to rebuild the Temple.

The sixth reason is to remind us of the binding of Yitzchak. Just as our forefather Yitzchak was prepared to sacrifice his life to sanctify God's Name, so should we be.

The seventh reason is to feel awe and reverence for our Creator, which will cause us to soften our hearts and bend our wills to His will. We should shake and tremble when we hear the shofar, as the prophet said, "If a shofar has been sounded in the city, shall the people not tremble?" (*Amos* 3:6).

The eighth reason is to remind us to prepare for the great and fearful Day of Judgment. It is thus written, "The great day of God is near, it is near and it is speeding more and more quickly... a day of shofar and blasting..." (*Tzefanyah* 1:14-16).

The ninth reason is to remind us to long for the great ingathering of the exiles, as it is written, "On that day, a great shofar will be blown, and those who were lost in the land of Assyria, and those who were dispersed in the land of Egypt, will come and bow down to God on the Temple Mount in Jerusalem" (*Yeshayahu* 27:13).

The tenth reason is to remind us to believe in and anticipate the resurrection of the dead, as it is written, "All you inhabitants of the world, all you who sleep in the earth: See mountains miraculously raised aloft like flags! Hear [God's voice] like the blowing of a shofar!" (*Yeshayahu* 18:3).

The Coronation of the King

Once, in connection with the first reason that we blow the shofar on Rosh Hashanah—that it marks the day on which God created man and revealed His absolute sovereignty over His world—the Maggid of Dubno related the following story about Rabbi Chayim of Volozhin.

When Rabbi Chayim heard the sound of the shofar rending the air, and saw its effect on his beloved congregation, he rejoiced and trembled at the same time. "Is it so simple," he asked, "to crown the Creator of the entire universe?!" Still, he set aside his trepidation and rejoiced for the great privilege of being able to celebrate the coronation of his Creator on such a holy day.

The Maggid illustrated this with a parable:

There was once a poor beggar who had a brother in a distant city. One day, news arrived that his brother had suddenly become very wealthy and admired. The poor man rejoiced, clapping his hands and dancing with all his strength.

People asked him, "What are you so excited about? Have you received a dime from your brother, that you are so happy? Who knows, when you go to visit him, he might even slam the door in your face and act like a total stranger!"

"It doesn't matter," the poor man replied. "Whether he gives or not, I am happy for him. He is rich now and no longer poor, as I am. I am just rejoicing in his happiness. If, in addition to this, he will help me when he sees me and save me from my dire straits, I will rejoice doubly..."

This is the meaning of the verse, "O God, King, we rejoice in Your invincible strength. O how greatly we exult in Your deliverance!" (*Tehillim* 21:2). First, we rejoice in God's awesome power, and that we are privileged to have such a great Father and King. Our Master is very great and infinitely powerful. When He finally delivers us—we will rejoice doubly.

Introduction to **Kochav Mi-Ya'akov**

Gidon's Shofar

In a discourse that he once gave before the blowing of the shofar, the Maggid of Rotzky spoke about Gidon. In the seventh chapter of *Shoftim* (the Book of Judges) we learn: When Gidon wished to surprise the camp of the Midianites in the dark of night, he took three hundred men with him and divided them into three divisions. He instructed each man to carry his shofar in his right hand and an empty earthenware pitcher in his left hand. Inside the pitchers they were to place burning torches.

The men went out and stealthily surrounded the entire Midianite encampment on three sides. At Gidon's signal, they all began to blow their shofars... they shattered their pitchers, and lit up the night with their torches. The Midianites were so terrified that they all began killing each other and running for their lives.

We also must act like Gidon, and thus ensure victory. Blowing the shofar is one component of victory; but something else is required as well. We must break the empty earthenware pitchers—these are our hearts! This is what David *Ha-Melech* meant when he said, "The [proper] offering to God is a broken spirit. O God, You will never reject a broken and contrite heart!" (*Tehillim* 51:19).

Break open the seal, remove the outer skin that prevents you from coming close to God! Reveal the innermost heart that beats within the breast of every Jew! It is a burning torch of love and awe that radiates holy light and emits Godly warmth!

The camps of our enemies will then be struck with terror. The Accuser and his legions will flee in every direction, as our Sages revealed to us: "The Accuser is thrown into a state of confusion when he hears the blasts of the shofar on Rosh Hashanah!" (*Talmud Yerushalmi; Tur, Beis Yosef, Orach Chayim* 585). Let us then call out as Gidon's soldiers did: "[Take] sword for God and for Gidon!"—to strike our enemies and silence our accusers!

Serigi Nefishi, *Derush* 3

Extinguishing the Fire

The Maggid of Rotzky delivered the following discourse before the blowing of the shofar one year:

The Talmud (*Rosh Hashanah* 16a) records an ancient tradition: "On Rosh Hashanah, the Holy One says: Declare verses of kingship, recollection and shofar blasting before Me. Kingship, in order to acknowledge My sovereignty over you; recollection, so that your recollection rises up favorably before Me; with what? With the shofar blast."

The meaning of the teaching is this: Similarly to a king of flesh and blood, Hashem unites His people under His authority. When the entire Jewish people unite in order to accept upon themselves His Kingship, the power of this unity causes them to be remembered favorably before Him. What actually brings them to this level of unity? The blast of the shofar.

By way of analogy, every town used to have a team of men who manned the fire station. If a fire broke out in the town, the man who was on duty would blast the siren and sound the alarm. Everybody would come running as fast as they could, for they all knew that no one man could fight a fire and bring it under control alone. When a fire broke out, everybody had to act together in order to extinguish it.

Our prophets have told us: "Behold, the day is coming. It will burn like a furnace, and all the arrogant and all the evildoers will be stubble. The day that is coming will burn them up..." (*Malachi* 3:19). "Behold, God will come with fire, His chariots with a storm wind, to render His anger with wrath, and His rebuke with flames of fire. For by fire God will execute judgment, with His sword, on all mankind, and the slain of God will be many" (*Yeshayahu* 66:15-16).

Our only chance of extinguishing the fire of Hashem's wrath is to unite!

But, the Maggid called in a piercing voice, even if all the townspeople gather together to extinguish the fire, they cannot! They will not succeed—unless they bring buckets of water! "Pour your heart out like water before the Lord!" (*Eichah* 2:19). "Let us lift up our hearts in our hands to the Supreme God in Heaven!" (ibid. 3:41). Let your tears flow in torrents, to extinguish the awesome fire of judgment that threatens to consume our people!

Serigi Tova, *Derush 2*

Proclaiming God's Oneness

Our holy teachers have told us that on Rosh Hashanah we are able to rectify and elevate all the "defective" prayers of the previous year. These include all our prayers which were mingled with extraneous or impure thoughts and as a result fell and became trapped in the "shells." These "shells" sustain themselves from the holy sparks in our prayers. As long as the holy sparks are trapped in the shells, the *Shechinah* (Divine Presence) is said to be in exile. On Rosh Hashanah, these prayers can be re-elevated and the *Shechinah* redeemed.

In his book, *Arvei Nachal*, the *Levushei Serad* explains this by way of a parable.

There was once a king who had many treasure houses in which he stored all the gold, silver, and precious gems in the kingdom. In one of his royal treasuries, the king kept his crowns; each day of the year he wore a different one! The royal seal was also kept there, and it was used to seal all official documents and decrees. The king appointed his beloved son over all his treasure houses and entrusted the keys in his keeping. He placed his father's seal on all official documents, and in addition, at the daily coronation ceremony, it was he who placed the crown upon his father's head.

Now, the king had a minister who was an officer in the royal army. This man secretly hated the king's son, for in his heart, he was jealous of the great distinctions which the king conferred upon him. He therefore devised a scheme.

He acted like a true friend and loyal confidant to the king's son, speaking intimately with the boy to win his heart. He did this on many occasions, and when he was sure he had his complete confidence, he slyly offered the boy his assistance in arranging the treasure houses and preparing the king's crowns. Because the king's son believed in him so unreservedly, he entrusted all the keys to his father's treasuries in his keeping.

One particular day, the king invited all his ministers to a festive meal. His son was to bring the crown for that day and place it on his father's head. He was also to hand the king his royal golden scepter in the presence of all the ministers and honored guests who were summoned to the meal. Meanwhile, the jealous officer, who had taken care to prepare every detail of the meal, stole away to the king's treasury. There, he smashed, broke, and bent every single one of the king's crowns!

When he returned, he said nonchalantly to the king's son, "Allow me to bring you the king's crown and scepter from the treasury, so that you can present them to the king."

The king's son agreed to wait on the steps of the royal palace, while the officer left to walk towards the treasury. A few moments later he was back. In his hands, he solemnly carried a velvet cushion; on the velvet cushion, lay the broken pieces of what had once been a crown! As he approached the king's son, the boy suddenly understood what was happening. He understood that he had been duped.

He was overwhelmed with shame. He had committed a serious crime. Against protocol and without permission, he had handed the royal keys over to this sinister, diabolic fiend.

He began to tremble and feel faint. In desperation, he hurried to his mother, the queen. After relating the whole story to her, he could no longer restrain himself. He broke down in a torrent of tears and cried out, "Mother! Please tell me what to do!"

This was her advice: "Quickly!" she cried. "Sound the royal horn to announce an enemy attack. The officer will immediately cast the broken crown to the ground and hurry off to assemble his soldiers. In the meantime, you can pick up the pieces and begin fitting them together again to fix the crown!"

"How will I put the pieces together in such a short time?" he asked.

"I have a special glue," his mother assured him. "It creates a permanent seal within seconds!"

The king's son followed his mother's advice, and succeeded in mending the crown in time. He crowned his father with the wondrous crown, and all present praised and lauded the king. The king was proud of his beloved son.

We are all God's children. He has given us His Torah, His treasure house of precious wisdom. The crowns in this treasure house are our prayers. Each day we are to crown Him with a different prayer. [God has placed numerous hints throughout His Torah (in the stories of Adam and Chavah, the Patriarchs, Moshe in Egypt, Israel in the wilderness) that the ultimate purpose of creation is the revelation of His Oneness through His beloved children, the nation of Israel. Our prophets and Sages took these hints and turned them into prayers, prayers for redemption. In the Torah, God says, *"Shema Yisrael*—Listen, Israel—I, God, am the Supreme Being. I, God, am the absolute Unity and Oneness behind all existence!" When we say the *Shema* we "unify God's Name," i.e., declare the Oneness of His Name. We then add, "May [the revelation of God's] Name—the glory of His kingdom—be ever increased in this world and for all eternity!" These prayers are what He wants from us. They are the crowns in His treasure house.]

But there is "one particular day" each year, Rosh Hashanah, when the King sits on His Throne of Judgment surrounded by His entire host of Heavenly ministers. The Heavenly Tribunal is convened. God's ministers stand to His "right" (mercy) and to His "left" (justice) to present their testimony, and God Himself sits as Supreme Judge. He expresses His satisfaction with His children for crowning Him with their prayers.

Among all God's servants and ministers who come to bow down before the Divine Throne is the Accuser. Knowing that he has very little chance against us, he disguises himself as our confidant and convinces us to hand him the keys to the king's treasuries. These keys are our ability to learn God's Torah with the pure intention of fulfilling His will, namely, to reveal His Oneness. In his hands, they are turned around to become the very opposite!

The Accuser is now able to enter the treasury and warp the crowns. That is, after taking away our ability to recognize the Torah's hints as to how to recognize God's Oneness, our prayers become woven with subtle ulterior motives. We no longer pray for redemption. If we still pray at all, we find it difficult to concentrate. We no longer understand what it is we are praying for! We no longer are aware of the One to whom we are praying! It isn't long before all kinds of extraneous thoughts enter the vacuum. Even if they are not altogether impure, these thoughts are prevented from rising up before God's Throne of Holiness. They are diverted by the Accuser for his own sinister purposes!

The Day of Judgment thus arrives, but we are sorely lacking. All the crowns are broken. All of a sudden, the gravity of the situation dawns on us. We are standing at the entrance of our King's palace, totally ashamed of ourselves for having besmirched His Glory!

But His Glory, the *Shechinah*, our Mother, is with us! And She advises us to take up the shofar and sound a battle cry against our enemies. This shofar has the special ability to confuse the Accuser. It reminds him of the ultimate redemption, his Day of Judgment. He is terribly frightened and confused by this, for the Redemption is his death warrant. It will signal the end, when he and his insidious hordes will be obliterated forever.

"But how will we weld our prayer crowns together in such a short time?" we ask. "Tears," she answers. The King will not forsake us if we truly cry out to Him. "O God, You will never reject a broken and contrite heart!" (*Tehillim* 51:19). With sincere regret and burning tears, we will repair the broken crowns and raise our prayers out of the realm of the "shells" to crown our King.

Based on this explanation, we can now explain the 47th Psalm which is recited seven times by the entire congregation before the blowing of the shofar:

Dedicated to the One who grants victory [on the Day of Judgment]. A Psalm by the descendants of Korach: Let all [angel-ministers of the] nations clap their hands [accusing us and rejoicing in their success at having duped us]. We must therefore blast [the shofar] and pray to God [in order to confuse the Accuser and let him know that his days are numbered]. [He must realize now] that God alone is Supreme and Awesome. He alone reigns sovereign over the entire world. [It is for this reason that, in the future,] He will subdue nations under us and place governments under our rule. [While the Accuser is still confused, let us therefore proclaim God's Oneness. He will then] elect us [and restore] our inheritance [the Torah], the pride of Ya'akov [our prayers] which He loves, Selah. God will then rise up [from His Throne of Judgment] with the blast. Almighty God [will sit on His Throne of Mercy] at the sound of the shofar! [For by crying out from the depths of our hearts and sounding the shofar] we cut through to God with piercing song, we cut through to our King with piercing song! For God alone reigns sovereign over the entire world. We must therefore wisely cut away [the forces of darkness, not wasting a precious moment before we return wholeheartedly to our God]. God reigns sovereign over the

nations! He has seated Himself upon His Throne of Holiness.
Right now the [angelic] ministers of the nations are assembling
[in Heaven] to join the people of the God of Avraham [as they
accept God as the sole Ruler of the world]. For God shields
the world [from the powers of evil]. He is greatly exalted.

Arvei Nachal 2:112

כָּל הָעַמִּים תִּקְעוּ כָף, הָרִיעוּ לֵאלֹקִים בְּקוֹל רִנָּה... עָלָה אֱלֹקִים בִּתְרוּעָה, ה' בְּקוֹל שׁוֹפָר

"Let all nations clap their hands... praise God with shouts of joy... God will [then] rise up amidst shouting, Almighty God at the sound of the shofar!"

Once, before his congregation began reciting the 47th Psalm
seven times in succession, the Maggid of Kutno told the
following parable:

There was once a great and mighty king. Every year he
celebrated the anniversary of his coronation with a formal
ceremony. For days in advance, hundreds of thousands of his
subjects could be seen converging on the royal city from all
the towns and villages of the kingdom. Excitement filled the
air. As the hour approached, everyone assembled in the
square outside the royal palace. They brought special torches,
burning with the finest olive oil. When the stars filled the
night sky, each person lit his torch. The spectacle was magnifi-
cent, as they burned brightly and lit up the entire square.

At the right moment, the king would appear on his balcony and see the multitudes of his subjects gathered below, and
the tens of thousands of torches that had been lit in his honor.
As trumpets blasted, the king's ministers stepped forward to
present him with his crown. After placing the crown on his
head, the king commanded that valuable gifts be distributed
to the people.

Once there was a famine, and every drop of olive oil was needed for food. That year, the multitudes were forced to light their torches with tar and pitch. In addition to not burning very brightly, these torches produced clouds of smoke. When the king came out on his balcony, the air was thick, ugly and suffocating. The little light that was produced by the torches was smothered by the billows of smoke that rose up from the square into the night sky. The king was extremely upset and angry.

Trumpets sounded, and the ministers stepped forth to present the king with his crown. Instead of accepting the honor, however, he shouted with rage, "What is the meaning of this?"

The entire assembly of men, women and children fell on their faces to beg forgiveness from the king. "We beseech Your Majesty!" they cried out. "Forgive us in accord with your abundant mercy! We are so poor and wretched that we spent our last pennies on these torches. We assembled here only to honor you, O kindly king. Have mercy on your people!"

The moral: Rosh Hashanah commemorates the day on which God created man and revealed His absolute sovereignty over His world. This is one of the primary reasons that we blow the shofar on this holy day. As Rabbi Sa'adyah Gaon wrote, just as trumpets and horns are blasted to celebrate the anniversary of the beginning of a mortal king's reign, so do we accept the sovereignty of the Blessed Creator on the anniversary of His "coronation" by blowing the shofar.

Long ago, when the Holy Temple stood in Jerusalem, we fulfilled the commandment of *aliyah la-regel* (pilgrimage), "to appear before the Eternal God, Master, Lord of Israel, three times each year" (*Shemos* 34:23). We gathered in Jerusalem in the hundreds of thousands. The air was filled with the excitement of coming close to God. For days and weeks we purified ourselves in order to be ready to stand in the courtyard of the Temple. As the Festival approached, we were filled with anticipation. Like David *Ha-Melech*, we yearned for only one thing: "To dwell in the House of God all the days of our lives! To behold the sweetness of God, and to seek [His closeness] in His Holy Sanctuary!" (*Tehillim* 27:4). Our fervor to serve our Creator rose to such a crescendo that our hearts began to burn with holy fire. We danced and sang and transcended all physicality. Like brilliant torches, our prayers rose up in flames of love for God...

We became aware of God's Presence in a way that was impossible to experience in any other place on earth. Many were lifted up into prophetic ecstacy. All together we sang: "Majesty and sublime honor are before Him! Strength and splendor emanate from the Abode of His Holiness... Lift up an offering and come into His courtyards. Bow yourselves down to God in holy fervor. Let the entire earth quake in His Presence. Let it be realized and proclaimed among the nations that God's reign [is eternal and] has never ceased. Only then will human society finally be established and vacillate no more. For He will submit all peoples to His straight judgment. The Heavens will then rejoice and the earth will be glad. The sea and all that fills it will thunder. The fields and all that fill them will exult. All the trees of the forest will sing for joy [before Him]! Before God! For He is coming [to reveal His Kingship]! He is coming to judge the earth. He will judge the world with justice and its peoples with His undeviating truth!" (*Tehillim* 96:6-12).

We sang: "Let all nations clap their hands... praise God with shouts of joy. For God alone is Supreme and Awesome. He alone reigns sovereign over the entire world... God will [then] rise up amidst shouting, Almighty God at the sound of the shofar!" (*Tehillim* 47:1-6).

Now, due to our unworthiness, our Temple is destroyed. The fire of holy devotion is almost extinguished in our hearts. An icy blanket of coldness has covered our prayers, and threatens to smother the burning embers of our Torah learning as well. As the Days of Awe approach, however, we have a chance to grab the almost dying torch. We attempt to light it, to revive the last dying sparks before it is too late. But the flames are dull. There is so much smoke and so little light! We are ashamed as we stand before our Father in Heaven. We ask Him to have mercy on us in our broken and wretched state. We ask Him to rekindle the holy fire of devotion that once burned so brightly in our hearts...

Gefen Yisrael, *Derush* 10

עֲרוֹב עַבְדְּךָ לְטוֹב, אַל יַעַשְׁקוּנִי זֵדִים
"Be a guarantor for Your servant, for good. Prevent the arrogant from oppressing me."

This verse is said before we blow the shofar. The Maggid of Dubno explained it with a parable:

A king appointed his son as governor over one of his provinces, with one condition: All taxes which were collected in these provinces were to be dispatched on a daily basis back to the king. At first, the son was meticulous in following his father's orders. Time passed, however, and he began to become lax. After all, he told himself, I am the governor of this province. Why should I relinquish all tax monies to the royal treasury? I shall hold them here and build up my own fortune!

It was no sooner said than done—he severed all contact with his father and ceased sending him the money.

His father issued him a warning: "If you do not desist, I shall come against you with a great and mighty army, and depose you!"

The son was foolish, however, and he sent a message back to his father: "I do not fear you. I have my own army." The truth is, he had a handful of palace guards armed with simple swords whom his father had sent along with him for protection...

The king arrayed his troops and marched toward his son's

province. The son went out to do battle against his father, surrounded by his band of trusty guards. When he saw tens of thousands of soldiers armed with heavy artillery, however, he suddenly came to his senses. He realized how foolish he had been to think he could provoke and fight such a powerful king.

He understood that there was only one way now to extricate himself from mortal danger. He would come before his father, fall at his feet, and beg forgiveness. But the king was surrounded by legions of rugged soldiers who had received orders to strike a blow against the rebel son and execute him!

"Let us take counsel," he said as he turned to his guards who were as confused and frightened as he. "How can I let my father know that I have repented, that I wish to surrender and submit myself to his authority?"

His chief adviser replied, "Command your soldiers to sound the call of surrender with their trumpets. When your father hears it, he will know that you have repented. His mercy, the mercy of a father, will then be aroused within his heart. He will order his soldiers to lower their weapons. You will then be able to approach him, to fall at his feet and beg forgiveness..."

We resemble that rebellious son. Our father has come to fight and crush our rebellion with a great and mighty army of accusers and prosecutors which we ourselves have created with our sins! These accusers block our way. They prevent us from coming before our Father, our King. We therefore sound the shofar—(particularly the *teruah* which is made up of a quick series of tiny broken notes that sound like uncontrollable sobbing)—as a sign of surrender. With the *teruah* we officially declare our regret and brokenheartedness for having rebelled against our Father's will. With this, we hope that He will silence our accusers and thereby prevent our enemies from oppressing us. This is the meaning of the verse we say before blowing the shofar: "Be a guarantor for Your servant, for good. Prevent the arrogant from oppressing me" (*Tehillim* 119:122).

Emes l'Ya'akov

שָׂשׂ אָנֹכִי עַל אִמְרָתֶךָ, כְּמוֹצֵא שָׁלָל רָב

"I rejoice over Your commandments as one who finds a great spoil."

The Maggid of Mezrich asked: What is the meaning of "a great spoil"? He answered with a parable.

A man is traveling in the wilderness when he happens upon a diamond mine. Everywhere he looks, he sees brilliant diamonds of all sizes glistening like the light of the noonday sun. All he can think is: "Countless diamonds! Indescribable wealth!"

He bends down eagerly to fill his pockets with enough diamonds to make him wealthy for the rest of his life. He spreads his coat out on the ground and tries to fill it with as many diamonds as possible. When he finally leaves that mine, he is probably the richest man in the world.

On the one hand, as he departs to make his way home, he is filled with joy at his attainment. On the other hand, he is troubled by a sense of loss: if only he had a wagon, he could take so much more...

This is the meaning of the verse, "I rejoice over Your commandments as one who finds a great spoil" (*Tehillim* 119:162). On the one hand, I am happy for the privilege of having learned Your Torah. On the other hand, I recognize my own failings. I am like a man who has found a "great" spoil but who is capable of grasping only the minutest part of its content. The Torah is like an ocean, whereas what I know is merely a drop. There is so much light, but I lack the vessels to contain it.

This is how the Maggid of Mezrich understood this verse, and in his humility he applied it to himself. But his vessels were in truth filled with diamonds! Have we even begun to fill ours?

Likkutim Yekarim 120

טוֹב טַעַם וָדַעַת לַמְּדֵנִי כִּי בְמִצְוֹתֶיךָ הֶאֱמַנְתִּי
"Teach me superior reason and knowledge in the merit of having performed Your commandments with pure faith."

The Maggid of Dubno offered the following explanation for why this verse, which emphasizes faith, is said before the blowing of the shofar:

On the one hand, it is important to perform the commandments with simple faith, not probing for reasons behind them and certainly not performing them only because of one's limited understanding of these reasons. [Even if a person's reasoning is correct to some extent, he may not base his performance of a commandment on this reasoning lest circumstances change and he feel justified in assuming that the reason no longer applies. Performing the commandments in faith means that we believe God knew what He was doing when He ordered us to perform them.] On the other hand, one who performs the commandments with pure faith is given deep insight into their true reasons and rewarded with enlightenment from above. This is the meaning of the Psalmist's request: "Teach me superior reason and knowledge in the merit of having performed Your commandments with pure faith" (*Tehillim* 119:66). This distinction can be illustrated with two parables.

A wealthy businessman was involved in a number of trade deals and was too busy to travel to the annual fair in Leipzig to buy certain merchandise. He commissioned a fellow merchant, and entrusted him with a large sum of money to go in his stead and make the purchases. Once the merchant arrived at the fair, he began buying various things and selling them at a profit. In the end, after accumulating quite a sum of money for himself, he bought the merchandise for which he had been sent to the fair and returned with it to the businessman.

It cannot be denied that he performed his duty, but it also cannot be denied that, in addition to his commission, he made some extra profit. The problem is that he did business with money which was not his own! When the businessman finds out about this, he is bound to be upset. The man misused funds; he was commissioned to act as an agent, and had no right to use his employer's money to make an extra profit. He not only acted wrongly with the businessman's money, but he also broke his trust!

The same can be said of one who performs God's commandments for reasons which he thinks he understands. In a sense, he is doing business with God's money and trying to make his own profit. What right has he to do this? God commissioned him to perform the commandments and guaranteed a suitable reward. His duty is to perform the commandments, and that is all.

David *Ha-Melech* thus said, "All of Your commandments are [to be performed in] faith" (*Tehillim* 119:86). Faith is closely associated with reverence for God. The more one places one's trust and faith in Him, the greater his awe and reverence, and vice versa. He therefore declared, "The highest wisdom is reverence for God" (*ibid.* 111:10). Shelomo *Ha-Melech* echoed this when he said, "Be not wise in your own eyes. Revere God and turn from evil" (*Mishlei* 3:7). Both David *Ha-Melech* and Shelomo *Ha-Melech* were aware of the dangers of relying too heavily on one's own logic when it comes to serving God, for His reasons are beyond our understanding.

In dividing the commandments into different categories, our Sages distinguished between *mishpatim* and *chukim*. *Mishpatim* comprise those commandments which are rationally understandable, such as the prohibitions against manslaughter, kidnaping, theft, bearing false witness, and the like. Such forbidden behavior destroys the fabric of society and hence the possibility of God dwelling among men (see Rashi on *Vayikra* 19:11-12). *Chukim*, on the other hand, are commandments for which no explanation is offered, such as the dietary laws, laws of family purity, sacrifices in the Temple, blowing the shofar, and so on, acts which we perform solely out of obedience to Him Who commanded them.* The truth is, however, that God's reasons for the *mishpatim* also transcend human intelligence. In this, they are not different from the *chukim!* Speaking of this, David *Ha-Melech* again said, "I have chosen the path of faith, placing Your *mishpatim* on par [with Your *chukim*]!" (*Tehillim* 119:30).

As stated, however, one who performs the commandments with simple faith is vouchsafed special illumination from Heaven. This is similar to four people who become ill and call on a great doctor for treatment and medication. The first asks no questions; he trusts the doctor, relies on his experience and wisdom, and takes the medicines which are prescribed for him until his health returns.

The second patient interrogates the doctor, inquiring about every medicine and the reason why it is being prescribed. The doctor unsuspectingly answers his questions. When this patient returns home, however, he decides, on the basis of his limited understanding of what the doctor has explained to him, not to take some of the medicines prescribed. He takes some and does not bother to take others; his condition worsens; and he eventually dies.

---

* Actually, the Talmud and Midrash are filled with profound explanations regarding all the *chukim*. Still, it is recognized that these explanations are no more than a ladder that can reach up but never attain that which lies totally beyond human comprehension. The paradigm for this is the commandment of *parah adumah*, the "red heifer" (*Bemidbar* 19), concerning which Shelomo *Ha-Melech* wrote, "I said, 'I will acquire wisdom'; but it is far from me" (*Koheles* 7:23; *Bemidbar Rabbah* 19:3).

The third patient also inquires as to the reasons for each medicine. The doctor tells him, "Look what happened to your friend. I have made a new rule: I no longer reveal the reasons for the different medications I prescribe. If you follow my instructions and take them as I have prescribed, you will become well. If not, I am absolved of all liability."

The fourth patient follows the doctor's orders with full trust in his medical knowledge. On a second visit, though, he asks about the reason for a certain medicine. The doctor sees that he is not trying to outsmart him and does not intend to rely solely on his own judgment. He therefore breaks the new rule and answers all his questions, willingly telling him all he knows about each medicine.

David *Ha-Melech* alluded to this when he said, "My only wish: may my paths be firmly established in observing Your statutes. Then I will not be ashamed when I probe deeply into all Your commandments" (*Tehillim* 119:5-6). If we observe all God's commandments as *chukim*, we will receive Divine assistance in understanding their deeper reasons. This is what we request when we take up the shofar to fulfill God's will: "Teach me superior reason and knowledge in the merit of having performed Your commandments with pure faith!"

Ohel Ya'akov, *Beha'alosecha*

The Call of the Shofar: Awake, You Sleepers

These are the words of Rambam (Maimonides) concerning the commandment of blowing the shofar on Rosh Hashanah:

"Despite the fact that blowing the shofar on Rosh Hashanah is a Divine decree [for which no reason is given, its penetrating sound] contains a message: Awake, you sleepers, awake from your sleep! O you slumberers, awaken from your slumber! Examine your deeds and return in *teshuvah!* Remember your Creator, O you who forget the truth [because you are mesmerized] by that which is transient and temporary, and waste all your years running after vanity and emptiness... Look to your souls! Better your ways and correct your actions. Let every one of you abandon his wicked ways and unscrupulous thoughts..." (*Hilchos Teshuvah* 3:4).

To Hear the Message of the Shofar

The Talmud (*Rosh Hashanah* 27b) states a law: "One who blows the shofar into a pit has not fulfilled his obligation." The reason, explains the Tur (*Orach Chayim* 585) quoting the *Ba'al Halachos Gedolos,* is that the commandment of the Torah is not fulfilled by *blowing* the shofar, but rather by *hearing* its call. For this reason, one who blows the shofar into a pit has not fulfilled his obligation, for he cannot be sure whether he is hearing its call or its echo. This is why the blessing recited on the shofar is not "*lisko'a ba-shofar*—to blow the shofar" but rather "*lishmo'a kol shofar*—to hear the call of the shofar." One must clearly hear the call of the shofar, not its echo.

The words *lishmo'a kol shofar,* explained Rabbi Ya'akov Yosef of Polnoy, mean much more than "to hear the call of the shofar." They imply that we must "understand" and "receive" something. They imply that we are to "hear the message" and "learn the lesson" that the shofar wishes to teach us. This message must not be deflected in any way; it must be direct and it must penetrate to the quick.

The Rambam alluded to this when he wrote, "Despite the fact that the blowing of the shofar on Rosh Hashanah is a Divine decree [for which no reason is given, its penetrating sound] contains a message: 'Awake, you sleepers, awake from your sleep! O you slumberers, awaken from your slumber! Examine your deeds! Return in *teshuvah!* Remember your Creator!'" (*Hilchos Teshuvah* 3:4).

This can be illustrated with a parable: A man who wanted to become a goldsmith moved to a distant city to learn the craft. When he was ready to return to his own town, the new goldsmith consulted his mentor and made a list of the steps he had to remember in order to practice his profession: First, place the gold in the furnace; then fan the fire with a bellows; then remove the gold with tongs; and last, shape the gold with a hammer and chisel.

On his return home he purchased all the necessary materials and carried out all the steps in his list. He completed the entire procedure, but... nothing happened!

Why? When the master goldsmith dictated the list to his disciple, he had not mentioned lighting the fire in the furnace. It was such a simple act that he did not think it needed to be said...

The same applies to the commandment of shofar: One who blows the shofar into a pit, i.e., into a heart which has not been ignited by hearing its call and taking its message to heart, into a heart which has not been awakened by its ringing blast, has not fulfilled the essence of shofar.

Tzofnas Pane'ach, *Va-era*

Tekiah, Shevarim, Teruah, Tekiah

We are commanded by the Torah to sound the shofar on Rosh Hashanah. Three types of calls must be made in order to fulfill the commandment. *Tekiah,* the first and last call, consists of one long unbroken blast. *Shevarim,* the second, has three medium blasts, each lasting two or three seconds. The third, *teruah,* consists of a minimum of nine short, staccato blasts.

The Talmud (*Rosh Hashanah* 34a) states that the sounds of *shevarim* and *teruah* represent two different kinds of crying. The three medium blasts of *shevarim* are likened to prolonged moaning, while the nine staccato blasts of *teruah* are likened to uncontrollable sobbing. The single, unbroken *tekiah* represents the respite that both precedes and follows the intense weeping of *shevarim* and *teruah*.

Based on the *Zohar* (III:98b), the Ari (*Siddur Ha'Ari*) states that the three types of calls also parallel the three Patriarchs, Avraham, Yitzchak, and Ya'akov. Avraham, who embodies the attribute of Divine Lovingkindness, parallels the initial, single, unbroken *tekiah*. Yitzchak, who embodies the attribute of Divine Justice and Punishment, parallels the two types of weeping, *shevarim* and *teruah*. Ya'akov, who embodies Divine Mercy, the perfect blend of love and justice, parallels the final *tekiah*. (In the *Siddur Beis Ya'akov* and *Siddur Otzar Ha-Tefillos*, the following correspondence is also given: *tekiah*—Avraham, *shevarim*—Yitzchak, *teruah*—David, and *tekiah*—Ya'akov.)

In his work *Arvei Nachal*, the *Levushei Serad* explains the connection between the three Patriarchs and the shofar, in the following parable.

An emperor who ruled over many kingdoms had an only daughter who was perfect in every way and whom he loved with all his soul. When she reached marriageable age, everyone waited for the emperor to choose a prince from a royal house to be her bridegroom. But the emperor thought otherwise.

Since all the kings in his domain were subservient to him, he saw no difference between them and the common folk. He therefore decided to wed his daughter to the son of his beloved and intimate friend who lived in a distant province and who worked tirelessly for the emperor with all his heart and soul...

The emperor had only one concern: his friend's son was ignorant of court manners and customs, and would not know how to conduct himself with the daughter of an emperor. He therefore had the young man brought to his court for a few years, until he was well-versed in court manners. The wedding took place, and his friend's son returned home with his new wife.

Even after all this, the emperor's actions continued to be

the subject of much controversy. Numerous antagonists spoke against the commoner who dared to marry the emperor's daughter. They sent agents out to secretly spy on the new prince and devise ways to expose his shortcomings, returning to the emperor with damaging evidence against his new son-in-law.

Being just and righteous by nature, the emperor could not ignore their accusations. He fixed a date for a hearing, and sent notice to his son-in-law, advising him to be prepared to defend himself against the charges. Over the years, a number of such hearings were held. Occasionally the charges leveled against the son-in-law were extremely grave, and his defense flimsy. Were it not for the emperor's daughter, who spoke on her husband's behalf to defend him against his enemies, all would have been lost. But in the face of testimony given by the emperor's own beloved daughter, the accusers were silenced and their accusations were put to rest.

Things went on like this for some time, until the couple had a serious argument. Being essentially a simple and un-learned man, the prince got angry and struck his wife a number of times. Not only did he show no remorse for the suffering and injury he was causing her, but he even threw her out of his house and cast her bed on top of the rubbish heap in his backyard...

A letter was not long in arriving from the emperor. In the letter, the prince was informed that this time extremely serious allegations had been brought against him, and that he was in grave danger. He must plan his defense very carefully and make sure to bring evidence in his favor, because his very life was now hanging in the balance. The emperor added that he was to bring along his wife, for she was his only daughter and it had been some time since he had had the pleasure of seeing her and enjoying her company.

As the prince read the letter, his heart pounded and he began to tremble uncontrollably. He broke into a cold sweat, his knees shook, and his teeth chattered. "Woe is me!" he began to groan. "What have I done! How will I defend myself now? On previous occasions, when lesser charges were leveled against me, I was saved only because my wife spoke up for me. Now, even if I placate her, even if I bring her back into my house and honor her in a way that befits her station— she is still black and blue all over! How can I face the emperor with her? But without her, I cannot appear before him either..."

He immediately went to his father and burst into tears in front of him. "Dear merciful and compassionate father, the time has come when you must save me!" he wept. "I have no one else to stand up for me. You are the emperor's dear and intimate friend. You have served him selflessly and fought for his honor all the days of your life. Surely if you stand before him and speak in my defense, he will listen to you!"

The father agreed, but when he beheld the emperor's daughter, he also began to weep. "Woe is me! How dare I come before the emperor and beg him to have mercy on you? Look what you have done to his daughter! The emperor will surely ask me how I can look upon his daughter's suffering with such indifference. His friendship towards me will be far outweighed by his love for his daughter!"

"Then what shall we do?" the prince cried.

"I will journey to the emperor," answered his father, "and ask him to postpone the trial for a while. In the meantime, you must placate your wife. Treat her with kindness. Get her medical care. Restore her natural beauty and thereby win her back. Convert her from an enemy to a friend. She will then accompany you as before, and together we will arouse the emperor's kindness and shut the mouths of the accusers!"

What is the message of this parable? The emperor is God, the Supreme King, the Holy One, blessed be He, whose greatness and power is infinite and without end, and before whom all Creation is as naught. The emperor's beloved only daughter is our holy Torah. She is perfect (*shalem*) in every way, as it is written, "She is a tree of life for those who grasp Her. Fortunate are those who support Her. Her ways are ways of pleasantness and all Her paths are peace (shalom)" (Mishlei 3:17). The accusers are the angels on high. When God was about to give the Torah to Moshe on Mount Sinai, it was these angels who protested, "God, our Master, Your Name is too powerful to rule on the earth. Establish it in the heavens above... What is mortal man that You think of him, and the finest human that You even consider him?" (Tehillim 8:2, 5). God overruled the angels, however, and preferred giving the Torah to His beloved nation, the children of Avraham, Yitzchak, and Ya'akov.

Every year these angels rise up against us and accuse us before God's Throne of Judgment: "Your children have sinned!" Out of love for us, God warns us ahead of time about the approaching judgment, as it is written, "He declares His word to Ya'akov, His statutes and His judgments to Yisrael" (Tehillim 147:19). He warns us to be prepared for Rosh Hashanah, the Day of Judgment. Only by repenting our wrongdoings can we hope to find favor in His eyes and transform the attribute of Divine Justice to Mercy and Lovingkindness.

Even when we are unworthy of finding favor in His eyes, we turn to the Torah, the daughter of the Emperor, beseeching her in our Selichos, "Plead for us!" After the Torah herself speaks in our behalf, the accusers of our people are silenced.

All of this is true, however, only when we honor the Torah as befits her stature as the daughter of the Holy King. When we argue and resist the Torah, mistreat her, cast her away, turn our backs on her, and revile her, what hope do we have? For the Torah is a complete spiritual structure, the counterpart of the Temple on high and of the human body below. Paralleling the body with its 248 limbs and 365 sinews and veins, the Torah has 248 positive commandments and 365 negative commandments. One who transgresses any of these, wounds his own soul and damages the Torah. When, in addition to this, he studies Torah for ulterior motives, such as the desire to win honor and power, he is casting her onto a rubbish heap, i.e. handing her over to the "shells" of evil which have no life of their own but merely live parasitically off the scraps of holiness which they are able to steal.

The Day of Judgment arrives. Our Father in Heaven warns us to be prepared. He expresses His desire to behold His daughter, the Torah we have learned throughout the year. This Torah learning is His Delight. With it, He sustains heaven and earth...

My holy brothers, children of Hashem, this must cause us to be gripped by uncontrollable trembling. Woe to us! How shall we not lament? How awesome is the Day of Judgment! It is at hand! How awesome is the Day of God's Rebuke! How can a person hope to escape unscathed? In previous generations we relied on our righteous *tzaddikim* who learned the Torah with unremitting self-sacrifice. What shall we do now? Our Torah learning cannot plead our case before the Holy One. It is too sorely lacking. It sits outcast on the rubbish heap, thrust away among the "shells." What shall we say? How can we hope to vindicate ourselves before God?

Now, more than ever, we must turn to our holy forefathers, Avraham, Yitzchak, and Ya'akov, as we say in the *Selichos*, "Rise up, you who sleep in [the Cave of] Machpelah, and come to my rescue! Cry out to God with me! With your righteous strength, persuade Him in my behalf!" The Patriarchs and Matriarchs are buried in the holy city of Hebron, in the Cave of Machpelah which Avraham purchased. We beseech them to appear with us before God and to speak in our behalf.

This is the connection between the three Patriarchs and the shofar. With the long, unbroken *tekiah*, we arouse our father Avraham, who embodies the attribute of Divine Lovingkindness. With the three measured blasts of *shevarim* and the nine staccato blasts of *teruah*, we arouse our father Yitzchak, who embodies the attribute of Divine Justice. With the final *tekiah*, we arouse our father Ya'akov, who embodies the attribute of Divine Mercy. And we beseech them to rise and speak in our behalf, for we have no one upon whom we can rely, except them. They are God's beloved. Surely, He will not turn them away empty-handed! And thus it was for many generations.

Even now, out of their great love and compassion for their descendants, our ancestors would be more than willing to speak in our behalf. There is only one problem. A true story will clarify.

Eliyahu *Ha-Navi* once appeared to a certain rabbi in the holy city of Safed. It was Rosh Hashanah, and the rabbi was a student of the holy Ari, Rabbi Yitzchak Luria. Eliyahu appeared to him and said, "For the sake of God, make sure to pray more strongly than ever. You must intend to sacrifice your very lives to arouse Hashem's mercy. For the accusation above has become so powerful that Michael, God's Angel of Lovingkindness who is appointed to speak on Israel's behalf, has been silenced!"

"But it is known that this year our Torah learning has intensified a hundredfold," the rabbi replied.

"The problem is," Eliyahu replied, "that most of that Torah was learned without pure intent. It has therefore been taken by the 'shells.' If the Accuser has his way, it will be used against you. He has brought it up to the High Court above. The little bit of pure Torah which Michael has brought with him is not enough to divert the impending catastrophe."

"And what does our father Avraham say?" the rabbi rejoined. "He is the bedrock of the Jewish people. Why does he not stand in heaven and plead our case?"

"Avraham admits that he is ashamed. Seeing what has become of the Torah, he is prevented from pleading for Divine Mercy. He is afraid that Hashem will ask him how he can look upon the disgrace and suffering of the Torah with such indifference. He is afraid that Hashem's affection for him will be far outweighed by His love for the Torah!"

When the rabbi heard this, he stood up with awesome fear

and trembling and cried out in a loud voice: "Hashem's people! Be strong! Let us gather strength! Let us do *teshuvah*. Let us return and repent all our sins between man and his fellow man and between man and God. For Hashem is sorely displeased with us. The accusers are gaining the upper hand. Our advocate in heaven has been silenced. God forbid, we are being judged guilty in the Heavenly court!

"But it is not too late. Repent! Return to Hashem. Vow to serve Him wholeheartedly in this life and in eternity. Affirm that all other thoughts and motives are hereby nullified. Repent with all your hearts. Even if you think you have been righteous, do not let this prevent you from pouring your hearts out and asking His forgiveness, not only for yourselves, but for our people, and for the holy *Shechinah*. Return now, before it is too late. Perhaps Hashem will withdraw from the fierceness of His Anger and revoke all evil decrees against His people!"

Thus he spoke and admonished his congregation and himself, until the hearts of all present were aroused to genuine weeping and supplication. And then Eliyahu *Ha-Navi* appeared to him again. This time, however, he informed him that with the power of their repentance, our father Avraham had been able to rise up to the Heavenly court and come before the Holy One, blessed be He. He had been successful in diverting the judgment against Israel until Yom Kippur! In the meantime, all would be given another chance to prove their resolve. Their Torah learning during the Ten Days of Repentance would be pure and sincere. In the merit of this, all the Torah which had been given over to the "shells" of evil would be extricated and elevated into holiness!

Arvei Nachal 2:108

The Musaf Service

הִנְנִי הֶעָנִי מִמַּעַשׂ

"Behold, I am poor in deed."

The Maggid of Lublin commented on these words which the *ba'al tefillah* says before the Musaf service: How should he see himself as he stands before Hashem pleading for the entire congregation? He should liken himself to a man whose legs have become paralyzed, God forbid, who awakens in the middle of the night and sees a reddish hue illuminating the night sky outside his window—a fire has broken out in the city! A fire has broken out! The house is constructed of wood, its roof is covered with straw, and the entire household is sleeping! Immediately he begins shouting loudly: "Get up, hurry, wake up! Run for your lives! Save me as well, take me with you as you escape!"

One who leads the prayers must know and recognize his insignificance. Like the great prophets of old, he is nothing more than an alarm to awaken the congregation to cry out and return in *teshuvah*, as it is written, "Cry out your lungs, do not hold back! Raise your voice like the shofar..." (*Yeshayahu* 58:1).

You are no more than a shofar which, in itself, has very little significance; it is only of value when it is used to awaken people to *teshuvah*. When they then awaken, they will save you as well...

Ohel Ya'akov

כִּי חוֹטֵא וּפוֹשֵׁעַ אָנִי

"For I am a sinner and a betrayer [of Your trust]."

Rabbi Moshe of Kobrin said: A *ba'al tefillah* really has no reason to be haughty. To what can he be compared? To a criminal who lived in a certain country... when the people of this country rebelled against their great and exalted king, the king was angered and decided to attack them with a massive army. As the king's army approached, the rebels realized that there was no choice but to surrender. They suddenly became afraid of the consequences of their actions. They knew, as well, that one of them would have to represent them, but they were afraid that the king would behead him.

But this criminal had already committed a grave and serious crime against the king. His fate had already been sealed once and for all. He said to his fellow countrymen: "Lay your fears to rest. I will go and try to placate the king. I have nothing to lose. My fate has already been decided..."

Toras Avos

בְּאֵין מֵלִיץ יֹשֶׁר מוּל מַגִּיד פֶּשַׁע
"No advocate to stand up against the prosecutor..."

Said the Maggid of Rotzky: To what can this be likened? Under normal circumstances, when a man is brought to trial, the judge may wish to intervene and suggest a compromise between the prosecution and the defense. When, however, the accused is charged with having disgraced the king, the judge may not intervene on his behalf. He may not compromise one iota on the king's honor. Only the king himself is allowed to forgive and grant pardon.

We have rebelled against Hashem and disgraced His honor. We come before His court, but there is "no advocate to stand up against the prosecutor." Not even Michael, Israel's advocate in heaven, may stand up for us when we have falsified our very mission as a nation. We have no choice but to ask the King Himself to intervene and champion our cause.

The Heavenly trial takes place in court, however, while the King is in His private quarters. How can we reach Him and request His intervention in our case?

Through the call of the shofar! It pierces the firmaments and sunders the curtains between us and our Father in Heaven. It carries our despair and our tearful cries up to the highest heavens. It prostrates itself before our King and lays all our prayers and supplications before Him. With it, the holy King will sweeten our judgment!

Serigi Tova, *Derush* 3

מִי יֵעָשֵׁר וּמִי יֵעָנִי

"Who will become wealthy and who will become poor."

The Maggid of Rotzky was called in to resolve a dispute between two Jewish merchants. After he heard their respective claims, he told them the following parable:

A certain man had a bank account with quite a large overdraft. Shabbos was approaching, and he needed money to make the necessary purchases. He went to the bank, made out a check to himself, and walked up to the teller. "I am very sorry, sir," was the reply, "but this account lacks the necessary funds to cover your check."

"What shall I do?" the man asked in despair.

"Perhaps you could ask the bank manager to initial the check."

But the man began pleading with the teller instead. "Please, do me a favor and have compassion. Don't turn me away empty-handed!"

The clerk paid no heed: "I'm sorry, but this is bank policy."

With no alternative, the man approached the bank manager, and explained that he had temporarily fallen behind. He promised to balance his books in good time, and the manager agreed to initial the check.

The man now returned to the teller's window, relaxed and sure of himself. Now that his check had the manager's initials on it, any clerk would be obligated to honor it.

The lesson: Merchants are constantly running after buyers and fighting among themselves. They act as though the keys to their livelihoods were in their hands. But our Sages have taught us that the key is in Hashem's hands alone. Nothing else will help. You must turn to Him, directly. You too will be required to justify your overdrafts, but at least you can rest assured that He will give you credit in the meantime.

A person's livelihood for the entire year is ordained on Rosh Hashanah. On Rosh Hashanah, he signs his check and presents it to the Holy One. He can then cash it with any "clerk" without the slightest problem. But he must first turn to Him, for it is to Him alone that we are obligated to plead. Everything depends upon Him!

Serigi Nefishi, Derush 8

כִּי לֹא תַחְפֹּץ בְּמוֹת הַמֵּת, כִּי אִם בְּשׁוּבוֹ מִדְּרָכָיו וְחָיָה

"You do not desire the death of the dead man, but that he return from his ways and live."

The Maggid of Dubno asked: Would we even consider for a moment that God wants the dead man to die? Why should God tell the prophet to inform us: "Do I wish the death of the wicked man? Let him only return from his [crooked] ways and live!" (*Yechezkel* 18:23).

This same question can be asked about a well-known *midrash* (*Bereshis Rabbah* 2:5). On the verses, "The earth was void and without form... God said: Let there be light!" (*Bereshis* 1:2-3), Rabbi Abbahu comments: "*The earth was void and without form* alludes to the wicked. *Let there be light* alludes to the righteous. But I am still not certain which of these God prefers! Does He prefer the actions of the wicked or the actions of the righteous? Then in the next verse we read, 'God saw that the light was good' (*ibid.* 1:4). Now I know that He prefers the actions of the righteous and has no pleasure from the actions of the wicked."

Here again, we can ask the same question. Is it even thinkable that God would prefer the actions of the wicked?

The answer should be clear from a *midrash* (*Shemos Rabbah* 7:4) concerning the plagues which God inflicted upon the Egyptians: A king once planted an orchard with fruit trees as well as non-fruit-bearing trees. His servants asked him, "What pleasure does the king have from these non-fruit-bearing trees?" He replied, "I need them just as much as I need the others. For without non-fruit-bearing trees, where would I get wood to burn for the bathhouses and the ovens?" The *midrash* now concludes: "Just as God's praises rise up from the mouths of the righteous in the Garden of Eden, so also do His praises rise up from the mouths of the wicked in Gehinnom!"

This is also the meaning of the *mishnah:* "All that God created in His world, He created only for His glory" (*Pirkei Avos* 6:11). That is, even that which seems intrinsically bad and without purpose was created for God's glory.

The Maggid then told a parable about two merchants: One of them would import merchandise from a neighboring country and pay all the customs duties at the border, while the other would concoct all kinds of schemes to elude the authorities and cross the border without paying.

One might think that it is only the first merchant, an upright citizen, who brings glory to the king, and that the second, an outright thief, brings disgrace. This would be correct, if the eyes of the king and his guards were not following the second fellow's actions very carefully. But if the royal police keep close watch on him, and intentionally allow him to slip by the customs officials, once, twice, even three times, and when they finally arrest him they collect all the taxes and fines for every time he cheated the government; and if they incarcerate him and publicly punish him, so that everyone will hear and take heed, it is possible to say that the king's glory is magnified no less, and perhaps even more, by the second merchant than by the first!

It is certainly true that God's glory is magnified by the righteous who perform His commandments wholeheartedly and with pure intent. As we learn from the above-mentioned sources, however, the same is true when the wicked are punished. What, then, is the difference between them? The difference is simple, and it is alluded to in the parable brought above: The righteous are like fruit trees. They give forth their produce while they are still alive and growing. The wicked are like non-fruit-bearing trees. They are useful only when they are cut down!

This is what God means when He says, "Do I wish the death of the wicked man?" Certainly, with his death, and with the punishments that will be visited upon him, God's Name will be sanctified. Still, God does not prefer to have His Name sanctified this way. He prefers that the wicked man only "return from his ways and live," by sanctifying God's Name while alive!

Ohel Ya'akov, *Va-Era*

בְּנַפְשׁוֹ יָבִיא לַחְמוֹ
"He earns his livelihood with his soul."

A person must be careful indeed that the livelihood he earns not be in exchange for his soul! The author of *Michtav Me-Eliyahu*, Rabbi Eliyahu Dessler, once witnessed a scene which brings this point home forcefully. He writes the following account:

Many years ago, while wandering around the cold northern countries, I beheld a pack of hungry wolves running through a snow-covered forest in search of food. When they found the carcass of a small animal, they began scrambling and pushing at each other in order to pounce on its flesh. In the mad scramble, though, not one of them could get at it. Instead, they bit at each other and fought with each other until they were all wounded and bleeding.

They fought over the carcass until they were strewn about on the snow without the strength to move. Only a few, the strongest among them, still waited to pounce on the carcass. Not a moment passed before these too were locked in mortal combat with one another. Again, they bit and tore at each other's flesh. In the end, one particularly strong one was victorious. Bloody and torn, he clenched the carcass in his jaws and fled.

I contemplated what I had just seen. I saw the victor running in the distance, leaving a trail of blood behind him... This blood, I thought to myself, is his soul, concerning which it is written, "He earns his livelihood with [in exchange for] his soul."

My attention focused on the remaining wolves. Their wounds were more numerous and severe than his. Their blood was oozing and their strength as well. What did they gain with all their fighting? Theirs was the disgrace of the loser. Their own friend had struck them and was sitting off at a distance enjoying the spoils. They were maimed and hungry. Having fought in order to satisfy their hunger, they were more hungry than when they began...

Now, when I contemplate the passion with which people go after material pleasures, I remember those wolves. In effect, their story is no more than an allegory for human beings. In human society, as well, the victor very often emerges a spiritual cripple. He is tired and exhausted, and his victory is not worth very much. His hunger for material goods will never really be satisfied. This is the portion of the victor. And the portion of the loser? Just consider that most people end up being losers in the competition, sacrifices on the altar of material aspirations.

The lesson: One who goes after purely material pleasures is the saddest of all creatures.

Michtav Me-Eliyahu

"...with his soul."

The famed Chasam Sofer, Rabbi Moshe Sofer of Pressburg, told the following parable.

Once there was a man who was always unemployed. He had never known success, and his wife bore the yoke of supporting the family. At times, unable to hold herself back, she would shout at him angrily, "Why don't you go out and get a job? Instead of wasting your life, why can't you support the family!"

But instead of looking for a regular job, he would seek one which would make him a rich man overnight. One day, he was told that if he made a long journey across the distant mountains, he would find diamonds in great abundance. If he were willing to endanger himself by going there just once, he would never need to work again! He decided to take the chance, and started off on his journey to the Black Mountains.

The Black Mountains were always covered with dark clouds and mist. Before starting out on his climb, therefore, he was advised to purchase a supply of candles. But in the store each candle cost ten dinars! The man was astonished.

Then he inquired about the price that diamonds fetched locally. He was shown a box full of diamonds: the entire box sold for pennies.

The man began to think: This is a real opportunity! If diamonds, which are sold here so cheaply, are worth so much more back home, why, these candles must be worth a fortune there!"

And so he bought all the candles the store had in stock. He worked day and night to make sure he acquired every single candle in town, and even hired wagons to transport the merchandise. He himself hurried ahead of them to tell his wife the good news.

"Nu?" his wife asked when she saw him. "Where are the diamonds?"

"I have a much more valuable commodity!" he exclaimed.

"Something worth many times the price of diamonds."

His wife waited to see this valuable merchandise. In the meantime, the wagons slowly made their way to his town. As the sun beat down on them, the tallow melted; then spoiled and began to stink. In the end, he even lost the few pennies he could have earned from the candles.

The man had lost all his money, his time, and the trouble he spent traveling. He lost everything he put into buying the candles, hiring the wagons, and paying their drivers.

"If you had at least brought home one bag of diamonds," his wife lamented, "even a single diamond... we would have been rich... But once a fool, always a fool..."

The moral: The soul descends to the "Black Mountains" of this world, a place of darkness and clouds, in order to learn Torah and perform a few commandments, with the goal in mind to end up with a few precious "diamonds," which are relatively easy to acquire. Of course, it is necessary to buy a few "candles," basic material goods which make it possible to live in this world. These "candles," however, are not ends in themselves, but only means. They are needed to help us see and gather more and more "diamonds." How pathetic is the person who spends his entire fortune on "candles"! In the end, when he returns to his place Above, he shows up empty-handed. The "candles" melt and stink, and he has nothing to show for all his effort...

Chasam Sofer on the Torah, *Shelach*

"...his livelihood with his soul."

It is known that this world is only a vestibule before the World-to-Come (*Pirkei Avos* 4:21). It is known that one of the things for which we collect "interest" in this world (while the "capital" is reserved for the World-to-Come) is the study of Torah (*Shabbos* 127a). It is known that one hour in repentance and good deeds in this world is better than all the life in the World-to-Come (*Pirkei Avos* 4:22). All this is known. Still, no one seems to have time to prepare for the next world, to acquire eternity for their souls. People are so completely involved in their business, in making a living, that the bread they earn is in exchange for forsaking their soul...

The Maggid of Dubno composed the following parable in honor of these unfortunates.

There was once a youth who, although not the smartest among his friends, nevertheless had an extremely good heart. He was hired as a servant in the home of one of the wealthiest men in a large city far from his hometown. One day, when he had some spare time, he decided to take a stroll through the city streets. He came to the public park, went in, and sat down on one of the benches.

The man on the other end of the bench studied him for a long time, noting that the boy was a stranger in town, young, good-hearted, and naïve. He came over to him and hugged him, crying, "My relative! What are you doing here? You are my own flesh and blood, one of my family!"

The lad was taken aback. He had never heard about having family in this distant place. He accompanied his new-found "relative" home, and was introduced to the "family." Out of the goodness of his heart, he began to visit them every day during his time off, and would help them with household chores and errands.

The neighbors could not help noticing the self-sacrifice with which the boy helped his relatives, and it was not long until they revealed to him that they were also his relatives! Simple-minded and good-hearted as he was, he rejoiced in finding so many new family members. He began to visit their homes daily as well, and to clean and run errands for them too.

The boy's employer noticed that he was absent from work more and more, and that he was run-down and exhausted. Since he understood the boy's nature very well, he realized what must be happening and decided to open his eyes. "I understand that you have found many relatives here," he began casually.

"Oh, yes, it is true!" the boy answered enthusiastically.

"And you, um... help them quite a bit?" the employer continued.

"Certainly! They are my family, after all."

"It's very nice that you are so kind to them, but tell me—what do you receive from them in return?" the employer inquired.

The boy was embarrassed at the question. "Oh, it wouldn't be right to take money," he protested. "After all, one must be devoted to his relatives. I only wish I could do so all my days!"

"But if you receive nothing from them in return," the employer continued, "and yet you give freely of your time and energy to them, who is to say that they really are your relatives? Perhaps, out of a desire to take advantage of the goodness of your heart, they have lied to you?"

The boy was taken aback. As he began to consider his employer's words, his eyes were opened, and he realized the sad truth. He had been tricked. He resumed working full-time for his employer whose bread he ate, in whose house he lived, and from whom he received his wages.

The moral: The world deceives a person into thinking that he has innumerable "relatives": his house, his store, his business, etc. He invests all his time and energy, thought and talent, in these relatives. In this way, they steal everything he has. But Shelomo *Ha-Melech* whispers in his ears, "What profit does a man have from all the work he does under the sun?" (*Koheles* 1:3). Certainly, your business dealings profit from you, but what profit do you receive from your business dealings? Perhaps, like those "relatives," they have deceived you, pulled you along, and taken advantage of you. When they are finished with you, they will leave you feeling totally empty

and dissipated. In the meantime, you have lost out by aban-
doning the Torah and the commandments which hold so
much material and spiritual happiness and good fortune in
store, in this world and the next. Do not earn your livelihood
in exchange for forsaking your soul!

Kol Negidim 96

וְכַחֲלוֹם יָעוּף
"[Life is] like a fleeting dream."

The Maggid of Kaminetz asked: Everybody knows that life is
like a fleeting dream, but who says that this is so bad? Can't
a dream also be good and pleasant, beautiful and enjoyable?
He answered with a chilling parable:

The angel of success was once traveling along when he
met the angel of dreams. They decided to travel to their
destination together. When they arrived at the outskirts of a
certain city, the sun was setting. "Night was created only for
sleep," said the angel of success, yawning. "Let us rest for the
night and start fresh in the morning!"

"You may work best during the day," the angel of dreams
replied, "but the night is my time. Sleep soundly while I go to
work—we'll meet in the morning."

In good spirits, the angel of dreams decides to play a
practical joke. He turns into the first elegant house he sees,
the house of one of the most prominent merchants in town.
Unannounced, he enters.

In the house, amidst the elegant furniture and crystal
chandeliers, there are signs of acute poverty. It has been only
a few weeks since the owner lost all his money and became a
pauper overnight. There is no bread to eat. Still, all the members of the family suffer silently. They hide their destitution
from the eyes of the world, hoping that good times will
return, and they will regain their former status. Nobody
would ever have to know what happened.

The angel of dreams comes to this merchant and grants

him a wonderful dream. He dreams that he has tremendous success in his business. He rises again to the heights of affluence. His store is stocked with the best merchandise. Customers stream in, order large quantities of goods, and pay in cash! As his business expands, his life circumstances improve. Smiles return to the faces of his children. He sits down to a sumptuous afternoon meal with them, before a table laden with all the delicacies in the world. He motions to begin the meal when all of a sudden one of his workers bursts into his house.

"What is the matter?" the rich man asks.

"Quickly!" the servant answers panting. "Thieves have broken into the store, and they're stealing all the money and looting the merchandise!"

The merchant jumps up and runs to his store. Right in front of his eyes he see the terrible sight. He raises his voice to tell them to stop, but the robbers jump on him and beat him relentlessly. He screams, "Save me, save me! All my money is lost, all my wealth is gone!"

His cries break the silence of the night and awaken the children, who also begin to cry. "Bread, bread!" they moan. "We are starving!"

The neighbors hear. One by one, they gather, enter the house, and are struck with the utter poverty. The rich merchant and his family are completely ashamed. The angel of dreams revels and rejoices that his plan has worked so well. He takes his leave of the agitated neighbors and humiliated family. He returns to the outskirts of the city and joins his friend, the angel of success. With a big grin on his face, he relates how he exposed the misery of the formerly wealthy merchant by means of a deceptive dream.

The angel of success scolded and rebuked him soundly. "You heartless fiend! How could you do such a cruel trick? Wasn't it enough that the wheel of fortune had turned against him? You had to come and add salt to his wounds, by exposing him to all his neighbors? How will you justify yourself in front of God?"

The angel of dreams also became incensed. He wouldn't allow the angel of success to exhibit such self-righteousness. "And you," he demanded, "do you think you are better than I?"

"Certainly," the angel of success answered. "For I grant happiness to people, true happiness—not imaginary, sham happiness—and while they are awake, not in their dreams!"

"Ha!" the angel of dreams cried. "You are actually a thousand times worse than I! My practical jokes last but a few moments. In his dream, that merchant felt as if his lucky star had shone. True, as a result of my dream, he felt embarrassment and shame, but it also made his poverty known to others so that they could help him. Now he and his family need no longer suffer the pangs of hunger. You, on the other hand—you self-righteous scoundrel—you claim to bring a person real happiness and prosperity, not imaginary. You make his head spin with thoughts of success. His business becomes his life. All day long he rushes around buying and selling. He has no rest or serenity. He accumulates tremendous wealth, real substance, tangible riches. And suddenly, the end comes! If the wheel of fortune does not turn on him and take his fortune away from him, death comes and takes him away from his fortune. The moment comes, he closes his eyes, and when he opens them again, in the next world, he realizes that all the success of a lifetime was nothing but a seventy-year-long dream. It was not a dream that lasted a few moments, while he was fast asleep, but a dream that ate up all the days and years of his life. Now I ask you, which of us is worse? Which of us is more cruel? Which taunts his victims more?"

Ateres Tzevi, *Derush Yud*

Verses of Kingship (Malchuyos)

לְדוֹר וָדוֹר הַמְלִיכוּ לָאֵ-ל, כִּי הוּא לְבַדּוֹ מָרוֹם וְקָדוֹשׁ

"In each generation they declare His Sovereignty, though He alone is exalted and holy."

Though we declare God's Sovereignty in every generation, we must know and recognize full well that we are totally incapable of grasping or understanding His true Sovereignty. He is "exalted" far beyond our grasp, "holy," transcendent and separate from anything we can know.

Our knowledge of Hashem resembles that of the child in the parable told by *Rabbenu* Bachyei ibn Pakuda in his *Chovos Ha-Levavos*:

Imagine your condition here on earth as being like that of a child who was born in a dungeon belonging to the king. The king took pity on the infant and ordered that he be provided with everything necessary for his well-being until he grew to full physical and mental maturity. In the meantime, the child had no knowledge of anything except the prison and all it contained. A royal officer would visit him regularly with everything he needed—candles for light, food and drink, clothing and shoes. He also informed him that he was a servant of the king, and that the prison and all it contained, as well as the food brought him, belonged to the king. The child was therefore obligated, explained the officer, to thank his royal benefactor and praise him.

The youth replied, "I praise the owner of the dungeon who has taken me as his servant, singled me out for all his bounties, and favored me with special notice and regard."

Said the officer, "Do not speak thus lest you sin. For the royal domain does not consist of this dungeon alone. The king's extended territories infinitely exceed this limited area. Nor are you his only servant, for he has countless servants.

Furthermore, the kindnesses he has bestowed upon you are insignificant compared to those he has bestowed upon others. The concern he has shown you is negligible compared to the concern he has shown others."

"I know nothing of what you have mentioned," the youth replied. "As for the king, I can understand only what I myself have experienced of his goodness and his sovereignty."

The officer then said to the youth, "Then say: 'I praise the supreme king to whose sovereignty there is no end and whose goodness and kindness are without limit. I am insignificant among the multitudes of his hosts. I am naught in relation to his omnipotence.'"

The youth now understood something of the king that he never understood before. His regard for the king's exaltedness grew. Reverence for him permeated his heart. Owing to the youth's realization of the king's exaltedness and his own utter insignificance, the royal goodness and kindnesses extended to him, as well as the gifts bestowed upon him, were magnified in his eyes.

Chovos Ha-Levavos 2:6

וַאֲנַחְנוּ כּוֹרְעִים וּמִשְׁתַּחֲוִים וּמוֹדִים

"As for us, we bow down, prostrate ourselves, and offer thanks..."

Said the Maggid of Horodna: The measure of all Divine service is the degree of submission a person experiences before the Holy One. In relations with our fellowman, one who bows down and submits himself demonstrates that he is below his fellow. Submission before the Holy One, on the other hand, reveals a person's greatness. The more he submits, the more exalted he is and the greater his soul. The Sages thus said: "A Jew who prays, bows at the beginning and at the end [of the *Amidah*]. A *Kohen Gadol* bows down at the end of each blessing. A king bows down and does not rise up for the entire prayer!" (*Berachos* 34b).

This is what David *Ha-Melech* meant when he said to his wife Michal, after he leapt and danced in honor of Hashem, "It was before God, Who chose me above your father and above all his house, to appoint me prince over God's people, over Israel"—that is, Who lifted me up to the greatest heights a human being can attain—"It is before God that I will make merry. And I will make even lighter of my own honor. I will be extremely insignificant in my own eyes" (II *Shemuel* 6:21). With this David showed his true greatness!

We see, then, that true submission is uplifting. This can best be understood with a parable.

A certain minister was very close to the king. Because of this, a rival official in the king's court hated him, and sought to denounce him before the king. This rival slandered him by spreading the false rumor that he was not from a noble family: that he had dared to lie about his lineage.

The minister sought counsel with a trusted friend, a wise and understanding man. "How can I protect myself against this charge?" he asked.

The wise man answered with a question: "And what is the truth? Are you of noble lineage or not?"

"I will tell you the truth," the minister answered. "I do not know myself if I am or not!"

The wise man said, "Let us therefore investigate this, and then we shall know where we stand."

They went to the royal registry and requested to be shown the records. As they sat down and looked through them, they discovered that the minister was indeed not of noble lineage. To make things worse, next to his family name was written the word *Mujik*, meaning "indentured servant"!

The wise man erased the word *Mujik*, and then wrote *Mujik* again in its place. "What have you done?" the minister asked. "As long as you are erasing the word, you should write *Noble Family* in its place!"

The wise man answered, "Do not think that we are the

only ones who will investigate your lineage. The accuser will slander you, and the authorities will examine these records. If they find the words *Noble Family* written over an erased word, they will suspect you! But now, when they see the word *Mujik* written over another word, they will suspect your accuser of having erased *Noble Family* and written *Mujik...*"

The moral: When a person submits himself before his Creator, he reveals the greatness and loftiness of his own soul. The more he submits, the greater he proves himself to be. This is the meaning of what we say when we bow in the *Aleinu* prayer: "As for us, we bow down, prostrate ourselves, and offer thanks before the Supreme King of all kings, the Holy One, blessed be He." In the merit of this submission, not only Israel, but the entire world will submit to the Holy One and be elevated beyond their present level. The *Aleinu* prayer thus continues telling how the time will come when "the entire world will finally be rectified and reach perfection under the sovereignty of the Almighty God. [At that time,] all mortals will call upon His Name, and all the wicked of the world will turn and return to Him. All the inhabitants of the earth will recognize [the truth] and realize: It is to Him alone that every knee must bend and every tongue must swear [eternal allegiance]... They will bow and fall down before Him. They will pay homage to the Glory of His Name. All will accept upon themselves the yoke of His Absolute Sovereignty."

Divrei Haskel 6

שְׁמַע יִשְׂרָאֵל ה' אֱלֹקֵינוּ ה' אֶחָד
"Hear O Israel: Hashem is our God, Hashem the One and Only."

The Maggid of Kaminetz told the following parable:
There was once a man who visited a hospital for the first

time. He saw sick people lying in their beds in all the wards except one. In that one, he saw patients leisurely eating a satisfying repast. He said to himself: This is the way to be healthy!

He continued on to the operating room. There he beheld patients undergoing difficult surgery. Doctors stood over them working frantically to amputate their limbs! He shuddered and said to his attendant, "What a difference between the doctors of the previous ward and this one! Those were compassionate, caring for the welfare of their patients and nourishing them with the finest foods. These doctors are wild men, abusing the patients placed under their care without the slightest compassion!"

The attendant smiled and replied, "You may be surprised to hear that the same doctor runs both wards. He is a specialist, the greatest in his field. He is compassionate and gracious, and the welfare of his patients is his only concern! There are, however, patients who require drastic surgery. This is the only way they can be treated and healed. The doctor therefore amputates their limbs, and does what he must do for their own good, in order to save their lives. Then there are the patients who are convalescing after surgery. Their treatment consists of total rest, eating and drinking..."

We are like this visitor. When we see what happens to some people, we are shocked. One is wealthy and the other poor; one is serene and the other bears affliction; but the holy Torah teaches us, "Hear O Israel," understand and know, "Hashem is our God." The Divine attribute of Mercy is alluded to in Hashem's four-letter Name (*Yod-Keh-Vav-Keh*), as well as the Divine attribute of Justice associated with the name Elokim. Both flow from the fact that "Hashem is the One and Only." He Himself is the Source of compassion, while the differences we experience depend upon us, His patients. Only He knows what we need for a complete recovery. Only He knows the root of our souls, the purpose for which we were born, our needs, and what is good for us!

Ateres Tzevi, *Derush 4*

אִם כְּבָנִים אִם כַּעֲבָדִים

"If [we are worthy to be judged] as Your children, have mercy on us as a father has mercy on his children! If as Your servants, our eyes are fixed on You until You absolve us and make our sentence [shine forth] like light..."

On the one hand we are Hashem's children, while on the other, we are His servants. How exactly are we to understand this difference? Rabbi Zalman Sender Kahana Shapira of Krinik clarified this distinction in a simple yet extraordinarily profound way.

Take a wealthy businessman in his prime who does not rest by night or day, and ask him: "What is the purpose of all this effort and activity? Why don't you live a quieter and simpler existence? The way things are now, you have enough money to last you for the next few hundred years!"

He will answer, "I have many children. I want to insure their future. I want to bequeath a well-founded and growing business to each and every one of them."

This is a logical answer. The entire business is for his children's welfare.

But what if he has no children? What will his answer be? Will he say that he has numerous administrators and clerks who rely on him for their daily bread? Does he run the entire enterprise for their sake? I think not. For one may hire an entire staff of workers for the sake of a business, but never run an entire business in order to employ a staff of workers!

This is the difference between children and servants. "If we are worthy to be judged as Your children," You surely created the entire world for our sake, as our Sages explained: "*Bereshis bara Elokim es ha-shamayim v'es ha-aretz*—For [the sake of Israel, who is called] *Reshis*—Beginning, God created the heavens and the earth" (*Bereshis* 1:1). Therefore, "Have mercy on us as a father has mercy on his children!"

But "if we are to be judged as Your servants," we are inferior and auxiliary to the world, to the "business," which was only created for the sake of those who do Your will! In that case, "our eyes are fixed on You until You absolve us and make our sentence [shine forth] like light."

Me'asef Derushei II:62b

"If [we are to be judged] as Your servants... absolve us and make our sentence [shine forth] like light..."

The Chasam Sofer also explained the difference between children and servants.

At the inauguration of the First *Beis Ha-Mikdash*, after the Ark of the Covenant had been placed inside the Holy of Holies by the *Kohanim*, and the Cloud of Hashem's Glory filled the Temple, Shelomo *Ha-Melech* knelt and prayed at great length. He spread his hands toward heaven and praised Hashem for the privilege of completing the Temple. He prayed and pleaded that Hashem hearken to the prayers of all who turned towards the Temple. When he concluded his prayer, he stood up and blessed the entire nation:

"Blessed is God who granted tranquility to His people Israel in fulfillment of all He decreed. For not one detail of all the good which He spoke concerning us, through His servant Moses, has failed to come true. May God our God accompany us as He accompanied our ancestors. May He not forsake us or abandon us, but incline our hearts to [serve] Him, to walk in all His ways, and keep His commandments, His laws and His judgments, which He instructed our ancestors. And may these words of mine, with which I have pleaded before God, be near to God our God, each day and night, *to judge the cause of His servant, and the cause of His people Israel,* as each day may require. So that all the inhabitants of the earth may know that God is the Ultimate Power. There is no other" (I *Melachim* 8:56-60).

The Talmud (*Rosh Hashanah* 8b) comments on the order of the sentence, "to judge the cause of His servant, and the cause of His people Israel." *To judge the cause of His servant* refers to Shelomo *Ha-Melech,* while *and the cause of His people Israel* refers to the members of the community. Rav Chisda said: We learn from this that when a king and a community await judgment, the king enters first. Why? You may say that it is not considerate to keep a king waiting outside. You may also say that he should enter first, before the Judge becomes angry [due to the sins of the community].

When we are worthy, when our deeds demonstrate that we are "a kingdom of priests and a holy nation," we are considered Hashem's children. We are then judged first and He "has mercy on us like a father has mercy on his children!"

However, if we become intermingled with the other nations of the world, and subservient to them, God forbid, the kings of the nations enter before us and inflame Hashem's anger. What shall we expect when our turn comes to enter? Who can withstand Hashem's displeasure? If we are to be considered "servants," how can we be sure that He will "absolve us and make our sentence [shine forth] like light"?

The Chasam Sofer answered with a parable:

A king once hired a tutor to instruct his son. One day, the king entered and found the tutor cruelly striking the young prince. The king became incensed at the teacher. Then, in the heat of his anger, he also raised his hand to strike his son, as if to say, "Why did you deviate from the right path to such an extent that you caused your teacher to strike you so cruelly?"

The boy cried, "Abba, Abba! You are angry at the teacher for striking me, and in the heat of your anger you wish to strike me as well! Why should I be beaten twice?"

This is our complaint as well. Hashem becomes angry at the nations when they inappropriately strike and afflict us. Is it then fair that, in the heat of His wrath, He strike us as well and judge us with terrible and uncompromising severity? This complaint is the secret key that transforms His attribute of Justice into Mercy. This complaint is the key to arousing His mercy until He "absolves us and make our sentence [shine forth] like [a beacon of] light"!

Derashos Chasam Sofer II:364

Verses of Recollection (Zichronos)

אַתָּה זוֹכֵר מַעֲשֵׂה עוֹלָם
"You remember the deeds of the world."

Said Rabbi Levi Yitzchak of Berdichev: It is well-known that Hashem remembers everything. There is no forgetfulness before the Holy One. "You remember the deeds of the world" thus is not a statement of fact, but of praise and thanksgiving.

This is similar to a father whose young son makes a wise remark for his age. Despite the fact that his own wisdom far exceeds that of his son, the father turns to the child to take pleasure in his wisdom. Out of love for the child, the father constricts his intelligence. Out of a desire to play with him and enjoy his presence, he lowers himself to the level of the child.

We turn to Hashem and say *"Attah—You."* You are so far beyond anything we can know or imagine, still, "You remember the deeds of the world," You lower Yourself, as it were, to enjoy us and delight in our meager endeavors to serve You.

Kedushas Levi, Rosh Hashanah

וְזָכַרְתִּי אֶת בְּרִיתִי יַעֲקֹב, וְאַף אֶת בְּרִיתִי יִצְחָק, וְאַף אֶת בְּרִיתִי אַבְרָהָם אֶזְכּוֹר
"I will remember My covenant with Ya'akov... with Yitzchak... with Avraham; and I will remember the Land."

The Maggid of Dubno said: "This is a famous question: Why does the verse enumerate the names of the Patriarchs in reverse order?" He provided two answers, both in the form of parables.

The first parable: A young lad was once standing in line at

the neighborhood market. The boy ahead of him requested a hundred grams of salted peanuts. The shopkeeper filled a small bag with peanuts, placed the bag on one scale and a hundred-gram weight on the other, and when the scales balanced, added three extra peanuts.

The young lad's mouth began to water. When his turn arrived, the shopkeeper asked, "And what do you want to buy, sonny?"

His mother had sent him to buy bread and milk, but before he knew it he had spit out the words, "Three peanuts!"

"Your mother sent you to buy three peanuts?"

"No," the lad replied, "but I saw you give the boy in front of me three free peanuts, and I want some too!"

The shopkeeper smiled. "Foolish boy! If someone buys a hundred grams, I gladly add a little extra. But if someone doesn't buy anything, should I give away gifts for free?"

The moral: We are not the only ones asking for favors in the merit of our forefathers. The children of Esav can plead in the merit of their father Yitzchak and their grandfather Avraham. The children of Yishmael and Keturah can plead in the merit of their father Avraham. How does Hashem avoid this? He arranges things in such a way that He only does favors in the merit of Ya'akov. In granting favors in the merit of Ya'akov, of course, He gladly adds in the extra merit of Yitzchak and of Avraham...

Indeed, the merit of all the Patriarchs is primarily an extra addition. When can a person enjoy this merit? When he pays cash, when he comes with his own merit. The Shopkeeper will then gladly add a little gift of His own, a little extra reward that goes beyond what he deserves. One who comes without a penny in his pocket, however, desiring only to receive a gift, will be disappointed...

But, the Maggid of Dubno went on, there is still another question we must ask: Why does this verse, which speaks of the merit of the Patriarchs, appear in the famous Verses of

Rebuke, wherein the people of Israel are warned of impending destruction and exile if they disregard the teachings of the Torah? The Maggid answered with his second parable.

A police unit on night patrol once noticed some suspicious activity, and surprised a pair of robbers in the act of breaking into a store. The two were brought before the judge and pleaded guilty. Could they have pleaded innocent even if they wanted to?

The judge had to pronounce their sentence. He asked one of the thieves about his past, and this thief told the judge that he had grown up in a broken home, with a father who had a criminal record. When he was only a youth he had gotten involved with crime.

The judge heard this and sentenced him to one month in jail and one year on probation. He then turned to the second defendant and asked him about his past. This fellow held himself in high regard, and rightfully so. His father was the rabbi of a certain city...

"Rabbi so-and-so is your father?" the judge asked, scarcely able to believe his ears. "He is the son of the great genius, Rabbi So-and-so..."

"That's right!" the thief answered with pride. Rabbi So-and-so was my grandfather. I learned in his yeshivah. I was even privileged to have seen *his* father, may he rest in peace. He was one of the greatest rabbis of the previous generation!"

"Unbelievable!" the judge exclaimed. "But let us return to the subject at hand. I sentence you to five years in jail and ten years on probation."

The thief was thunderstruck. "How can this be?" he protested. "My friend got one month and I got five years? We stole together, and we were caught together! Why are you discriminating against me?"

"How can you compare the two of you?" the judge retorted. "Your friend is the son of a thief. He was born into thievery. He is like the boy whose father washed him, anointed him, fed him, gave him wine to drink, hung a money pouch around his neck, and left him standing at the door of a brothel. What could the boy do but sin? (*Berachos* 32a). But you? You grew up in a house filled with Torah and the fear of Heaven. You went to learn at the side of your illustrious grandfather. You were even worthy of seeing your father's grandfather, whose name is never mentioned without trembling. You had all the ingredients needed to become upright and loyal. You could have been beloved in the eyes of Heaven and in the eyes of man. If you have now forsaken the good path and chosen the company of criminals, you yourself are responsible. Your punishment is therefore that much greater!"

At the end of the prophecies describing the punishments which would be visited upon the people of Israel, Hashem wished to inform us of the reason for such severe measures. He said: In and of themselves, the sins you commit are enough to warrant punishment. But they are seven times worse when I remember My covenant with Ya'akov! What a remarkable father you had! And what of My covenant with Yitzchak? What a marvelous grandfather! And what of My covenant with Avraham? What a phenomenal great grandfather! How could you turn out like this?

Ohel Ya'akov, *Bechukosai*

הֲבֵן יַקִּיר לִי אֶפְרַיִם אִם יֶלֶד שַׁעֲשׁוּעִים,
כִּי מִדֵּי דַבְּרִי בּוֹ זָכוֹר אֶזְכְּרֶנּוּ עוֹד

"Is Efrayim a precious son to Me, [or] an adorable child? [Even] when I speak [harshly] of him, I cannot help but remember him. As a result, I am deeply moved for him. I will surely have compassion and take pity on him!"

The Maggid of Dubno explained and clarified this verse with the following parable:

Imagine a father holding his baby. What a precious child! He smiles—and the father smiles back in delight. The baby gurgles—and the father melts in rapture. Then the father turns his attention to the baby's older brother, who has arrived home from school. He tests the boy on what he has learned, asks him questions, savors his answers, and takes delight in his precociousness. The son knows that it is worth learning his lessons well, for he loves to please his father....

One day, the little boy's mind wandered during his lessons. On the way home, he was worried: Since he hadn't listened, he wouldn't know the answers to his father's questions. "What will I answer Father? If I can't, he will surely be disappointed. What shall I do?" He thought, and came up with a solution.

When he came home his father asked him what he had learned that day.

The boy tried to put on a grin from ear to ear.

"Answer me, son. What did you learn today?"

"Gagaga..." the boy gurgled.

"Why are you doing this?" his father asked, puzzled.

"It's very simple, Father. I cannot answer your questions today, but I didn't want to disappoint you... I've noticed that when my little brother smiles at you and gurgles, you are delighted. So I thought that today I'd please you in the same way..."

"Ah, now I see," the father said, and sighed. "But you must understand the difference between yourself and your baby brother! He is an infant, and doesn't even know how to speak yet, let alone to learn! Gurgling and smiling are all he can do. But if *you* gurgle like a baby, it just looks silly. You are capable of learning, and therefore you can't please me with anything less!"

This is similar to the Talmud's comparison (*Bava Kamma* 92b) of two verses in the Torah. Immediately after the Exodus, as the children of Israel traveled towards the Red Sea, it says,

"God went before them by day with a pillar of cloud to guide them along the way, and by night with a pillar of fire to illuminate [the way] for them, so they could travel by day and by night" (*Shemos* 13:21). Later, after the incident of the golden calf, God promises, "I will send an angel before you to safeguard you on the way and bring you to the place I have prepared" (ibid. 23:20). The Talmud exclaims: When we were young, we were considered mature enough [to walk on our own]. Now that we have grown old, we are treated like children [who need an angel nursemaid]!

When we were young: When Hashem was about to bring us out of Egypt and we were still sunk in forty-nine levels of Egyptian uncleanliness, He required only two acts from us—that we slaughter the Passover lamb, and perform circumcision on all males. These two acts were sufficient to clear the way, to prepare us, as it were, to experience the revelation of His awesome Presence on Mount Sinai. *Now that we have grown old:* After we received the Torah, on the other hand, one transgression (not protesting against the mixed multitude when they worshiped and danced around the golden calf) was sufficient to act as a barrier between us and the Divine Presence, that is, to cause His direct Providence to withdraw from us and be replaced by a lower, more indirect level, namely, an angel.

The Talmud (*Bava Kamma* 50a; *Yevamos* 121b) finds a further allusion to this dialectic in a verse describing Hashem's judgment: "A devouring fire goes before Him; round about Him a storm wind rages exceedingly" (*Tehillim* 50:3). Based on the similitude between the words *se'arah* (stormwind) and *sa'arah* (hair), the Talmud states: The Holy One is exacting to a hairsbreadth with His righteous ones who stand about Him.

Moshe spoke of this when he comforted his brother Aharon after the deaths of his eldest sons, Nadav and Avihu: "This is exactly what God meant when He said, 'I will be sanctified among those close to Me, and I will be glorified in the midst of [this] entire nation'" (*Vayikra* 10:3). The very fact

that Nadav and Avihu had been punished so severely for a
relatively minor infraction convinced Moshe of their greatness.
"Now I know," he said to Aharon, "that they were [destined
to be] greater than you and I" (Rashi, *ibid.*).

The opposite is true of those who distance themselves
from Hashem. Like small children, they are rewarded for the
smallest good deed, as the Talmud (*Chullin* 92a-b; Rashi, *ibid.*)
records: The descendants of No'ach (ancient mankind) originally adopted thirty ordinances, but observe only three of
them to this day: 1) [Although they practice homosexuality]
they do not write marriage contracts for two males, 2) [al-
though they eat from the carcass of an animal that died natu-
rally] they do not weigh out such meat in their stores, 3)
[although they are jealous of the Jewish people] they cannot
help paying lip service to the Bible.

For Israel, such "good deeds" would not be worthy of
mention. Much more is expected of us.

Shelomo *Ha-Melech* also alluded to this dialectic when he
said, "The more wisdom, the more outrage. He who increases
knowledge, increases torment" (*Koheles* 1:18). That is, the
wiser and more knowledgeable a person becomes, the more
outrage and torment people will heap on him if he fails to act
according to the dictates of wisdom. Similarly, on the verse,
"Anger is preferable to smiles" (*ibid.* 7:3), the Talmud (*Shabbos*
30b) explains: "The anger the Holy One directs against the
righteous in this world [for their minor misdeeds] is preferable
to the smiles He smiles at the wicked in this world [for their
good deeds]."

The fact that God directs His "anger" against the righteous
shows that He has not given up on them. On the contrary—as
one expects more of a grown child, He expects more from
them. The opposite is true of His "smiles" towards the wicked.

We can now re-read our original verse: "Is Efrayim a
precious son to Me [or] an adorable child?" Is Israel like a
precious and wise son, from whom God expects much, and

whom He punishes when he fails to live up to His expectations? Or is Israel like an adorable little child, a baby with
whom one plays, and from whom nothing is expected in
return?

The answer is: "[Even] when I speak harshly of him, I
cannot help but remember him." After receiving the Torah,
Israel is considered a grown son. Hashem is therefore exacting
to a hairsbreadth with the Jewish People. He expresses His
displeasure with them, and rebukes them for the slightest
infraction. This very rebuke, however, reminds Him, as it
were, of the special qualities they manifested when they first
received His Torah. It also arouses the original love He once
had for them when they were still His "adorable child." "As
a result, My heart is deeply moved for him. I will surely have
compassion and take pity on him!"

Kol Yeshorer 6

"Is Efrayim a precious son to Me... I will surely have compassion and take pity on him!"

Said the Maggid of Dubno: The Jewish People are called
Hashem's children. He created the world for their sake. Even
when they are not found worthy in His eyes, He loves them
and has compassion on them. This means, as the following
parable shows, that nothing can nullify His love for them.

There was a man whose only son was not a gifted student.
When the boy's teachers told the father that he had great
difficulties with his studies, the father hired private tutors who
worked very hard to educate the boy properly. They were
paid handsomely.

This man owned a store, where he employed a young boy
who served the many customers. The boy was bright, performing his duties faithfully and diligently, and his employer
was pleased with his work.

One day, though, the man turned to his worker and said,

"My competitor's worker receives the same salary as you do, but in addition to his regular work in the store, he puts his employer's accounts in order and balances his books every night."

"I'm sorry to tell you," the worker replied, "that I don't know how to do accounting."

"Well then," the man replied, "if that's the case, you must terminate your job here at the end of this month, for an offer has been made to me to employ him as my worker. That way I'll be able to save myself the trouble of balancing my own books."

"I would like to understand," replied the offended worker. "Just because I am not proficient in accounting, you are firing me? Is that fair? Why, you yourself have a son who is below average in his studies, yet you willingly spend a fortune on extra tutors to educate him—and with little success!"

The man smiled at the question. "What is the comparison?" he answered. "My relationship with you is one of employer and employee, and no more. When I was satisfied with your work, I valued you as a worker. If I am able to employ a better worker, the privilege is mine. The relationship between a father and child, on the other hand, is unconditional. Since it does not depend on performance, nothing can ever abrogate or nullify it. On the contrary—the less hope there seems to be, the greater the love and compassion!"

Ohel Ya'akov, *Balak*

וְתֵרָאֶה לְפָנֶיךָ עֲקֵדָה שֶׁעָקַד אַבְרָהָם אָבִינוּ אֶת יִצְחָק בְּנוֹ

"Let the binding of his son Yitzchak on the altar appear before You..."

The Maggid of Warsaw asked: What is so special about the *Akedah*, the binding of Yitzchak? The Jewish people have been bound and sacrificed countless times during periods of religious persecution. Countless "altars" have been built and countless Jews have given their lives and their children's lives to sanctify God's Name! What makes the *Akedah* of Yitzchak so unique and different from all of these?

He answered with a parable: A king once appointed his close friend as the ruler of one of his provinces. The new governor expended every effort on behalf of the citizens of his province. He also imposed high taxes on them which were collected and transferred to the king's treasury. He fought the king's wars and subdued the king's enemies, subjugating them under the king's sovereignty. Because this governor served the king with all his might and dedicated himself completely to his service, he was beloved by the king as well as by all his subjects. All, that is, except the king's ministers—for they were jealous of his accomplishments. Nevertheless, they were unable to discover anything with which to ruin his standing with the king. They were forced to bide their time and await an opportune moment.

The moment arrived when the king expressed his desire to reward the governor for his dedicated service; he would give the governorship over the province to his descendants forever. Here the enemies found the tiniest crack through which to inject their poisonous slander.

They spoke before the king: "This governor never intended to serve the king, but only his own aspirations for power and wealth. See how he enjoys the acclaim of his subjects and the love of the king! He rides upon the heights of fame and fortune, honor and glory. See how his soldiers jump at his command, serve him with blind loyalty and submission. Why, he acts like an emperor, an all-powerful dictator in his province. Why reward him with additional honor and everlasting power? He has been given enough, especially in view of the fact that he is interested solely in his own aggrandizement!"

The king listened, and replied: "No one can deny that this man's actions have been good and upright. You, however, claim that you can judge his heart and discern the true intent behind his actions, and you wish to denounce him for this.

Fine, then—let us test his heart!"

The king wrote out a royal proclamation in which he commanded the governor to build a paper bridge over the river that separated his province from the royal capital. He was then to cross over the bridge with his troops.

The governor received the command and trembled. What can this mean? he thought to himself. My soldiers are in the service of the king; they have conquered the king's enemies and subjugated them before his majesty. If I command them to cross over such a bridge, they will all drown, the king will lose his finest troops, and his enemies will stage an uprising. The entire kingdom will be endangered!

Yes, they will all drown! These precious soldiers have served the king so loyally, brought him riches. How can he bear to see them lost? But the king's word, nevertheless, is law. I have dedicated my whole life to him. Shall I now transgress his command?

He commanded his engineers to design and "build" a paper bridge. He arrayed his troops at the foot of the "bridge." They saw the "bridge" and understood that they were being commanded to cross it—to cross it and to drown.

The governor stood before his soldiers, who were to him like his own sons. "You know that you are more precious to me than my own soul," he began. They knew. "You know, as well, that I have dedicated my entire life to the service of our king. I have always been prepared to die for him." They knew. "If you were commanded to go out to the field of battle and give your lives for him, would you not do so willingly and gladly?" Yes, they would. "If so, and if his wish is that you go up on this bridge, and if our sole desire is to please him, then go up, my brave children, cross over!"

The soldiers began moving toward the bridge as one man. Suddenly, a courier came galloping with a message from the king, calling out: "Stop! Stay where you are! Stand at attention! Let no man dare go up on the bridge. No one is to move from his place!"

He rode up to the governor and handed him a letter. In it, the king decreed that he and his descendants would rule in this province forever after. No slander or accusation would ever undermine their position! This is the meaning of the verse, "God says: No weapon fashioned against you shall be successful. Every tongue that accuses you in judgment you shall indict. This is the heritage of God's servants, and their vindication from Me" (*Yeshayahu* 54:17).

The moral: Our father Avraham was God's most loyal servant. He taught his contemporaries about the Almighty and spread the light of belief in the One God everywhere he went. He taught about God's goodness and kindness, and he embodied that goodness and kindness in his every act. As a result of this, he was beloved above in heaven and below on earth.

Avraham taught that God loves man and abhors human sacrifice. But just as He was about to confer His eternal covenant on Avraham and his children forever after, the Accuser denounced Avraham. As the Talmud (*Sanhedrin* 89b) explains: It is written, "It came to pass after these words, and God tested Avraham" (*Bereshis* 22:1). After what words? The words of the Accuser. He spoke before the Holy One, saying, "Master of the universe, You granted this old man a child at the age of one hundred, yet, of every feast which he has made, he could not find one dove or one pigeon to offer You?" The Holy One replied, "[You claim that] he did it all for his son [and not for Me]. But if I were to tell him to sacrifice his son, he would not hesitate!" Thus, "And God tested Avraham. 'Avraham!' He said to him... 'Take your son, your only one, whom you love, Yitzchak, and go to the land of Moriah. Lift him up there as an elevation-offering on one of the mountains I shall indicate to you'" (*ibid.* 22:1-2).

Having been commanded by Hashem to sacrifice his only son, Avraham was confused. What shall I do? he thought to himself. If I sacrifice him, I will not only be killing him with my own hand. I will be false to the faith of all those who follow after me. If I take my son and sacrifice him, all my efforts to discourage human sacrifice will have been in vain. What will come of all my work? Where shall I flee in my disgrace? All my efforts to awaken people's hearts to perform acts of kindness with each other in God's Name will be ruined!

But Avraham strengthened his heart and said: Come what may, I will never transgress the command of my God. So he took his son, built an altar, and took the slaughtering knife in hand. Only at the last moment did God's angel appear and say, "Avraham! Avraham!... [God commands you:] Do not harm the lad. Do not do anything to him. Now I know that you are truly God-fearing, for you have not withheld your only son from Me!" (ibid. 22:11-12).

God then promised him, "I have sworn by My own Essence that, because you performed this deed and did not withhold your only son, I will surely bless you and increase your offspring like the stars of the sky and the sand on the seashore. Your offspring will inherit the gates of their enemies. All the nations of the world will be blessed through your descendants because you obeyed My voice" (ibid. 22:16-18).

The Maggid of Warsaw concluded: We can now understand why we always mention the merit of Avraham who bound his beloved son Yitzchak! Nevertheless, if we truly wish to be redeemed in the merit of the *Akedah*, we must also act accordingly. That is to say, we must always be prepared, like Avraham, to nullify our own will in the face of God's will. We must not devise spurious arguments in order to challenge or circumvent His will. When we then hearken to His word with complete and wholehearted faith, we can emulate our forefather Avraham and ask in his merit: "Let the binding of his son Yitzchak on the altar appear before You!"

Chomas Ha-Da'as v'Ha-Emunah 16

וְזָכַרְתִּי לָהֶם בְּרִית רִאשׁוֹנִים

"And fulfill Your promise to [redeem] us: I will remember the covenant [I made] for them with their first ancestors..."

When is it possible to ask to be redeemed in the merit of the Patriarchs? The Maggid of Dubno answered this question with a parable.

The rabbi of a city, an extremely wise and holy man, married his son to the daughter of a wealthy businessman in a distant city. It was not long before this businessman passed away, leaving his entire fortune to his son-in-law. The young man took over the business and at first was very successful. In no time at all, however, the wheel of fortune turned. It was not long before he lost everything.

Although he could still afford to feed and clothe his family, when his own daughter came of age he was simply unable to provide her with a proper dowry. He therefore returned to his home town, and there, in memory of his sainted father, the community welcomed him with great honor and presented him with a generous sum of money, more than enough for the dowry.

Some years passed, and when this rabbi's second daughter came of marriageable age and a match was made, he pledged to provide a sizable dowry. For a second time, he set off for his hometown; but as luck would have it, the similarity to his first visit stopped here. He fell deathly ill while travelling on the way. His face was pallid and spotted with pox; his mouth became twisted and deformed; his voice changed and his hair fell out.

With his last ounce of strength, he made his way on foot towards his home town. He was penniless and exhausted, his clothes and shoes had worn out, he looked ghastly. But as he walked, a single flicker of hope burned brightly in his heart. He yearned to arrive at his destination and be honored as he had been the first time. He strengthened himself with this hope at all times. He remembered every detail of his previous visit, went over it in his mind by day and in his dreams at night.

He finally arrives. He stands tattered and ravaged at the gates of the city. He enters and walks the familiar cobblestone streets. He passes his illustrious father's house. He stands at the door of the study hall of his father's yeshivah. He looks inside, sees it filled from wall to wall with students. He enters and leans weakly against the door. He waits to be welcomed. Where are the shouts of joy? Nobody turns to him. No one welcomes him. He approaches them and stretches forth his hand. They rebuff him. "But I am the rabbi's son!" he cries. They don't believe him. They just stare at him and then return to their studies...

He breaks down and begins to cry. He calls out in a broken voice, "Dear God! How unbearable is my pain! Nobody even recognizes me. 'I am like a stranger to my brothers, an alien to my mother's children'" (*Tehillim* 69:9).

The moral: It is true that we are children of Avraham, Yitzchak, and Ya'akov. But when we ask to be answered and saved in their merit, we must first be identifiable as their children! Our father Ya'akov was the pillar of truth, Yitzchak was the pillar of reverence, and Avraham was the pillar of kindness. The Talmud (*Yevamos* 79a) thus gives a sign: Whoever has mercy on others is surely a descendant of our father Avraham. The same can be said of the qualities of the other Patriarchs.

Now that we have become so estranged from their qualities, however, we are scarcely recognizable as their descendants. We must strive to recover those precious qualities, then, and say, "When will my deeds resemble those of my ancestors, Avraham, Yitzchak and Ya'akov?" Otherwise, how can we expect to be redeemed in their merit?

Ohel Ya'akov, *Emor*

_____ THE PALACE GATES

כָּתְבֵנוּ בְּסֵפֶר הַחַיִּים, כַּכָּתוּב וְאַתֶּם הַדְּבֵקִים בַּה' אֱלֹקֵיכֶם
חַיִּים כֻּלְּכֶם הַיּוֹם

"Inscribe us in the Book of Life, as it is written: 'And may all you who bind yourselves to Hashem your God be vouchsafed eternal life today!'"

Said the Chasam Sofer: This is similar to a builder who assembles a pile of lumber for building a house. As long as the house is being built and the lumber remains stacked in a pile, this is an open invitation to any thief. A watchman must therefore stand guard over the beams. Once the house has been completed, however, no one would dare steal a beam from the wall or roof of a building!

Each individual Jew may be likened to a beam in a building. Alone, he is exposed to all kinds of dangers, but when the entire Jewish people stand as one, when each individual is attached to his fellow, and the entire congregation of Israel is bound together, and all of them together are bound to their blessed Creator—they are all shielded and protected, like the beams in a great edifice.

There is only one problem. The Talmud (*Kesubos* 111b) itself asks, regarding this verse: Is it then possible to bind oneself to the Divine Presence? Is it not written (*Devarim* 4:24), "Hashem your God is a consuming fire"? Rather, if one marries his daughter to a Torah sage, does business with Torah sages, and uses one's possessions to benefit Torah sages—in short, if one keeps the company of and attaches oneself to the sages who emulate the Divine—it is considered as if he has bound himself directly to the Divine.

The verse thus says, "And you who bind yourselves to Hashem your God are *all* of you vouchsafed eternal life today," that is, when you join together as one, you shall be shielded and protected forever!

Derashos Chasam Sofer II:346

"'And may all you who bind yourselves to Hashem your God be vouchsafed eternal life today!'"

Regarding the verse (*Devarim* 13:5), "You shall follow Hashem your God, fear Him and keep His commandments, obey Him and serve Him, and bind yourself to Him," the Sages ask: "Is it possible to follow after [and bind oneself to] the Divine Presence? Is it not written, 'Hashem your God is a consuming fire'? (*ibid.* 4:24). Rather, follow after (emulate) His qualities. Just as the Holy One clothed the naked, so should you clothe the naked... Just as He visited the sick, so should you visit the sick... Just as He comforted mourners, so should you comfort mourners... Just as He buried the dead, so should you bury the dead...." (*Sotah* 14a). In a similar vein, they state further, "Just as He is merciful and compassionate, so must you act mercifully and compassionately" (*Shabbos* 133b).

The Maggid of Dubno illustrated this with a parable.

There was once a great and profound Torah sage, who would solve any difficulty he found, and whose novel insights involved building entire structures based on a wide range of sources. He had a son who was a yeshivah student.

He once asked him, "What are they presently learning in the yeshivah?"

"We are in the middle of such-and-such a subject," his son replied.

The father asked his son one or two questions to which the son provided superficial answers. Seeing that his son had not penetrated to the depths of that subject, he asked what other subjects had been covered recently. The answers were again superficial, indicating that his son's understanding of his studies was weak indeed. It would be necessary to guide him, to teach him how to look deeply into a subject, to penetrate to the depths of the *halachah* (law). The father took his own notebook (on the subject the son was studying) and gave it to him. He hoped that the boy would see how he had proceeded systematically, taking every subtle point into consideration, until he had arrived at his present understanding. The boy returned an hour later with the notebook, his eyes shining.

"Now," the father exclaimed, rubbing his hands together in anticipation, "what have you got to say?" And he asked to hear the boy's criticisms, questions and clarifications. Perhaps, he thought, his son would pose a particularly difficult problem. Perhaps he would strengthen his father's argument with additional proofs. One way or the other, he would be happy. For this is the way of Torah!

"What have you got to say, son?"

"What can I say? You're a genius, Father!"

There was no end to the father's disappointment. He certainly did not need his son's approval. His only desire was to guide his son in the proper path of looking deeply, to show him that he could do the same as his father!

In His Torah, Hashem revealed just a little bit about Himself and His ways. He is merciful and compassionate. He is kind, patient and long-suffering. We are very moved by this and exclaim, "Who is like Hashem our God? He is kind to the wicked as well as to the good!" But Hashem replies, "Do I need your approval? My intention is that you follow in My ways and emulate Me. You be kind as well. I will then delight in you and you will find favor in My eyes. I will decree long life for you and inscribe you in My Book of Life forever."

Kochav Mi-Ya'akov, *Haftarah of Vayikra*

אִם תָּקוּם עָלַי מִלְחָמָה בְּזֹאת אֲנִי בוֹטֵחַ

"If an army encompasses me, my heart is not afraid. If war rises against me, I trust in this one thing."

Asked Rabbi Zev Wolf of Zhitomir: "'I trust in this one thing' —What is this one thing?" He answered with a parable.

In a thick forest separating two large cities lived a band of thieves who attacked and robbed people. If a poor farmer drove his wagon, loaded with hay, through the forest, they let him pass unharmed. If a wealthy merchant passed through in a carriage full of merchandise, he could be certain of being attacked unless he hired armed horsemen to protect him.

Now, who would imagine that such a wealthy merchant would bemoan this fact and say: "What a shame I am not a poor farmer moving slowly through the forest with a wagon-load of hay!" On the contrary—he is thankful for the privilege of transporting the kind of expensive merchandise that draws the attention of the robbers. He will therefore make sure to protect himself so that he may travel through the forest in peace.

This is the meaning of: "If they rise up to battle me, I trust in this one thing." That is, if I must battle with the Evil Inclination and his henchmen when they attempt to ambush and undermine me on my path through life, this battle itself will make me happy and fill my heart with trust. Why? Because evil is only interested in me when I carry expensive merchandise. It is only jealous when I possess a treasure for which it is worth fighting. This recognition gives me the strength to go on even when I feel I am losing.

Or Ha-Meir, *Rimzei Rosh Hashanah*

לְךָ אָמַר לִבִּי בַּקְּשׁוּ פָנָי אֶת פָּנֶיךָ ה' אֲבַקֵּשׁ

"In Your behalf, my heart has whispered [to me]: Seek My Presence. O God, I seek [only to be found worthy of] Your Presence!"

The Maggid of Kovno saw a double meaning in this verse. On the one hand, almost imperceptibly, our heart whispers to us in a still small voice to seek out the Presence of the Divine in all the different aspects of our lives. At the same time, our heart sends a secret message to Hashem Himself to come into our lives. The message reads: "You have planted a soul within us which is a veritable reflection of Your Presence, an interface between us and Infinity. Please rescue this soul before it is overwhelmed by life's vicissitudes." In this sense, the verse can be read: "My heart has said to You: Seek my inner [soul]. O God, I seek Your reflection within me!" He explained this with the following parable:

A prince once strayed from the proper path and angered his father with his wicked deeds. The king was finally forced to banish his son from the royal palace. The boy ended up in the house of a villager who worked him mercilessly.

After suffering this way for a few months, the prince took account of himself and his actions. He regretted having angered his father. He wished to return home but felt terribly embarrassed. Ashamed to ask forgiveness directly from his father, he wrote him a letter: "I have fallen ill and request that you come to me as soon as possible. My soul is about to expire. Please come before I breathe my last breath..."

Upon receiving the letter, the king did not hesitate for a moment. He ordered his carriage prepared, and immediately drove off. When he arrived, he was quite surprised to see his son so healthy and strong, chopping wood in the villager's yard! On the one hand, he was happy about this. On the other hand, he was extremely irritated at the boy. "Why did you lie to me?" he asked.

The prince answered with wisdom. "Father, heaven forbid, I did not intend to fool you. It is true that my body is healthy and I am physically fit, but my soul is the sensitive soul of the son of the king. Every day I spend here in this village, my soul suffers and becomes more ill. In a few days, my soul might leave me completely. When this happens, I fear it will be replaced by the brutish soul of a farmer..."

This describes our condition. We are the beloved children of the Blessed Holy One. When we angered Him with our deeds, He banished us to wander among the nations. Instead of repenting immediately, we assimilated with the gentiles and adopted their ways. Little by little, we lost our uniqueness. Our Divine soul, the reflection of the Divine within us, began to abandon us.

We want to return to our Father in Heaven before it is too late, but we are ashamed to ask His forgiveness. We therefore say, "Come and see how sick we are. It is not a physical illness. Thank God, we are physically fit. Rather, our souls are about to expire! Look down from heaven and save us before it is too late!"

This is what David *Ha-Melech* meant when he cried out: "My heart has said to You: Seek my inner [soul]. O God, I seek Your reflection within me!"

Ateres Tzevi, *Derush* 3

Tashlich—Casting Away Sins

מִי אֵ־ל כָּמוֹךָ נוֹשֵׂא עָווֹן וְעוֹבֵר עַל פֶּשַׁע

"Who is a God like You, Who pardons sin and passes over crime for the remnant of His heritage..."

This verse describes the Thirteen Attributes of Divine Mercy. It is said three times on the afternoon of Rosh Hashanah while standing near a body of water and shaking out our pockets to symbolically "cast our errors into the depths of the sea."

Rabbi Levi Yitzchak of Berdichev saw a double meaning in the words *nosei avon,* which can be translated as "pardons sin," or literally as "raises up sin." The Berdichever chose to concentrate on the second meaning, explaining thereby why Hashem would want to "raise up" or "inflate" our sins into crimes...

If a father were to see a stranger doing something wrong, he would not necessarily wish to get involved by rebuking him. In most instances, his natural instinct would be to ignore the person unless he thought that such reprimand could influence him and discourage him from doing what he was doing. He would hardly act the same way, however, with his own child. He would reprimand him and even magnify the severity of the act many times over in order to motivate his son to abandon it on his own. This severe reprimand would actually demonstrate the father's love for the child and his readiness to pardon him.

This is the meaning of "He raises up sin," that is, He enlarges and inflates the sin (and makes it seem like the biggest crime in the world) in order to reprimand, to warn and to frighten us into realizing the gravity of our actions and where they could lead. Immediately after this, however, He "passes over our crime" and pardons our sin!

Kedushas Levi, Rosh Hashanah

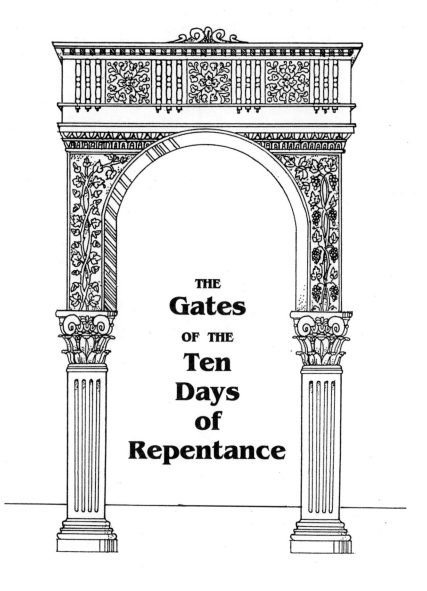

THE
Gates
OF THE
**Ten
Days
of
Repentance**

"Seek God when He can be found"— these are the Ten Days of Teshuvah.

The Talmud (*Yevamos* 49b) quotes an ancient tradition that the evil king Menashe set up a mock court to try his grandfather, the prophet Yeshayahu, to execute him on spurious charges of being a false prophet. One of the questions he put to Yeshayahu was: Your teacher Moshe said, "Who is like Hashem our God [who answers us] whenever we call upon Him?" (*Devarim* 4:7), yet you have said, "Seek Hashem when He can be found, call upon Him when He is close at hand" (*Yeshayahu* 55:6). That is, it seems that your statement contradicts that of Moshe by implying that there are times when God is not found and not close.*

The Talmud shows how the apparent contradiction between Yeshayahu's and Moshe's statements may be resolved: "Seek Hashem when He can be found" refers to the individual, while "Whenever we call upon Him" refers to the community. And when can the individual "find" Hashem most easily? Rav Nachman said in the name of Rabbah bar Avuha, "During the Ten Days of *Teshuvah* which begin with Rosh Hashanah and end with Yom Kippur."

The Maggid of Dubno explained this with a parable.

The residents of a certain country once rebelled against their king. Furious, the king threatened to send his army against the country to crush the rebellion. Knowing that this would spell their downfall, they hurriedly sent an ambassadorial party to request the king's pardon. The gates of the palace were opened before the distinguished members of the party.

---

* The Talmud relates that Yeshayahu understood very well that anything he said would be held against him. He therefore uttered a Divine Name and disappeared into a cedar tree. Menashe's soldiers proceeded to cut down the tree. When they reached the place level with Yeshayahu's lips, his soul departed. He was vulnerable in this particular spot because he had once used his lips to slander the People of Israel, as it is written, "I dwell in the midst of a people with unclean lips" (*ibid.* 6:5).

They were allowed to enter and state their case before the king. In the end, the king agreed to honor their request. He granted full pardon.

In the royal city, there was a certain poor man who had fallen behind in his tax payments to the crown. The government authorities were about to foreclose on his possessions. He too decided to come before the king to request that his debt to the crown be waived. Somehow he managed to steal past the guards at the gate to the outer courtyard of the palace. Immediately upon entering, however, he was spotted and expelled by the king's guards. Undaunted, he stood at the gate and proclaimed his case: "Where is the justice and the fairness? They rebelled against the king and deserved to have been tried and hanged. My sin is minuscule in relation to theirs. What is not paying taxes compared to rebellion against the crown? There, an entire country rebelled. I am just a single individual. If the king can pardon such an enormous sin done by so many people, will he not consider pardoning a negligible offense committed by one man? Why should they be allowed to enter while I am pushed outside?"

"True," he was told, "but they sent a distinguished party composed of men whom the king respects. You, on the other hand... you had better return home before you make more trouble for yourself..."

Still not satisfied, the poor fellow waited outside the palace gates for the king to take a ride in the royal carriage. When he finally spotted the monarch, he cried out, "Oh, please save me, your majesty!"

The king ordered the carriage stopped, and the desperate man poured out his heart. Out of pity for his bad fortune, the king pardoned him.

The lesson: During the entire year, God's Presence, as it were, is in heaven above. The gates of prayer are closed. In addition, "guards" surround these gates and obstruct those prayers which are not worthy of rising up and entering before

His Throne of Glory. When an entire community prays, however, there are certain righteous and learned individuals before whom no wall or door is closed. In their merit, and in the merit of their faith and purity, the prayers of the community enter and are accepted.

During the Ten Days of *Teshuvah*, on the other hand, the Holy One leaves His Heavenly abode and descends in His chariot, so to speak, into our very midst. At this time, He accepts all prayers, even those of individuals who might otherwise not be considered worthy. The prophet Hoshea spoke to such individuals when he said (in the singular), "Return, O Israel, to Hashem your God" (*Hoshea* 14:2), that is, return during the Ten Days of *Teshuvah*, while Hashem is still accessible, for "you have stumbled because of your sins" (*ibid.*) and may not plead before Him when He returns to His Heavenly abode immediately after Yom Kippur.

But then the prophet turned to the community and spoke (in the plural) and without any time limitation. He declared, "Take with you words and return to Hashem" (*ibid.* 14:3), at any time, for the "wall" that obstructs the prayers of the individual from reaching Hashem cannot stand before the outpourings of the community together with its righteous members. Rather, "Say to Him: Forgive all sin and take the good" (*ibid.*). Ask Him to consider the good deeds of the righteous among them. In their merit, He will forgive the sins of the entire community and pardon them.

Ohel Ya'akov, *Acharei Mos;*
Kochav Mi-Ya'akov, *Haftarah* of *Vayetze*

We have not come before the Holy One— but He has come to us...

"Seek Hashem when He can be found, call upon Him when He is close at hand" (*Yeshayahu* 55:6). The Talmud (*Yevamos* 49b) explains: "Seek Hashem when He can be found... During the Ten Days of *Teshuvah* which begin with Rosh Hashanah and end with Yom Kippur." The Maggid of Lublin illustrated this with the following parable:

A prince once had a son for whom he foresaw greatness, and he wished to give him authority over certain of his provinces. Although he trusted in his son's astuteness, he thought it best to prepare the boy before letting him assume the responsibilities of power. Accordingly, he decided to send him to the royal city to study in the finest educational institutions in the land. He had fitting living quarters prepared and hired the best instructors available. He also provided him with a sizable sum of money for his needs. Before the boy's departure, the prince took him aside and spoke the following solemn words: "My dear son, you are more precious to me than my own soul. I will miss you while you are gone, and therefore I want to hear from you regularly. I will want to know how you are faring and how you are progressing in your studies. Promise me that you will write me whenever possible: during your trip, when you arrive at your destination, after you get settled, and throughout the entire period of your absence. I want to know how you are at all times."

The boy promised and took leave of his father.

He set out on his journey, passing through several towns along the way. One night when he stopped at an inn, the innkeeper immediately discerned that a naïve and sheltered youth with large sums of money in his purse had fallen into his clutches. He decided he would not let such prey escape easily. He received the boy with honor fit for aristocracy. He served him meticulously and cared for his every need, addressing him with clever words intended to win his trust. He fed him the finest foods, and served him the oldest wines, which brought on drowsiness and then deep sleep. The boy awakened with a ravenous appetite. He ate, drank, and again fell deeply asleep. Again he awakened and again he ate and drank. This went on for quite some time.

All the while the innkeeper catered to his every whim. He

made him feel that everything was all right, that he did not have a care in the world, and that doing nothing was the best way to pass the time. In return for such special treatment, the boy opened his purse generously to the innkeeper for each day's service. Somehow, he completely forgot why he had stopped in the inn and what his destination was to have been.

Meanwhile, the prince sat in his palace waiting for a letter from his son. A week passed. Two weeks. No letter or courier came. Not a sign of life appeared on the horizon. The prince sent messengers to the royal city, to the room that had been prepared in advance for his son's arrival. They were informed that the boy had never arrived. An investigation was launched, but no one was found who knew the boy's whereabouts. He had disappeared and was nowhere to be found!

The prince was beside himself with worry lest his son had met misfortune. He decided to set off himself and follow his son's trail. Who knows what might have happened? he thought. Perhaps the boy was attacked by a band of robbers and kidnapped? Perhaps he became ill on the way? Perhaps he fell and broke his leg? Perhaps he was stricken with convulsions and died?

He located the driver who had taken him to the neighboring city. He located the inn in which he had stayed his first night. He located members of the caravan with whom he had traveled to the next city. Here he lost the boy's trail. From here, it seemed, he had traveled on his own. The prince continued traveling.

It wasn't long before he felt weak from hunger. He saw an inn on the way and entered. And who did he see but his own beloved son! There he was, lounging at a table full of delicacies. The innkeeper was catering to his every whim, serving him and flattering him!

The boy saw his father and began to tremble. He stood up and ran to his father, falling at his feet, and cried, "Oh, Father, Father, take me out of here! I am a prisoner of this innkeeper's flattery. I am a hostage to his delicacies and fine wines. They confounded my senses until I became oblivious to everything else. I forgot where I came from and where I was going. I even forgot you! I forgot to write to you, to fulfill my promise to you!"

Our condition during the entire year differs very little from that of this captive rich boy. Our Father, too, sent our souls down to this world to fulfill a mission, to honor Him by learning His Torah and performing His commandments. He prepared proper living quarters for each of us and great teachers to instruct us in the way of God. We strayed from the proper path, however, and turned into the inn of the Evil Inclination. God created this force so that we could earn eternal closeness to Him by overcoming it. In the meantime, it manages to make us forget our mission and our destiny. It schemes only to steal our most precious possessions, our souls. It deceives us and deludes us. It makes us feel we no longer have any connection with our Father in Heaven, and certainly no obligation to fulfill our vows towards Him. As a result, we forget how to come before our Creator when we need Him most.

But our Sages have told us that during the Ten Days of *Teshuvah*, Hashem comes to us. "Seek Hashem when He can be found, call upon Him when He is close at hand... during the Ten Days of *Teshuvah* which begin with Rosh Hashanah and end with Yom Kippur." Our Father comes to the inn in search of His children. Should we not tremble in His presence and fall at His feet? Should we not call out from the uttermost depths of our souls, "Behold our affliction and wage our battle!" Behold how the Evil Inclination has caused us to fall asleep in exile. Rescue us from his clutches and take us to our Holy Land, to the place You have prepared for our ultimate benefit, to our teachers who will instruct us how to fulfill our mission...

Ohel Ya'akov

קְחוּ עִמָּכֶם דְּבָרִים וְשׁוּבוּ אֶל ה׳

"Take with you words and return to Hashem."

Rabbi Yisrael Meir Ha-Kohen, the Chafetz Chayim, asked: Which words shall we take with us? He answered with one of his most famous parables.

A poor man once met a wealthy member of the community and requested a loan. He explained that he was offered the chance of renting a small store in which he could honorably earn a living. If the wealthy man would agree to lend him the required down payment, he would rehabilitate himself and establish himself once and for all.

"I will be happy to help you," the wealthy man replied, "but right now I am on my way to an important meeting. Come to my office in two hours, and you will receive the sum you need."

The wealthy man hurried his meeting in order to be home for his appointment. He prepared the amount that had been agreed upon and waited for the poor man, but the latter did not show up.

The wealthy man left his home in the afternoon for another appointment. As he was walking, the poor man stopped him again and said, "If you could only lend me the sum we spoke about, I could establish myself with an honorable livelihood. You would be fulfilling the mitzvah of 'When your brother becomes impoverished and cannot support himself, come to his aid and help him survive...'" (*Vayikra* 25:35).

"Well said," the wealthy man replied, "but didn't we already set up an appointment this morning? I waited for you and you didn't come... But let us not dwell on the past. Right now, I am on my way to meet with someone. Come to me in another hour and I will give you the money I promised you."

An hour later, the wealthy man sat waiting in his home. Again, the poor man did not show up.

The next morning, as the wealthy man was on his way to the synagogue to pray, he was met again by the poor man.

Again he pleaded, "The store is still for rent. If you would only lend me the required sum..."

"Look here," the wealthy man replied, "yesterday I waited for you in the morning, and again in the afternoon. You never came! You always encounter me in the street, by chance, and you never take the trouble to come and get the money. It seems that you do not really mean what you say. Your heart is far from your mouth. If you were really in such need of money, surely you would take the trouble to come and pick it up."

We are not very different from the poor man in this story. Before proclaiming Hashem's Oneness in the *Shema* every day, we ask, "Our Father, our King... be gracious to us and teach us... have mercy on us and imbue our hearts [with the ability] to comprehend and discern, hearken, learn and teach, safeguard and practice, and fulfill all the teachings of Your Torah out of love [for You]! Enlighten our eyes with Your Torah. Bind our hearts to [You through the performance of] Your commandments! Unify our hearts [and minds] to love and fear Your Name!" In the *Shemoneh Esreh* we ask, "Grant us knowledge, understanding, and intelligence." At the conclusion of the *Shemoneh Esreh*, we request, "Open my heart with Your Torah so that my soul will run to do Your commandments [of its own accord]!" In *u'Va l'Tziyon* we ask, "May He open our hearts [and minds] with His Torah and instill His love and His awe within our hearts to perform His Will and serve Him wholeheartedly."

Undoubtedly, Hashem wants to answer and fulfill our requests. He says, "I will certainly help you. Just come to My house, to the *beis midrash*, the study hall and the yeshivah, and I will enlighten your eyes with the light of My Torah. Whoever comes to be purified will be assisted from Above!" We, however, make the requests but do not trouble ourselves to come and receive the treasures that await us.

This is what the prophet meant when he said, "Take with

you words and return to Hashem!" (*Hoshea* 14:3). Which words shall we take? The very words we pray when we ask for Hashem's blessing. Take these words *seriously*. Come to Hashem and bring them along with you. His only desire is to fulfill them!

Shem Olam

כִּי יְשָׁרִים דַּרְכֵי ה׳ וְצַדִּיקִים יֵלְכוּ בָם וּפוֹשְׁעִים יִכָּשְׁלוּ בָם

"Hashem's ways are upright; the righteous will walk in them, but the disdainful will stumble in them."

Said the Maggid of Dubno: It is known that "The precepts of God are upright, gladdening the heart. The commandments of God are radiant, enlightening the eyes" (*Tehillim* 19:9). How is it that wicked people stumble in them? Why are the commandments a yoke and a burden for such individuals? He answered with a parable.

There was once a rich and charitable man who provided shelter for the homeless and food for the hungry. Tables were always set in his home and a staff of servants was always ready to provide delicious meals and fine drink for anyone in need. One day a certain poor man once showed up, and was invited in. He sat down to partake of the meal, and stuffed himself with fish, pheasant and quail. Afterwards he wandered out of the house just as he had come in.

All of a sudden he felt ill. Attacked by a sharp pain, he collapsed, unconscious. The servants saw him fall and immediately called an ambulance. He was taken to the hospital, where the doctors found him in critical condition: a serious kidney condition had been inflamed as a result of eating so much rich food. The wealthy man felt very bad when he heard this, and he hurried to the hospital to visit the poor fellow. When the poor man saw him, he whispered with his last ounce of strength, "Murderer..."

The wealthy man lifted his hand and said, "You are pre-
sumptuous. You may ask the countless other poor people who
have eaten at my table if my meals are good and healthy or
not. When you arrived at my doorstep, however, you were
already seriously ill. Why complain to me? I never had sick
people in mind when I prepared my meals..."

This is what the prophet meant by "Hashem's ways are
upright." The proof of this is that "the righteous will walk in
them"—they not only stay perfectly healthy but constantly
increase their strength and vigor. For them, the Torah and its
commandments become an elixir of life (*Yoma* 72a). "The
disdainful," on the other hand—those who have ruined their
spiritual immune system through neglect and outright con-
tempt—"will stumble in them." They are not worthy, God
forbid, and so the Torah becomes an elixir of death for them.

The lesson: One need only strive to improve oneself, and
the precious light of healing contained in the Torah will do the
rest.

Kochav Mi-Ya'akov, *Haftarah* to *Parashas Vayetze*

"Hashem's ways are upright..."

The Maggid told another parable with a similar message. This
parable is known to have made a profound impression on
Rabbi Menachem Mendel, the Kotzker Rebbe.

One Friday afternoon, a number of merchants were returning to their home town after spending the week away from
their families. Their wagon was delayed on the way a number
of times, and the hour was late. They finally arrived at their
destination a few minutes before the Sabbath. As they drove
through town, one of the merchants jumped from the wagon
to run home and prepare in honor of the Sabbath. He called
to the driver, "I'm in a hurry and have no time to unload my

things. If you will just bring my bag to the house, I will pay you for your trouble."

He arrived home and managed to bathe quickly and get dressed in his Sabbath clothes. He had just finished when the driver stepped into his study, out of breath and sweating profusely. "Those steps!" the driver complained, wiping his brow. "They're backbreaking!"

"But there must be some mistake," the merchant interrupted. "You must have accidentally switched my bag with someone else's."

"How can you tell?" The driver looked at him in surprise. "You haven't even seen the bag I brought! Go into the next room and see for yourself!"

"That's not necessary," the merchant replied, smiling. "It's enough to see you panting and sweating in order to know that you brought the wrong one. Mine contained only a few pieces of clothing—it is very light!"

The driver understood his mistake. He had hauled a heavy bag up the stairs for nothing. In the end, he did not even receive payment for all his effort.

The lesson: There are those who complain about the difficulty of observing the commandments. To such people, the prophet says in the name of God, "It is not Me you have called upon, O Ya'akov; nor is it for Me that you have wearied yourself, O Israel" (*Yeshayahu* 43:22). If you are weary after having done a commandment, as if you have expended all your energy and depleted your strength, it is a sure sign that your worship was not genuine and pure. Why? As the Psalmist says: "The precepts of God are upright, gladdening the heart. The commandments of God are radiant, enlightening the eyes" (*Tehillim* 19:9).

Kochav Mi-Ya'akov, *Haftarah of Vayikra*

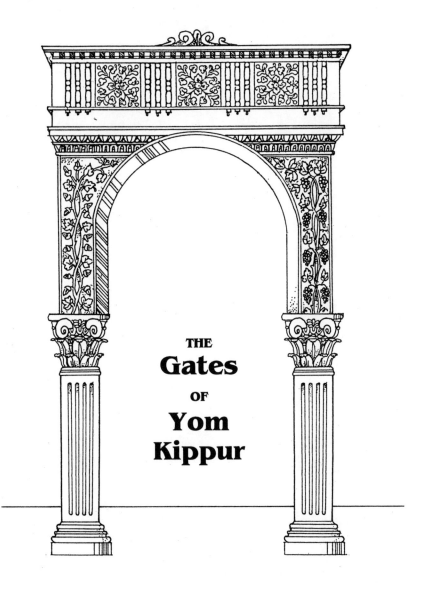

THE
Gates
OF
Yom
Kippur

Vidui—Confession

The Difference between
Confession and Accusation

Speaking before a congregation on Yom Kippur, the Maggid of Dubno quoted a verse in which the Psalmist speaks of the effect of Moshe's extraordinary love and self-sacrifice for his people: "[God] thought to destroy them had not Moshe—His chosen one—stood in the breach before Him, to turn His wrath back from destruction" (*Tehillim* 106:23).

The Midrash (*Shemos Rabbah* 43:1) likens this to a king who sat in judgment on his son. Seeing that the prosecutor was biasing the king with his allegations against the boy, the boy's tutor stepped in and had the prosecutor removed. He then stood in his place and spoke favorably about the boy. Thus, too, when Israel made the golden calf, the Heavenly Accuser stood up to prosecute them within [the Heavenly court] while Moshe stood without. What did Moshe do? He stood up, thrust the Accuser out, and stood in his place, as it is written, "He stood in the breach before him," in place of the breacher himself [i.e., the Accuser] who had preceded him.

In a slightly different version, the Midrash (47:9) continues: Moshe acted wisely. First he mentioned their sin and only then pleaded for pardon. First he began to accuse Israel, as it is written, "The people have committed a terrible mistake by making a golden calf!" When the destroying angels saw Moshe doing their work, they left of their own accord, saying, "Why should we accuse? Let Moshe do it for us!" Moshe waited for them to leave and then said, "Now, if You would, please forgive their mistake."

In this same way, whoever confesses and admits his mistakes effectively prevents all Heavenly accusers or earthly enemies from harming him. Like the destroying angels mentioned above, they will say, "Why should we accuse? He is detailing everything he did without us!"

But, the Maggid of Dubno added, an obvious question must be asked: What do we really gain by confessing our sins? What is the difference between a person admitting that he did wrong, on the one hand, and being accused of the same things by an avowed enemy, on the other hand? The difference is... in the melody, in the way the words are said. A parable will clarify this.

There was once a merchant who traveled to Leipzig for the great fair and remained there a short while after the fair ended. When he finally was ready to return home, he purchased a fine and expensive suit for his son. The family rejoiced upon his arrival home. The son's happiness was especially great, both for his father's return and the suit he received. He immediately dressed up in the suit and went out to show it off to his friends. Some of them were impressed; some rejoiced with him in his good fortune; and some were jealous. While they were all walking along together, however, the boy slipped and tumbled headlong down a muddy embankment. He was unhurt, but the suit was completely covered with mud.

One of the boys immediately called out, "I'm running home to tell your father what you did to your new suit!"

The distraught boy knew that his father was bound to be very angry; so, without losing a moment, he ran home himself in order to get there first. "Father, Father!" he cried. "Look what happened to me! Look at my new suit!"

His father's mercy was immediately aroused. "Don't cry," he comforted his son. "The suit can be cleaned, and if not, I will buy you a new one."

What is the difference between the slander of a jealous enemy and one's own confession? The melody. The way the words are spoken... This is what David Ha-Melech meant when he said, "Depart from me, all you evildoers, so that God will hear the voice of my weeping. [So that] God will hear my plea. [So that] God will accept my prayer. All my enemies will then be ashamed and panic-stricken. They will repent, [but] at that moment they will experience [unbearable] shame" (*Tehillim* 6:9-10). All Heavenly and earthly accusers will be silenced and depart, and our confession will be accepted, if only our pleas for pardon are accompanied by genuine weeping and sincere regret.

This is also the meaning of the verse, "It is something that is very close to you. It is in your mouth and in your heart, so that you can do it" (*Devarim* 30:14). When can it be done? When the heart joins the mouth in confession!

Ohel Ya'akov, *Emor*

Ten Confessions on Yom Kippur

Why did the Sages institute so many confessions? The great Kabbalist, Rabbi Yosef Gikatilia, likened our sins to the rope tied to a pail which is lowered into the well to draw water. At first the rope is very strong, but after repeated usage it begins to unravel. Finally, it snaps and breaks, and the pail drops into the water.

Such are our sins. At first, they are tenacious and unyielding. When one repeatedly requests pardon for having committed them, however, his connection to them begins to loosen and unravel until it finally breaks. This is the meaning of the verse, "I will obliterate your crimes like a thick [rope] and [disperse] your sins like a cloudy mist" (*Yeshayahu* 44:22).

Sefer Ha-Meshalim 53

אָנוּ קְשֵׁי עֹרֶף וְאַתָּה אֶרֶךְ אַפַּיִם

"We are stiff-necked, but You are patient and slow to anger."

What kind of a claim is this? Just because we are stiff-necked, should God forgive us?

The Maggid of Dubno asked the same question about

Moshe's words to God: "If I have found favor in Your eyes, God, let my Lord go among us. This nation may be *stiff-necked*, but forgive our sins and our mistakes, and make us Your own" (*Shemos* 34:9). What is the justification? Is this a proper defense? For this very reason itself, God Himself had already declared, "[You will thus go to] a land flowing with milk and honey. I will not go with you, however, since you are a *stiff-necked* nation, and I may destroy you along the way" (*ibid.* 33:3). Moshe seemed to have turned the source of the problem [of God's wanting to distance Himself from us] into the very reason why His Presence should accompany us! How did he expect to get away with such a thing? This can only be understood with a parable.

There was once a peddler who purchased an entire lot of remnants of cheap cloth in various colors and patterns. These remnants were good for mending and patching old clothes, for a small patch could be used to save an entire garment. Thus the merchandise promised to bring in a good profit. The peddler loaded up his wagon and headed for the capital, thinking, "The people of this city are well-off, so they will surely buy my merchandise at a good price."

But when the people in the capital saw his merchandise, they weren't interested. One man explained to him, "Please don't be offended, but here, people wear silk and satin; and when a garment is torn it is thrown away, never to be worn again! If you want to find customers for your goods, travel to the small towns and villages. There people wear old and simple clothing—and it's all full of patches!"

Moshe ascended to Heaven and found it written in the Torah that God is "merciful and gracious, patient and slow to anger, [with] infinite lovingkindness and truth, preserving lovingkindness for thousands of generations, forgiving sin, rebellion and error, and cleansing [them]" (*Shemos* 34:6). Such qualities are extremely useful for fixing up any fault or defect, and "patching" any rip or tear. Moshe said to God, "Master of the world, here in Heaven there is no one to buy this won-drous merchandise of Yours. Here, everyone is dressed in garments of light and glory. Their cloaks are never torn or soiled. 'If I have found favor in Your eyes, God, let my Lord go among us' and put His qualities of mercy to use on earth. 'This nation may be stiff-necked'—their clothes are torn and ragged—'but [for this very reason] forgive our sins and our mistakes, and make us Your own!'"

The same is true of us: We are stiff-necked, but that is all the more reason for You to be patient and slow to anger with us!

Ohel Ya'akov, *Ki Sissa*

לוֹמַר לְפָנֶיךָ... חָטָאנוּ

"We are not so arrogant and stiff-necked as to say... that we are completely righteous and have not erred. Rather, [we admit that] we and our ancestors have erred."

When Moshe Rabbenu stood up to pray for Israel and entreat forgiveness for them, he began with the confession, "The people have committed a terrible mistake by making a golden calf" (*Shemos* 32:32). Why did he emphasize the enormity of the sin? The Maggid of Dubno explained with a parable.

There were once two friends who were inseparable. They were both poor, and therefore found it fitting to stay together while begging from door to door as well. Once, one of them became ill with a highly infectious disease. His friend feared that if the truth were known, he would be quarantined in a hospital for incurables, where his condition might worsen until he died, alone... "No!" the loyal friend decided. "He will stay with me and I will take care of his every need." And so it was. Everywhere they went, he found comfortable lodging and hid the fact of his friend's illness. He went begging alone from door to door for enough money to pay for food and lodging for them both.

One night, upon returning to their room, he heard that a famous doctor had come to spend the night at the inn. He immediately went and called on the doctor. In confidence, he divulged the whole story. "You understand," he confided, "that I would never agree to abandon him in the condition he is in, but perhaps it would be possible to alleviate his condition somewhat..."

"Alleviate his condition!" the doctor exclaimed. "Why not have him cured completely? Why have you not spoken up until now? Come, let us examine your friend!"

They went down to their room, and the man told his sick friend, "Show the doctor all the scabs on your body, and tell him about your disease."

"Heaven forbid!" cried the sick man in horror. "I mustn't speak about it lest my secret become known. Make the doctor leave at once—before he puts me away for the rest of my days!"

"Calm down," his friend replied. "We have kept our secret from everybody, but this man is a doctor: he can help cure you! You can tell him everything!"

In the same way, Moshe was Israel's true and loyal friend. When they were infected by the poison of the serpent and seduced into worshiping the golden calf, he broke the stone tablets in order to divert attention away from their sin. He then risked his life to plead on their behalf. None of this was sufficient to atone for and cleanse them of their sin, however, until he stood before God and detailed the entire episode. In acting thus, he was teaching us that complete atonement can be gained only when the enormity of a sin is acknowledged. This is why he said, "The people have committed a terrible mistake by making a golden calf."

Ohel Ya'akov, *Ki Sissa*

"Rather, [we admit that] we and our ancestors have erred."

The Talmud (*Yoma* 87b) states that the phrase "*Aval anachnu chatanu*—Rather, we have erred,*"* in which we admit and take responsibility for having done wrong, is the *sine qua non* of genuine confession. The Alter of Kelm was bothered by this. A *chet* is an error, a mistake. How can confessing and acknowledging one's errors also cover more serious transgressions which might have been done purposely and with bad intent?

He answered that the word *chet* carries an additional connotation. This is brought out in the verse describing the fighting men of the tribe of Binyamin: "There were seven hundred chosen men, left-handed, every one of whom could sling stones at a hair, and not miss" (*Shoftim* 20:16). "And not miss" is *v'lo yachti* in Hebrew. We learn from this that *chet* involves some lack, deficiency, flaw, or imperfection within us that makes us "miss the mark" and stray from the straight path. Admitting our *chet* is therefore a fundamental prerequisite of true confession because it refers to something extremely basic and essential at the root of all sin. Instead of detailing the different levels of sin and transgression, therefore, we say: "Woe to us, that we are filled with such imperfections, which have brought us to commit all these sins!"

Based on this, the Alter of Kelm explained how the first man, Adam, God's own pristine creation, who fell and sinned by eating from the Tree of Knowledge of Good and Evil, could have said in his confession, "The woman whom You allotted to me offered me from the tree, and I ate" (*Bereshis* 3:12). Many have seen this statement as outright slander, an obvious attempt to rationalize his guilt and place all the blame on Chavah! This is not necessarily the case. On the contrary, it can be seen as a cutting admission of his own guilt, a true confession. In reality, Adam was saying, "Master of the world, I have committed an actual sin by eating from the tree, and I can certainly confess and repent for having done so. But the root cause for my sin still lurks within me. It is this dreadful imperfection which allows me to succumb to temptation and persuasion. As long as this root cause exists within me, what good will it do to pluck or cut off every new stalk that sprouts? What good is it to confess and repent for every new little sin that peeks its head above the surface? If I repent for one sin, another one will surely pop up in its place! If, however, I can get to the root of my imperfections and fix that—all the sins that could possibly have grown out from that root will automatically be eliminated!" [The verse now can be re-read as: "The woman whom You, in Your wisdom and kindness, allotted to be with me and share my life—she offered me from the forbidden tree. It was not her fault. On the contrary, I should have said no. But, because of my own weakness, I succumbed and ate."]

Chochmah u'Musar 1:74

"...we and our ancestors have erred."

In the days when the *Beis Ha-Mikdash* stood, the *Kohen Gadol* would detail his confession. He would distinguish between inadvertent error (*chet*), intentional transgression (*avon*), and blatant rebellion against God's sovereign authority (*pesha*). We, on the other hand, include everything under the general heading of *chet*, which, as we mentioned earlier, implies a fundamental lack or flaw, a "missing the mark."

Asked the Maggid of Dubno: Why did the *Kohen Gadol* have to detail each different type of sin, whereas we, filled with imperfections as we are, group them under one general heading? He answered with a parable.

A certain man was very sick. He lay in bed immobile as a stone, blind, bald, covered with painful boils and festering sores from head to foot, one arm in a splint and one amputated, one leg in traction and another amputated. One day, he heard the sound of people shouting and running in the streets. He began to cry out, "Hey! Hello! Can anybody hear me?"

One man answered, "Yes—what do you want?"

"Tell me, please," the sick man pleaded, "what has happened? Why is everyone running and shouting?"

"An awful catastrophe is about to befall us," the man replied. "They are all running for their lives!"

"Woe is me!" the sick man moaned. "I am lying here, totally immobile! What tragedy is about to occur? I have been left alone and no one has told me a thing! Who is threatening us? How did the whole thing develop? Come, sit by my side, tell me all the details. I want to know about the whole thing!"

"I'm sorry, but this is not the time to satisfy your curiosity," the man replied. "I don't have the time to chat! Besides, what does it matter to you anyway? If you were healthy, there might be some justification for your question. You would have to know, for example, whether you should arm yourself in order to confront the coming disaster. You would have to know where to flee, and which places were safe and which dangerous. Since you aren't healthy, however, and can't do anything to help yourself, all these things need not concern you. You should have one request: to be rescued from here, and quickly. The rescue team will already know where to take you. Once you're there, you'll have plenty of time to ask questions..."

The lesson: When the *Beis Ha-Mikdash* stood in Jerusalem and the Sanhedrin judged the nation, it was appropriate to use a special order of confession in which we detailed each different kind of sin. This explains why the *Kohen Gadol* referred to each category of sin separately: "Your people Israel have erred (*chet*), deliberately disobeyed (*avon*), and obstinately violated (*pesha*)." The reason for this is obvious. The penalty for a sin depended on two things: the kind of sin and the degree of evil intent or lack of it that a person had at the moment he committed a crime. The system of penalties provided a gauge as to the relative severity of various sins. Certain grave sins were punishable by one of four levels of capital punishment, by corporal punishment (flogging), and/or by various gradations of animal offerings. There were guilt offerings (*asham*), expiation offerings (*chatas*), and offerings which were completely burnt on the altar (*olah*). [In a sense, the slaughter and burning of an animal represented a vicarious taste of death for the sinner. Sacrifice thus never served as an end in itself, but merely as a means to arouse a person to repentance. No sacrifice could atone for sin unless it was accompanied by repentance.]

Now that the Temple no longer stands, we are like the sick man in the parable. Our entire national body is devastated. God knows, we have suffered terrible losses of life and limb. Yeshayahu described our condition aptly when he lamented, "Ah, sinful nation, a people laden with iniquity, offspring of evildoers, children who deal corruptly... How much more punishment do you require, seeing that you continue to rebel? The entire head is sick, and the entire heart faint. From head to foot there is nothing sound in [the national body], only wounds, bruises, and festering sores. They have not been pressed out, or bound up, or softened with ointment" (*Yeshayahu* 1:4-6).

Now, without the Temple and a Sanhedrin, and no way to atone for specific sins, we are left with prayer. Sincere prayer takes the place of sacrifice, as the prophet foretold: "We will offer the words of our lips instead of calves" (*Hoshea* 14:3). With this in mind, we therefore repeatedly call out throughout Yom Kippur: Master of the world, we have erred! We have gone off course! We are full of flaws and imperfections! Quickly, rescue us! Restore us to our Land, rebuild our Temple, and there we will serve You with love and awe, as in days of old and years gone by!

Ohel Ya'akov, *Ki Sissa*

אָשַׁמְנוּ, בָּגַדְנוּ

"We are guilty. We have been ungrateful..."

Guilt (*ashmah*) is not as contemptible as ingratitude (*begidah*). This is made clear in the following parable by the Maggid of Dubno.

A craftsman whose work was highly prized and sought after once fell into debt and required a loan. He approached a wealthy patron of his and solicited monetary assistance. The latter responded generously and provided the craftsman with the entire sum he had requested.

When not specified otherwise, a loan is for thirty days. The first month passed, and a second, however, and the craftsman still did not repay his loan. Three months passed. The patron sent a letter requesting that the loan be repaid. No answer. He had the craftsman's tools impounded as security. These were expensive tools with which the craftsman made his living. The patron had no doubt that the craftsman would now make every effort to obtain the money to repay his debt and reclaim his tools.

How great his exasperation and displeasure when he heard that the craftsman had simply switched jobs without reclaiming his tools, without attempting to repay the loan, and without even apologizing! What audacity!

The lesson: Our Father in Heaven provided us with an abundance of good. When we failed to repay this goodness in kind by learning His Torah and fulfilling His commandments, He decided to take our Temple from us as collateral. The Sages found a hint for this in the word *mishkan*. In the Torah, the tabernacle that Moshe built in the wilderness is called the *mishkan*. The word *mishkan* (literally, "dwelling") refers to the in-dwelling of the Divine Presence; but it also means "collateral" or "security." On the basis of this double meaning, the Sages saw in the verse "These are the accounts of the *mishkan*, the *mishkan* of testimony" (*Shemos* 38:21), an allusion to the two Temples which would be taken from Israel as "collateral" on account of their sins. (Rashi *ibid.*)

The Holy Temple was the place where heaven dwelled on earth. It was the source of our life and livelihood. Since it was destroyed, there is never a day that isn't worse than the previous one (*Sotah* 9:12). We don't realize it today because we cannot imagine that the world was ever any different than it is now. The destruction of the Temple was equivalent in its time, however, to the expulsion of Adam and Chavah from the Garden of Eden. When the Temple was destroyed, our Sages tell us, the world became black, purity disappeared from the world, and great men were no longer to be found. Since that day, an iron curtain has been placed between us and our Father in heaven (*Berachos* 32a). We paid dearly when the Temple was appropriated as collateral for our sins. In doing so, Hashem wished to awaken us to the gravity of our plight. "Look!" He was telling us. "See how your source of livelihood has been taken. Purify yourselves, do everything you can to reclaim what is rightfully yours. At least ask My forgiveness! Plead before Me to rebuild the Temple, and restore My Presence to Zion in mercy!"

How great was His displeasure when He beheld our brazen ingratitude, when we turned our backs on Him and went about our lives as if nothing had happened. Then, we were no longer guilty of just having sinned; we were guilty also of lack of appreciation of what we had lost. We were guilty of blatant ingratitude, of completely ignoring God!

Ohel Ya'akov, *Pekudei*

גָּזַלְנוּ

"We have stolen."

The Talmud (*Sanhedrin* 108a) quotes Rabbi Yochanan: Behold the power of *chamas* (theft, oppression, cruelty)! The people of the generation of the Flood were guilty of every conceivable sin, but their fate was not sealed until they began stealing and oppressing. This is the meaning of the verse, "God said to No'ach, 'The end of all flesh has come before Me. The world is filled [as a cup is filled] with *chamas* (violence) through them. I will therefore destroy them with the earth'" (*Bereshis* 6:13).

As the Torah itself implies, the generation of the Flood was steeped in sexual depravity and idolatry. Why was their fate not sealed until they began stealing and oppressing? Why should theft be considered worse than anything else?

The Maggid of Dubno explained the difference between theft and all other crimes. For example, a righteous judge sees a Jew eating pork in public. He will certainly be enraged and have the man flogged. His indignation will stem from his sense of justice. A Jew just does not do such things.

If the same judge sees another man stealing the last crumbs of bread from a beggar, he will have him flogged also. In this case, however, his indignation will stem not only from his sense of justice, but from his sense of compassion as well. It is in this sense that we can understand how Hashem wished to punish the generation of the Flood, but restrained His wrath until they began stealing and oppressing. It was then that the cup of the world became filled to overflowing.

Kol Ha-Tor 39a

עָוִינוּ

Avinu—"We have sinned intentionally."

The prophet *Yeshayahu* writes, "The Lord has poured a spirit of distortion (*ivim*) into her" (*Yeshayahu* 19:14). Rashi comments: "*Ivim* is the name of a sickness which causes mental disorder." *Metzudas Tziyon* relates *ivim* to *ivus* (distortion) and *akimus* (crookedness). The concept of *avon* thus involves a kind of progression from *chet*. *Chet* is the initial error or mistake. As the rabbis have said, it is a spirit of folly which enters a person and blinds him. When one first makes a mistake, there- fore, it is necessary to correct it immediately, to banish the spirit of folly and come back to one's senses. When this is not done, a certain distortion takes place. Similar to the perception of patients who are mentally disturbed, our perception be- comes twisted. We no longer view reality as it is, but begin to rationalize our vice and think of it as a virtue. We are then willing to sin intentionally in order to satisfy our desires. It does not bother us any more. The distortion has set in and become part of us.

The Maggid of Dubno illustrated this progression with a parable.

A man was once walking in the forest with his children. As they went further and further into the dense woods, they lost their way. Eventually they ran out of the few provisions they had brought with them, and were forced to eat roots and wild grass which were as bitter as wormwood. Their stomachs protested such repulsive fare, and they suffered unbearable cramps. Nevertheless, for lack of anything else, they contin- ued to eat. They knew that they must stay alive and continue on, hoping to emerge from the oppressive darkness and find their way back home.

One day, one of the children announced happily to his father, "Today I ate one of the shrubs in the forest and it tasted sweet! My stomach didn't hurt at all!"

Instead of rejoicing, however, the father began to cry.

"What's wrong, Father?" the boy asked in wonder. "Why are you crying?"

"My son, I am very distressed," the man replied. "Know that as long as these plants and shrubs were bitter to us and harmful to our stomachs, it was a clear sign that we were still civilized human beings unable to digest food fit for animals and insects. But the moment it is no longer bitter, and our stomachs adjust to it, this is a sign that we have become accustomed to the wild and are like savages and animals, no longer human and part of civilization!"

The lesson: As noted, sin causes distortion. It is likened to a spirit of folly which enters a person and causes him to perceive things which are evil as good, and vice versa. When this spirit is not evicted forthright, and the sin is repeated, twice, three times, and more, it seems like the most natural thing in the world (*Yoma* 87a). There is no greater distortion than this.

This is alluded to in the words of the Psalmist: "My soul has been sated with evils; my life-force nears the netherworld" (*Tehillim* 88:4). That is, when does a person know that he has reached the lowest level of existence possible, that his life is nearing the netherworld? When his soul no longer protests the evils he has committed, but is "sated" and "satisfied" by them!

Ohel Ya'akov, *Va-yelech*

סַרְנוּ מִמִּצְוֹתֶיךָ וּמִמִּשְׁפָּטֶיךָ הַטּוֹבִים, וְלֹא שָׁוָה לָנוּ
"We have turned away from Your good commandments and laws, and it has not profited us."

In its most perfect sense, says the Rambam (*Hilchos Teshuvah,* Ch. 2), repentance consists of four elements: changing one's ways, sincere regret, confession to God, and resolve not to repeat the sin. All of these are included in the prophet's admonition, "Return, Israel, to God your Lord (1), for you have regretted your sin (2). Take along words (3), and return to God. Say to Him... 'we will no longer make gods out of the works of our hands (4)'" (*Hoshea* 14:2,4).

In our confession, as well, we express a desire to change our ways. We pound our breasts and admit having done wrong. [By pounding our breasts, we point to our hearts and thus acknowledge that it was our desires that misled us into doing wrong.] We ask that Hashem assist us in our resolve never to repeat our sins. We also express sincere regret by admitting, "We have turned away from Your good commandments and laws, and it has not profited us."

But, the Maggid of Dubno asked, what does "it has not profited us" mean? If a man sitting in jail reviews his deeds and the price he has had to pay for doing them, and comes to the conclusion that "crime does not pay," is that enough to warrant saying "it has not profited us"? And if it had profited him, if he hadn't gotten caught by his fellow human beings, would he still regret having defied God? No, such regret is not enough. It is not sufficient to observe that one has not benefited in the least by having tried to circumvent or defy God's will. This is still missing the point. We must understand the correct reason for being remorseful.

A true and penetrating realization of "it has not profited us" would go something like this: Look at yourself. Look how you've gone and exchanged eternity for a passing fancy. Did you, a mere mortal, think you could defy God? How could you have been so dense? Did you think He wasn't real just because He transcended your minuscule idea of who He was or ought to be? Be thankful now that He is what He is. He is all there is. He alone gives you life. He alone sustains you at all times. Even when you were busy thinking that He didn't exist, He did not cease sustaining you for a moment! What made you such an ingrate? Was it your desires, your desire to be a somebody, to gain people's recognition, to make them like you, to have power over others, or a million and one other excuses? Is that what distorted your perceptions and made you think that He wasn't as close to you as your very soul? That would make sense. Unconsciously, you felt that in order to establish your own sense of selfhood you had to deny and revolt against His. Is this how you went off course and became so insensitive to your soul? Well, now it is time to wake up. Now you know that it was all to no avail!

The Maggid then told a parable about this.

There was once a brutish man who was an ignoramus and behaved accordingly. For some odd reason, good fortune shone its face on him and he became very wealthy, one of the leading members of his community. When his daughter reached marriageable age, two possible matches were offered to him. One was the son of a man known to all as "the Informer." This was a cruel, black-hearted Jew who found a way of getting close to the government by informing on his fellow Jews. If so-and-so had illegal merchandise in his store, the Informer would gladly notify the authorities, for a price. If so-and-so had built a house without authorization from the city planning commission, the Informer would be on hand. In this way, he caused his Jewish brethren plenty of harm. People kept their distance from him and his activities. The authorities, on the other hand, rewarded him amply for his devoted "services." He received a percentage of every fine they collected at his instigation. By the time his son was ready to get married, he had managed to accumulate a nice fortune. His status in the community, though, was as lowly as could be.

The Informer's son was proof that the apple does not fall far from the tree. The boy was wicked and cruel; he was friendly with the *goyim* and imitated them in his actions. Now, the Informer's son was being offered to the brutish man who had suddenly become wealthy as a match for his daughter! The Informer was also willing to put up a nice dowry. He would buy the couple a house and furnish it. He would foot the tab for the entire wedding. In short, he was willing to pay for everything.

The brutish man was deliberating about this match when a second offer came his way: the rabbi's son. The rabbi of this town was highly respected. His son, as well, was brilliant, talented, even-tempered, upright, decent, and graced with excellent character. In short, a real catch.

The brutish man, who had recently become wealthy, expressed his surprise to the matchmaker: "Why would the rabbi agree to have his son marry the daughter of a man like me?"

"You are aware," the matchmaker replied, "that the rabbi's

salary is meager. He also has a number of daughters who have reached marriageable age. He has therefore agreed to this match on the condition that he will not be required to lay out any money. You will pay for the wedding and the wardrobe. You will purchase the house and furnish it. You will pay for everything."

What could he say? This match was still incomparably more attractive than the first. "Fine, I will pay for everything," the man agreed. "The rabbi need only provide a suit for the groom—nothing more!"

The matchmaker went to the rabbi to deliver the message. He returned shortly thereafter with an answer: "The rabbi does not agree to your terms. The stipulation was that you pay for everything. He is not willing to buy his son a suit."

The brutish man became incensed. "This is mere pettiness. He is being stubborn for the sake of being stubborn. I will not agree to it. I am going to marry my daughter to the son of the Informer!"

"As you wish," the disappointed matchmaker replied. And he returned to the rabbi to tell him what had happened. He also tried to persuade the rabbi not to ruin a perfectly good match because of a trivial thing like a suit. "After all," he explained, "the fellow is willing to spend so much on everything else. Why pass it up?" But the rabbi stood on principle and the matchmaker was unable to budge him.

The story spread. Friends of the brutish man were shocked. "How can it be," they challenged him, "that you are willing to refuse a perfectly good match because of a silly suit? And what do you get instead? The son of the Informer? You will be the laughingstock of the town. People will scoff and mock you. And your poor daughter—she will be heartsick forever!"

Their words penetrated his heart, and he decided to go to the rabbi himself. "Rabbi," he said, "I accept your conditions. I will pay for the suit. Let's shake hands and drink a l'chayim! Mazal tov, my dear in-law, mazal tov!"

But his outstretched hand remained suspended in midair. The rabbi shook his head and answered solemnly, "I am sorry to inform you that I cannot let my son marry your daughter. I hereby regret having gotten involved in the first place. I was sorely mistaken."

"Why?" asked the bewildered man.

"I will tell you," the rabbi replied. "When the match was first brought to my attention, I was under the impression that you had instructed the matchmaker to seek out a scholar with good qualities since it was your desire that your daughter marry into a Torah family. I was under the impression that Hashem had endowed you with wisdom to utilize your wealth to support the Torah, to support your son-in-law's studies, until he would become a great leader of our people. It was with all this in mind that I agreed to have my son—who is, thank God, a fine young man and a promising scholar—marry your daughter.

"But when the matchmaker told me of your intention to refuse the match with my son because of a suit, and take the Informer's son instead—a boy who is already infamous for having committed every sin in the book—I changed my mind. Even if you promised me all the wealth in the world, I would never agree to having my son marry your daughter. Clearly, if you do not recognize the value of Torah and those who learn it, my son has no place in your house!"

The moral: People who regret their actions and lament, "We have turned away from Your commandments, and it has not profited us," because they did not gain anything from doing evil, are acknowledging that they have no concept of true spirituality and holiness. Their decisions are biased by trivial material concerns. If they could only find a way of "making crime pay," they would be the first to rationalize their consciences away.

We, however, make sure to say, "We have turned away from Your *good* commandments and laws." We understand how precious they are. We appreciate their value. We therefore regret not having adhered to them. We regret the irreplaceable spiritual loss. It is this loss that we lament when we say, "It has not profited us!" This is genuine regret.

Ohel Ya'akov, *Shelach*

"What does God require of you, but to fear [with] God your Lord."

The Maggid of Mezrich told a parable about a boy whose father warned him not to go barefoot in the street, lest he be injured. The boy joined a group of unruly children, however, with whom he ran around barefoot. In no time at all a thorn did indeed stab his foot.

At first, the boy hardly felt it, but his father saw it and was concerned that it would become infected. He wanted to remove it, but the child would not allow him to touch it for fear that the extraction might be painful. The father held his son in his lap, however, and removed the thorn with a knife, against his child's will. The boy cried out in pain.

In the child's opinion, his father acted cruelly toward him, because the pain of extraction was greater than the pain of the thorn in his foot. In truth, however, this was kindness, not cruelty, for if the thorn had not been removed a far more painful and dangerous infection would have developed.

We can see, therefore, that the father's fear cannot be compared to the son's. The father feared infection and abscess. The son feared the pain of having the thorn removed, and considered this a punishment for disobeying his father. The father was not concerned with this, since his son's pain was only momentary, and removing the thorn was ultimately for the boy's own good.

Man's fear is not the same as that of God. Man generally fears punishment, but God is sorrowed by the actual sin which causes a person to sink into impurity. Once the sin is done, God does not hesitate to exact punishment. After all, the punishment is meant as a remedy, to cleanse man and restore his spiritual stature. Man should strive to make his fear the same as God's.

This is the meaning of the verse, "What does God require of you, but to fear את God your Lord" (*Devarim* 10:12), understanding *es* to mean "with." That is, your fear should be one *with* God's fear—the same as His. He is concerned lest you sin and injure yourself spiritually. This should be your concern as well. This is the true meaning of "fear of Heaven."

Likutei Yekarim 244

"We have turned away from Your good commandments and laws, and it has not profited us."

The holy Rabbi Chayim of Zanz told the following story: It was the custom of a certain priest to rail in every sermon against the curse of drunkenness. He was unrelenting in disparaging the members of his parish, which consisted mostly of farmers, from ruining their lives, wasting hard-earned money, and damaging their ability to think clearly. One Sunday morning in particular, he spoke so convincingly that everybody was in tears. As a result, the majority of the flock vowed not to overdo their drinking.

Not one day passed, however, before the first drunk was lying in the street. The other farmers were called to the scene, and they dragged him to the priest's home. He would determine a proper punishment.

The priest was genuinely perplexed by the spectacle that met his eyes. "What a powerful lure this accursed drink exerts! It drags a man down to the abyss of depravity and causes him to lose all semblance of humanity!"

"What is his punishment?" all present demanded to know.

Here again, the priest found himself in a bind. "How can I pronounce a man's sentence without having stood in his shoes and been faced with the same test? I have never tasted a sip of liquor in my entire life. I have always been careful to keep away from it. In order to punish a man, I must first be intimate with the test he was unable to withstand. If one of you will please bring me a glass of whiskey, I will drink it and know!"

They hurried and brought it to him. The priest tasted it with the tip of his tongue. The bitter sting of the alcohol burned his tongue and caused his face to screw up in contortions. He spit it out in disgust and said, "You wish me to decide this man's punishment? What greater punishment could there be than one sip of this accursed drink? He has already punished himself sufficiently by imbibing it, not to mention the loss of his senses and the sickness that resulted from it!"

This is what we mean when we say: "We have turned away from Your good commandments and laws, and it has not profited us." That is, all year round we grovel in our sins and wallow in their defilement. After taking stock of ourselves during Elul and the Ten Days of *Teshuvah*, we understand the bitterness of sin and the depth of depravity to which it leads. We therefore call out: Master of the world! What need is there to punish us further? It is enough of a punishment that we have turned away from Your good commandments and laws without having gained the slightest benefit or advantage. Can there be a greater punishment than this?

Mekor Chayim

"...and it has not profited us."

A parable from the Maggid of Vladislav: An elegant carriage once stopped in front of an expensive jewelry store on the main street of one of Europe's large cities. A distinguished looking woman stepped down from the carriage and entered the store. She introduced herself as the wife of one of the professors at the university. She had come to purchase a selection of jewelry for her upcoming birthday. Price was of no consequence. Her husband would pay whatever was required of him. She was only to make her selection and bring it to him.

A buyer such as this does not come along every day. The proprietor himself stepped up and showed her a selection of the store's finest jewels, with stunning settings of the largest diamonds. The distinguished buyer showed herself to be a person of fine taste. She selected the most beautiful and costly jewels in the store and requested that they be packaged as a gift, with the bill attached.

"Now, if you would be so kind to accompany me to my home," she said confidently, "I will show the jewels to my husband and he will write out a check for the entire sum on the spot."

The jeweller nodded in agreement. They stepped out of the store and up into the carriage which proceeded to make its way to the expensive part of town where the aristocracy lived. The carriage stopped in front of one of the more impressive mansions. As they ascended the marble steps, the jeweller glanced at the bronze plaque on the door. It read "Professor So-and-so," as the woman had said.

She rang the doorbell and the servant answered. "I have come with the jeweller," she announced. The servant bowed and ushered them in. They walked across the soft carpets. The woman accompanied him to a spacious parlor, and then left to show the jewels to her husband, promising to return shortly with a check.

He waited. Five minutes passed. Ten. A quarter of an hour. The woman still had not returned. The jeweller was perplexed: How long does it take to write a check? Who knows, maybe the professor was busy. Perhaps he was in a meeting with someone. Twenty minutes passed. Half an hour. Finally he decided to find out what was happening. He stood up and went out into the corridor. The servant was there. "Perhaps you can direct me to the professor's study?" he asked.

"Right over there, sir," the servant said as he pointed to the next door.

The jeweller stepped over to the door, knocked, and was invited in. As he entered he saw an elderly gentleman sitting at his desk, who motioned him to enter and sit down.

"You must be the professor?" the jeweller inquired.

"Yes, I am he. Please take a seat," the elderly gentleman said.

"But where is the woman?" the jeweller asked in wonder.

"It is all right; she explained everything to me. Sit and we will talk," the professor replied.

"What is there to talk about?" the man replied indignantly, still not sitting down. "I happen to be the owner of the most exclusive jewelry store in the city. Your wife bought some of my most expensive pieces. I accompanied her here, and I now request that you give me 40,850 dinars without further delay," he said, visibly agitated.

A smile crossed the professor's lips. It was an understanding smile, a comforting smile. "Yes, I know, I know. Sit down and tell me how it all began..." he said very sympathetically.

An eerie suspicion stole across the jeweller's mind. "How did it begin? How did what begin?" he asked distrustfully.

"This condition of yours. You can be frank with me. As you know, I am a psychiatrist. The woman told me the whole story when she was here this morning. She told me about a man who thought he was a seller of precious stones, who was pestering her with wild accusations that she owed him a fortune of money for jewels which he insisted she had purchased from him. I told her to bring him in if she could, and I see she has succeeded. Oh, my! What's happened? Wake up! Help, bring water!"

The door opened. The servant looked upon the jeweller, who lay sprawled out at his feet. He had fainted!

This is exactly how the Evil Inclination works, the Maggid concluded. He takes all our most precious possessions from us. He takes our superior qualities. He takes our Torah learning. He takes all the wonderful mitzvos which we might have performed. And he promises to pay us a fantastic price: happiness, contentment, and satisfaction, if we will only follow him. Then we go ahead and unsuspectingly deposit all our jewels into his safekeeping, only to fin out that he has slipped quietly away, leaving us with nothing... only the realization that it was all to no avail...

Siach Eliezer 19b

וְאַתָּה צַדִּיק עַל כָּל הַבָּא עָלֵינוּ
"You are therefore justified with regard to all that befalls us."

Said the Maggid of Dubno: To what can this be likened? To a man who summoned a well-known textile merchant to court. He stood before the judges and declared indignantly: "I have been cheated. I have been robbed. I have been extorted! I bought three yards of fabric from him. I paid for three yards of fabric. And when I returned home, I found only two yards! I have obviously fallen into the clutches of a cheat, a thief and a scoundrel. He took my money and made off with the goods!"

The judges turned to the shopkeeper and asked, "What have you got to say for yourself?"

"I refuse to stoop to his level and answer his accusations. I turn to you judges, however, and ask: I have been in business for decades. Thousands of customers make their purchases from my store every year. Ten of thousands of yards of fabric have been sold. Has one person ever complained? Has one customer charged me with taking even one penny falsely? And now this fellow shows up—I had never seen him before in my life—he buys a few cents' worth of merchandise and makes a big fuss for nothing. The accusations he has leveled against me are false. He is only coming to tarnish my reputation, to play a prank and to cause discord."

The moral: God created the world and all that is in it. He also governs everything with integrity in the best possible manner. The sun and the moon never change their courses. Trees blossom and give fruit. Lions and leopards, birds and butterflies—all are constantly supported and sustained without the slightest inconvenience. The only creature who suffers and groans, who struggles and who knows privation, is man. This must tell us something! It tells us that man is the cause of his own troubles.

This is the meaning of the *mishnah* (*Kiddushin* 4:14): "Rabbi Shimon ben Elazar says: 'Have you ever seen a wild animal or bird who works for a living? And yet, though they do not work, they make a living without the slightest aggravation. Now, when you consider the fact that they were created solely to serve me, and I was created solely to serve my Creator, should I not expect, all the more so, to make a living without the slightest aggravation? Rather, I have been at fault and deprived myself of a livelihood.'"

Kol Rinah vi-Yeshuah 44b

עַל חֵטְא שֶׁחָטָאנוּ לְפָנֶיךָ בְּאֹנֶס וּבְרָצוֹן
"For any error we may have committed before You, whether under duress or willfully."

It is rather surprising that we confess for having acted under duress. Surely, it is a well-known principle that "God acquits those under duress of liability" (*Bava Kamma* 28b). Similarly, the Sages said, "The Holy One does not expect the impossible [literally: does not act like a tyrant] with His creations" (*Avodah Zarah* 3a). The Maggid of Dubno explained this with a parable.

A passing traveler knocked at the door of a village inn as the sun was setting. He was weary from traveling all day, and he was hungry as well, not having eaten since dawn. The innkeeper politely welcomed him and let him in. He set down food and drink before him, and prepared his bed. He was more than happy to fulfill the mitzvah of welcoming a guest into his home, a mitzvah, the Sages say, which surpasses welcoming the Divine Presence! (*Shabbos* 127a).

In the dark of night, the traveler awoke. One thought kept bothering him, giving him no rest. He knew that the innkeeper stored barrels of wine, mead, and vodka in the room next to his. There was more than enough there to satisfy an army. It was too good to be true, a chance not to be passed up!

Silently, careful not to cause a stir, he rose up from his bed and felt his way in the darkness until he was inside the next room. There, he continued groping for one of the barrels, when suddenly his hand touched a shelf. Before he knew what was happening, the shelf tipped, and dozens of bottles and cups came crashing down. The traveler, overwhelmed by the clatter, panicked and lost his footing on the broken glass. The innkeeper and his family were immediately on the scene, holding lamps and staring, until they realized what had happened. Silently they led the guest, cut and bruised, to his room, where they locked him in for the rest of the night.

In the morning the innkeeper made up a bill charging the traveler for every last bit of damage. The town judge was notified and a hearing was hastily arranged. The traveler stood before the judge and said, "I plead innocent. It was not my fault. The inn was completely dark. I could not light my lamp lest I awaken the innkeeper and his family and disturb their sleep. As for the shelf—it was loose, and overloaded with bottles and mugs. It was blatant negligence on the part of the innkeeper to keep it like that!"

The judge looked at the innkeeper and then at the traveler. He said, "You are right. If you had gotten up in the middle of the night with a dry throat and felt your way around in the dark in order to find a flask of water to satisfy your thirst, and if you had then inadvertently touched the shelf and the whole thing fell—you would not be culpable. But if you intended to steal—that is, if, as is clear from the facts, you wished to repay the innkeeper's generosity by sneaking in and drinking his wine and his vodka—then you are entirely culpable. You must therefore pay even for that which occurred under duress!"

The moral should be obvious...

Ohel Ya'akov, *Vayishlach*

עַל חֵטְא שֶׁחָטָאנוּ לְפָנֶיךָ בְּדַעַת וּבְמִרְמָה
"For any error we may have committed before You, knowingly and deceitfully."

The Evil Inclination can sometimes convince a person to do something wrong knowingly. At other times, he may deceive him into thinking that there is nothing wrong with the act.

The Maggid of Kelm illustrated this with a parable.

Two men once quarreled bitterly with each other. After a time, they made peace. That is, one of them made peace and the other pretended to do so. Deep in his heart he fanned a flame of hatred and malice, and only waited for the opportunity to teach his dear old "friend" a lesson. After all, he reasoned, he felt slighted. He could not easily forget the fights, the arguments, and especially the name-calling. For that alone, he swore to himself, he would take revenge.

He investigated and traced down a gang of counterfeiters. It is always difficult to produce counterfeit coins and banknotes, but the hardest part is circulating them, passing them off in large quantities. Policemen and detectives were stationed throughout the city. Their eyes and ears were open twenty-four hours a day. The slightest wrong move could prove disastrous. And pity the counterfeiter who is caught! The gang lived in constant danger. The bitter man came to them and offered to buy a sizable quantity of banknotes. They agreed on a price and the deal was closed.

He now turned to his "friend," who was a merchant. He bought a large quantity of merchandise, for which the merchant thanked him with all his heart. True, he thought, in the past we had some difficulties, but that is all over now. I was mistaken about him. He didn't even try to bargain. He left me with an excellent profit, and on top of it all, he paid in cash!

The cash, of course, was counterfeit. And the bitter man was not willing to leave it at that. Cheating his old friend was not enough; he ran to the police and denounced him.

The merchant's gratitude was not long-lived. His life turned black when the police came to arrest him as a counterfeiter. Before he knew it he was thrown in jail...

This is exactly the way the Evil Inclination acts with us. On the surface, to all appearances, he is our friend. He even provides us with "quality" merchandise. About so-and-so, it is a mitzvah to speak *lashon ha-ra* (slander). After all, he is a wicked man. It is also permitted to lie to so-and-so. Even a little theft is okay once in a while. In sum, he is sly. He serves his mitzvos to his prey on a silver platter. And all the while, he smiles with glee...

But what kind of person can this "friend" deceive? Only one who is not familiar with counterfeit mitzvos. A merchant with a sharp eye will know right away with whom he is dealing. He will know which bills are phony and which are real. He will be on guard and never be fooled. The same is true of mitzvos. When we learn Torah, we become wise to the cunning wiles of the Evil Inclination.

David *Ha-Melech* alluded to this when he said, "I will thank You with uprightness of heart, when I have learned Your righteous judgments" (*Tehillim* 119:7). When can I be sure that my heart is upright, and that the Evil Inclination has not deceived me? When I learn the righteous judgments of the Torah and attain mastery of God's Law.

Tochachas Chayim 23b

וְעַל חֵטְא שֶׁחָטָאנוּ לְפָנֶיךָ בְּהַרְהוֹר הַלֵּב
"For any error we may have committed before You with the thoughts of our heart."

Said the Maggid of Kovno: When the Temple stood, the expiation offering (*chatas*) and guilt offering (*asham*) were required for serious transgressions. The elevation offering (*olah*), on the other hand, was required for sinful thoughts. At first glance, this seems inverted. The *olah*, which was completely consumed on the altar, should have been required for serious transgressions which were actually committed. The *chatas* and *asham*, which were eaten by the *Kohanim*, should have been required for sinful thoughts. A parable, however, will clarify why this is not the case.

A prince had to leave his estate for a period of time. He allocated all the jobs to be done, among his faithful servants. One was given responsibility over the fields; another was to oversee the orchards; one was appointed over the stables, and another over the cowshed; one was to manage the house, and another was given charge over his office, in which the keys to all his treasuries were stored.

When the prince left, however, all of his servants neglected their duties and spent their time instead drinking in the local tavern.

When he returned he found havoc. The fields were full of weeds and thorns, the horses had run away, the cows had disappeared, the house had been broken into. Utter chaos reigned. He administered a hundred lashes to each of his servants, except the one who had been appointed over his office: he was to receive two hundred!

The fellow complained, "But I did exactly the same as all the others! Why should I be punished doubly?"

The prince replied, "Each one of them was negligent in one specific area. One neglected the fields, one the orchard, one the stable, and one the cowshed. You, on the other hand, were responsible for all my keys—your negligence resulted in all my treasures being stolen."

We can now understand why an *olah* is required to atone for the thoughts of our hearts.

Ateres Zahav

וְעַל חֵטְא שֶׁחָטָאנוּ לְפָנֶיךָ בְּחִלּוּל הַשֵׁם

"For any error we may have committed before You by desecrating the Divine Name."

We are generally unaware of how a single seemingly insignificant deed can cause the Name of Heaven to be sanctified or—God forbid—profaned. The following story about the Chafetz Chayim, told by Rabbi Eliyahu Lopian, illustrates that such is indeed the case.

Once, on my travels abroad on behalf of the yeshivah, I found myself in a certain city, calling on a number of wealthy patrons, soliciting contributions. Everyone I met told me that it was worth approaching a certain wealthy gentleman who generously supported a number of Torah institutions. Despite the fact that he was not observant, he never refused to make a sizable donation.

I took note of their suggestions but decided not to approach him. The Torah, I thought to myself, should not be supported by those who profane it. As Avraham said to Avimelech, "Not a thread nor a shoelace! I will not take anything that is yours! You shall not [be able to] say, 'It was

I who made Avram wealthy!'" (*Bereshis* 14:23). Upon hearing my decision, however, my listeners urged me to change my mind. They were concerned lest the wealthy man hear that I had rejected him on account of his life style and actually discontinue his support of the various local Torah institutions. They requested that I at least visit him. In deference to their request, I was persuaded to meet them half way. I would visit him, but I would not accept any money from him.

I made my way to his home, accompanied by the leaders of the community. Though I had been informed about his non-observance, I was shocked by what I saw. Not a sign of Jewishness in the entire household, let alone in its owner! He received us cordially. I opened with a question which sent chills down the spines of my companions. "Would you be so kind as to tell me what connection you might possibly have with our holy yeshivos? Why are you so generous in your donations to causes which seem so different than your own? Please do not be offended by my questions. The truth is, since I was informed to what extent the local Torah institutions depend on your donations, the question gives me no rest."

The wealthy man smiled and replied: "I am not at all offended. The question is in place; its answer involves an interesting story which is well worth hearing...

"When I was a young man, shortly after I became bar mitzvah, my father sent me to apply to the yeshivah of the Chafetz Chayim in Radin. When I approached the *Mashgiach* with my request to be accepted, his sharp eyes discerned that I was already infected with the fever of 'emancipation,' and that it might be contagious. He refused to admit me into the yeshivah. His impression was, in fact, a correct one, and I, for my part, was not sorry at all. Only one thing bothered me: it was already evening, and the train would not be leaving until the next morning. Where would I spend the night?

"In my distress, I turned to the Chafetz Chayim himself for permission to sleep in the yeshivah that one night.

"'Definitely not,' he answered me. 'A student who is not

fit to be admitted into the yeshivah is not fit to stay there even for one night!'

"'If that is the case,' I said in despair, 'what shall I do? Where shall I go? Should I spend the night in the train station?' And, let me remind you, this was the middle of winter. Everything was covered with snow. It was a cold night!

"'Heaven forbid!' the Chafetz Chayim exclaimed, hugging me warmly. 'Perish the thought! You may not stay in the yeshivah, but you may certainly stay in my house!'

"He took me in hand and brought me to his home. He served me a wonderful meal and prepared a comfortable bed for me. He brought sheets, blankets and a pillow. He urged me to get into bed and go to sleep.

"Of course, I could not fall asleep. The events of the day kept passing through my mind's eye. I thought about the *Mashgiach's* opinion of me. How correct he had been, how discerning! But what amazed me most was the way the Chafetz Chayim had treated me. He was an elderly man, a saintly man, while I was a young boy, eager to throw off the yoke of Torah, a complete stranger in his world.

"I was still musing when I heard the door of my bedroom opening slowly. My eyes, which had already become accustomed to the dark, discerned the small figure of the Chafetz Chayim quietly entering. He thought I was already asleep. He stood by the bed and breathed in and out a few times, to test the temperature of the room. His breath condensed into vapor. 'It is freezing in here...' he whispered. 'Maybe the boy is cold.' He deftly slipped off his coat and spread it out carefully over my blanket. Then he tiptoed out of the room..."

The wealthy man fell silent. The whole house was still. He waited a few moments and added, "Rabbi, believe me, that coat, that mantle of the Chafetz Chayim—*it still keeps me warm.* And it gives me a special feeling of warmth and love for all the yeshivos. It constrains me to donate again and again..."

heard from **Rabbi Y. Rottenberg,** a student of Rabbi Lopian

עַל חֵטְא שֶׁחָטָאנוּ לְפָנֶיךָ בְּטֻמְאַת שְׂפָתָיִם

"For any error we may have committed before You by impure speech."

The great Kabbalist, Rabbi Yosef Gikatilia, asked: What does the mouth that utters filthy speech resemble? He answered with a parable.

The king had a silver goblet which his silversmith had specially crafted for him. One day one of the king's servants took the goblet and—in the king's presence—urinated in it! Needless to say, his punishment was very severe. And worst of all, he had ruined the beautiful goblet: the king would never use it again!

When God created man with numerous limbs and organs, He assigned a function to each. The eyes were to see, the ears to hear, the hands to work, the legs to walk. But it was to the mouth that He gave authority over all the limbs. Speech is man's highest faculty. Like a king sitting on his throne to whom all are subservient, all the limbs of the body are subservient to the mouth. The mouth was created to praise its Creator, to make His wonders known, to judge righteously, and to teach human beings how to serve God.

If a man uses his mouth to utter filthy speech, how will he ever use it to mention God's awesome Name?

Sefer Ha-Meshalim 117

עַל חֵטְא שֶׁחָטָאנוּ לְפָנֶיךָ בְּיֵצֶר הָרָע

"For any error we may have committed before You with the Evil Inclination."

What insidious force is behind almost every problem that plagues mankind? The Torah tells us: "The *yetzer* (inclination) of man's heart is *ra* (evil) from his youth" (*Bereshis* 8:21). "And God saw that man's wickedness on earth was very great.

Every *yetzer* of [man's] innermost thought was solely for evil, all day long!" (*ibid.* 6:5).

Asked the Maggid of Lublin: Seeing that the Evil Inclination is the cause of all our troubles, isn't there any way of overcoming it? Yes, there is, he answered, but with one condition. And he explained with a parable.

The parents of a young boy passed away and left him a sizable inheritance. Lacking experience, he turned to his uncle and asked his advice. His uncle answered him, "I am prepared to handle all your affairs for you and do business on your behalf with your money. I propose that you give me your money, and I, for my part, will contribute my experience and expertise. We will then split the profits between us, fifty-fifty."

The boy was delighted with his uncle's suggestion. "It is certainly in my interest to place my money with you rather than with some stranger!"

He deposited all his assets in his uncle's keeping and returned home without a worry.

A month passed. It was time to pay a visit to his uncle to receive a report of how much he had earned.

"I invested the money in a certain commodity, but its value unexpectedly dropped," his uncle informed him sadly. "You must expect certain losses from time to time, you know. I will bear half of it with you."

The boy was satisfied with the explanation. After all, he thought to himself, fortune is likened to a wheel that constantly revolves. A person may lose on one investment but gain on another!

At the end of the following month, he visited his uncle again and was told that the money had been invested in a certain company owned by a wealthy merchant. Robbers had attacked the merchant, however, and taken all the money: Everything was lost. He was not to let this upset him, though, his uncle said, because he himself would bear half the loss. He felt partially responsible for what had happened. Have patience, he advised his nephew, for the wheel is bound to turn, and the profits will come rolling in!

A month later, his uncle himself made a trip to the fair to purchase a warehouse of the best merchandise at a good price. Profits were guaranteed. But then a fire unexpectedly broke out in the warehouse and all the merchandise was lost. The boy was very upset to hear this. He was even struck with pangs of conscience: It's terrible, he thought to himself, that my uncle should sustain such tremendous losses because of me! My bad fortune is the cause of all this. In addition to the trouble he is going through, all for my sake, he is also carrying half of all the losses. The proof is that his private investments are successful, while everything he does with my money fails!

The boy approached one of his father's old friends to consult him. "Something doesn't smell right here," the man told the boy. "Wait a few days. I will investigate the matter and get back to you."

He suspected that the uncle was a fraud and a scoundrel—that while he reported calamities and losses to his nephew, he was busy investing the boy's money in his own successful business enterprises and raking in the profits for himself. Not only was he not letting the boy in on any of these profits, the friend thought indignantly, but each month he was probably taking half of whatever was left of the original inheritance!

He investigated the matter and was surprised to find that he was mistaken. The uncle really had suffered the losses he reported: the robbers had stolen; the value of the merchandise had fallen; the fire had broken out. Nevertheless, he was not willing to give up so easily. He continued his detective work, for he was certain something was amiss...

When the boy came to him again, a few days later, his father's friend had solved the mystery. "Listen to me," the man began. "You began with a large inheritance, and even though you have sustained some heavy losses, you can still invest the remaining money in successful business endeavors, and see plenty of profit."

"But where should I invest?" the boy cried. "Everything I have done so far has failed because of my bad luck!"

"You are mistaken," the man said. "I have discovered that somebody has been there all along to make sure your luck was bad. Your uncle, it seems, was always at odds with your father. Not only that: he hated him with a passion, I have been told, although your father never knew it. And now that you have fallen into his hands, he is doing everything he can to take revenge!"

"I can't believe it!" the boy cried.

"I knew that this would be difficult for you to accept, but the evidence I have gathered is indisputable. You must know now that as long as your uncle has access to your money, he will continue to lose month after month until there is nothing left. He ships merchandise along roads where he is sure it will be robbed. He buys merchandise whose market price he knows is about to plummet. He will make sure a fire breaks out in every warehouse you buy. And in every instance he will be only too glad to bear half the losses; he would sacrifice more than this just to make sure you end up a pauper! Therefore, know and never forget: as long as your money is in his hands, you will continue to fall. You do not stand a chance unless you recognize your uncle for who he is. You thought he was your father's friend, you thought he had your best interests at heart. But he is a fraud and a scoundrel! He hates you and wishes you harm!"

In our confession, we ask to be pardoned "for any error we may have committed before You with the Evil Inclination." The root cause of all our problems is our constant habit of succumbing to the Evil Inclination. We naively entrust our most precious treasures into his "safekeeping." Oh, he dresses up in many disguises; he masquerades as our loving uncle and our best friend. But he is out to harm us. Nevertheless, he can be overcome. The only condition is that we be as alert

and cautious with Uncle *Yetzer* as we would be with a poisonous snake!

Sefas Ha-Yeriah, Kedoshim

וְעַל חֵטְא שֶׁחָטָאנוּ לְפָנֶיךָ בִּפְלִילוּת

"For any error we may have committed before You with [faulty] judgment."

Faulty judgment involves the inability to make proper decisions. A person with faulty judgment confuses right and
wrong. He mistakes light for darkness and darkness for light.
He decides that a vice is a virtue and a virtue a vice. What is
the source for this? The Maggid of Kelm answered with a
parable.

The *yetzer ha-tov* (Good Inclination) once called the *yetzer
ha-ra* (Evil Inclination) to appear before the Heavenly tribunal.

"He's a liar and a cheat!" the *yetzer ha-tov* contended before
the court.

"The truth is that *he* is the one who is leveling spurious
charges," the *yetzer ha-ra* replied. "He is jealous of my success.
And anyway, I don't know what he wants from me. Both of
us do our jobs!"

"No, no! It isn't true," the *yetzer ha-tov* shouted. "It isn't an
equal competition in the least. He has all the advantages. I do
my work all right, but he steps in every time to ruin whatever
I do!"

The *yetzer ha-ra* turned to the *yetzer ha-tov* and asked,
"What exactly are you referring to?"

The *yetzer ha-tov* calmed down and answered: "When you
mislead a Jew into slandering another Jew, for instance, I
stand on the sidelines and grit my teeth. I wring my hands
and begin to shudder. I cannot even interfere! You can make
him do whatever you want. Nothing constrains you!

"And when I bring a Jew to the synagogue, to pray with
the congregation and listen to the Torah reading, I find you
there distracting him with all kinds of decoys, luring him into

all kinds of conversations, making him forget to answer *Amen*, putting him to sleep, and generally diverting his attention! It isn't fair!

"Your expertise is in making people lie, gossip, and ridicule all that is sacred. I specialize in learning Torah. Why, therefore, when I am finally successful in getting a person to sit down to study a *mishnah* or page of Gemara, why do you distract him with daydreams and fantasies, make him remember things he forgot to do, and clutter his mind with all kinds of schemes? Where is the justice?

"And why, when a person is about to commit a sin, must I stand on the sidelines and let you take control of his mind? Whereas when a person is about to perform a mitzvah, which is my department, you insinuate yourself and bring all my efforts to naught?"

"You are wrong," the *yetzer ha-ra* insisted. "Your hands are not so clean and lily-white! You also encroach on my territory. You yourself said that slander is my expertise. Why is it, then, that people are constantly making the excuse that 'So-and-so is a wicked man and it is therefore permitted to slander him to make sure people stay away from him and not learn to be like him'? Isn't that encroaching on my territory, using my weapons for the sake of a mitzvah?

"You yourself accused me of distracting people from Torah study. But is it fair that a Jew can close his book to do a favor for someone else and claim that you gave him permission to do so? Isn't that overstepping your bounds?"

The *yetzer ha-tov* heard this and shuddered with indignation: "Wicked one, scoundrel, hypocrite! Slandering people and justifying it with the excuse that they are wicked, or closing a book with the pretext that one must do a favor for someone else, are your doing, not mine! Of course it is permitted to speak up about a wicked person, and one must close the Gemara to do something for someone that no one else can do. But *you* are the one who supports and prods a person to do these very 'mitzvos' even when they are not called for or justified! What have you got to lose? You let people perform such 'mitzvos' as long as they get good practice speaking slander and closing their books in the process!"

This is the meaning of the *mishnah:* "Ben Azzai said: Run to do [even] a light mitzvah, and flee from sin. For one mitzvah leads to another mitzvah and one sin leads to another sin. For the reward of a mitzvah is a mitzvah, and the reward of a sin is a sin" (*Pirkei Avos* 4:2).

Why does Ben Azzai give reasons for performing mitzvos and disavowing sins? Isn't it enough that we are commanded to do so? And furthermore, what is a "light" mitzvah? Are we so audacious to think we know the difference between a mitzvah which is important and one that is less so?

This is not the intention. Rather, a light mitzvah is a mitzvah done without pure intention, such as for the sake of receiving a compliment or to gain some advantage. In view of the fact that the *yetzer ha-ra* specializes in enticing a person and making it "easy" for him to perform such a mitzvah, we might feel justified in fleeing. Ben Azzai comes to teach us, however, that a person should not refrain from doing such a mitzvah, even if it is not done with the most altruistic intentions. The reason for this is: One mitzvah leads to another, better mitzvah. Eventually, one will begin doing mitzvos the way they are supposed to be done, with pure intention and for the sake of Heaven.

Conversely, one should flee from a sin, any sin, even one which is done "for the right reasons," and in a way which seems permissible. The reason for this, again, is simple: One sin leads to another.

In summary, the line between what is right and what is wrong is not always clear-cut. Without some degree of objectivity, the line becomes easily blurred. The wisdom contained in our Torah, on the other hand—and this includes the wisdom that has been passed down to us in these very parables—provides us with the objective yardstick with which to measure our own underlying tendencies and motivations. The only remedy for false judgment is the commitment to learn true judgment, that is, the Torah.

Tochachas Chayim 26b

עַל חֵטְא שֶׁחָטָאנוּ לְפָנֶיךָ בְּצָרוּת עָיִן

"For any error we may have committed before You with a begrudging eye."

The Maggid of Kamenitz called upon one of the wealthy members of his community, in order to solicit funds for the poor. As they were talking, a poor man knocked on the door and presented a letter from the rabbi of his city, explaining how the poor man's house had burned down, leaving him penniless, and how it was a mitzvah to come to his aid and put him back on his feet.

The wealthy man gave him a small coin, but the poor man was not satisfied. He complained that it was not enough, and asked for at least one more coin.

The wealthy man was irritated by this. "All these roving solicitors are a traveling plague," he complained to the Maggid. "I have no rest from them. While one is still talking, another one shows up at the door. This one's house burned down, and that one went bankrupt. This one wants to marry off his daughter and that one's luck soured. They all come to me, and they're never satisfied, always asking for more! They are leeches!"

Seeing that the poor man was humiliated by this outburst, the Maggid broke in and said: "Let me tell you about something that happened to me when I was traveling to a certain city. It was summertime, and the heat was scorching. The horse pulled our carriage at a snail's pace while the sun beat down on us. Finally, as we approached the city, swarms of flies and mosquitos surrounded the horse and attacked him. They bit his back and sucked at his belly until he bled. The poor horse swiped at them with his tail, and the driver swatted at them with his whip to drive them away, but the quenched ones merely made way for the thirsty ones.

"The driver, a simple but upright Jew, halted the wagon, turned to me and said, 'Rabbi, I know that God is good and kind, and I once heard that He did not create even one thing for naught. Why, then, did He create these pernicious flies? Why doesn't He have pity on this poor defenseless horse? Why does He allow them to suck its blood?'

"'If you had read some books on nature,' I replied, 'you would not complain about God's ways. You would know what a favor these flies and mosquitos are probably doing for your horse and for you! You would sing God's praises and thank Him! It is written that certain tribes in Africa draw blood from their horses every month. They are sure that the horses will die unless they do so! Certain veterinarians investigated this phenomenon and concluded that this procedure was necessary only because there were no insects there to suck the animals' blood! Now you can understand that if these flies were not here, you might well have to hire a veterinarian and pay him to draw your horse's blood, and then let the horse rest for a week to get his strength back! Instead, for all we know, God has sent you a free veterinarian to heal your horse while he works!'

"When the wagon driver heard this, he lifted his hands up to heaven and exclaimed, 'I thank You, Hashem, for the favor You have done me and my horse. Please forgive me for saying what I said about You without knowing!'"

Now the Maggid turned to his host, the wealthy man, and said, "I repeat the same words to you about your complaints that so many poor people come to you and bother you. If you could only understand God's ways of running the world, you would also ask to be forgiven for what you said. You would never call them leeches. You would understand how great a favor they are doing you by 'leeching your money' and 'sucking your blood.'"

This is what the Midrash means when it says: "Any door which does not open to the poor will surely open to the doctor." If Heaven decrees that a certain amount of a person's earnings must go, it is better that it go to support "leeches" such as this man rather than be spent on doctors...

Ateres Tzevi, *Derush* 8

"...with a begrudging eye."

The Rizhiner Rebbe was staying at the home of a certain wealthy gentleman on one of his visits to a neighboring town. The wealthy man complained about the multitudes who came to his house in order to see the Rebbe: the mud on their shoes made a terrible mess.

Hearing this, the Rebbe told his host the following story. Once a poor villager went to the city to work and earn money for Passover expenses. On the night of his return home, laden with purchases, his horse and wagon fell into a pit which had been made muddy by the spring rains. A wealthy man, passing by, heard his cries, and helped his own driver to extricate the villager. He roped the latter's wagon to his carriage, and accompanied the poor man to his hut. On beholding the abject poverty in which the villager and his family lived, the wealthy man gave him several hundred rubles.

When the wealthy man died and was brought before the Heavenly tribunal, it came out that his demerits far outweighed his merits, because of certain business dealings. He was about to be sentenced to purgatory when, suddenly, an angel of mercy appeared and asked that the Heavenly scales be used to determine whether the worth of his good deeds outweighed his sins. When consent was given, the angel placed the poor villager and his family, whom the wealthy man had saved, on the scale of good deeds. This did not suffice. The horse and the wagon were added. They still did not suffice to weigh the scales to the side of merit. Then the angel placed the mud and the mire, from which the wealthy man had rescued the villager, on the scale of good deeds. This caused the scale of good deeds to be tipped over to the side of merit. In this way the wealthy man was saved from purgatory!

The host understood the Rizhiner's hint and complained no more about the mud on the shoes of his visitors.

עַל חֵטְא שֶׁחָטָאנוּ לְפָנֶיךָ בְּקַלּוּת רֹאש

"For any error we may have committed before You by acting lightheaded and flippant."

The following parable of the Maggid of Lublin stresses the importance of taking seriously our "business trip" to this world, as opposed to wasting precious time in lightheadedness and frivolity.

There was once a young scholar who was supported by his father-in-law, until he decided that it was time to go out and make a living. He would go into business on his own.

His father-in-law was happy with this decision, and he loaned the young man a large sum of money to get started with. The young man, in turn, lost no time in traveling straightaway to the fair in a neighboring town to buy merchandise.

Upon arriving there, he turned into the first inn he saw. He rented a room and left his belongings there while he went out to stroll around the city. His head spun. What colors! What noise and tumult! Stands and booths had been set up at every corner. He saw taverns and gambling tables, clowns and magicians, fortune tellers and sorcerers. In the midst of the bewildering sea of sights, sounds, smells, and colors, he saw a familiar face: it was his uncle, an old and experienced merchant. "You see, Uncle, I am also a merchant!" the young man greeted him proudly.

"Very good!" his uncle replied with a robust laugh. "What business do you wish to begin?"

"I have decided to buy and sell textiles, and I've come to purchase materials," the young scholar answered.

"And where are you staying?" his uncle asked.

The young man told him where his inn was.

"Let us be sure to meet again before the fair ends," his uncle said. "And good luck!"

They parted. The young scholar continued to stroll around, overwhelmed by the sheer immensity of the fair. In the meantime, his uncle went to the other textile merchants, and requested that they approach his nephew. Each one came to the inn and offered a choice of fabrics to the young man, who examined, compared prices, and chose a selection.

When his uncle guessed that one merchant had finished trading with his nephew, he sent him other merchants, who offered him additional buys. In this way, he was kept busy with one merchant after another until he had spent all his money on merchandise. When nothing was left to pay for his room in the inn, he made preparations to return home. Last of all he sought out his uncle to say goodbye.

"It's a pity," he said with a sigh. "I spent the whole time selecting and buying merchandise, and never had a minute to enjoy the fair! I hardly even rested, because I was busy with merchants the entire time!"

His uncle smiled and said, "I'll let you in on a secret. It was I who sent all those merchants to you, so as to keep you busy!"

"But why, Uncle?" the young man asked in surprise. "Why did you want to keep me so busy? And why did you bother them for nothing? Surely you see that if they hadn't come to me, I would have gone out to the fair and found them selling their wares at their stands. And I also would have been able to enjoy the sights of the fair."

"I want you to understand," his uncle said, "that this was the very reason I sent them to your room at the inn. You are young and inexperienced, and this is your first time at the fair. The temptation is very great to spend all one's money on vanities: a penny here and a dime there, a game here and a game there. You could have easily lost all your money and returned home with nothing to show for your journey. That is why I sent all the merchants to you—to keep you occupied all day with the very thing you had come to accomplish, namely, to buy the best merchandise at the cheapest prices, so that you could return home and succeed in your first business venture!"

The moral: The Mishnah (*Makkos* 3:16) states: Rabbi Chananyah ben Akashya says: The Holy One, blessed be He, wished to refine Israel and add to their merit. He therefore gave them much Torah and many mitzvos, as it is said, "For the sake of [Israel's] righteousness, God desired that the Torah be vast and comprehensive" (*Yeshayahu* 42:21). The question naturally arises: If one wishes to add to his friend's merit, would he weigh his friend down with strict commandments and warnings?

It is as we have said: God sent man down to this world to acquire "merchandise" with which he will be able to do "business" in the next world with sizable profits. And what is this merchandise? The Torah and its commandments. Since this world resembles a fair, however, and offers endless amusements and distractions which can tempt one and prevent him from fulfilling his Divine mission, God has therefore surrounded him with good merchants (the Sages) who pressure him to buy more and more of their merchandise (the mitzvos). In this way, he will not waste his time here in lightheaded frivolity.

Thus, if the reason for so many mitzvos is to prevent one from wasting his time, how great is the sin of a person who defies God and wastes his life in frivolity!

Yerios Ha-Ohel, *Kedoshim*

עַל חֵטְא שֶׁחָטָאנוּ לְפָנֶיךָ בְּשִׂנְאַת חִנָּם
"For any error we may have committed before You by causeless hatred."

Shelomo *Ha-Melech*, wisest of all men, wrote, "There are six things which God detests, and seven loathsome to His soul: haughty eyes, a lying tongue, hands that shed innocent blood, a heart that devises wicked thoughts, feet swift in running to do evil, a false witness who inflates lies, and one who sows discord among brethren" (*Mishlei* 6:16). The verse does not list six items followed by another seven, but rather six followed by one. As such, it would seem more logical to say, "and a seventh which is loathsome to His soul" instead of "and seven..." Based on this seeming inconsistency, however, the Midrash (*Vayikra Rabbah* 16:1) remarks: "The seventh weighs heavier than all the others put together; and all are punished with leprosy!"

Why such a punishment? Punishment is supposed to fit the crime. In what way does this punishment fit these crimes? The Maggid of Dubno explained that the common denominator of all these sins is hatred of other human beings. Leprosy makes the one who hated others loathe himself. Just as a mourner mourns for close relatives who have died, the leper must mourn for himself. As the Torah says, "When a person has the mark of the leprous curse, he must tear his clothing, go without a haircut, and cover his head down to his lips. 'Unclean! Unclean!' he must call out [about himself]. As long as he has the mark, [it is a sign that] he is still unclean. Since he is unclean, he must remain alone. His place is outside the camp" (*Vayikra* 13:45-46). Again, the Maggid asked, why does the Torah write, "He must remain alone. His place is outside the camp"? Why not just, "He must remain alone outside the camp"? Why the seemingly superfluous word *mekomo*, 'his place'? He answered with a parable.

A child was sitting at a meal to which his father had invited some other people. The guests, his father's friends, were not to the boy's liking, and he whispered to his father, "When will they leave? I want to be alone!"

His father scolded him: "If that's the way you feel, *you* get up and leave! It is better that you should be the one who goes outside and is alone, than that they should be sent out in your honor..."

This applies to one who is poisoned by hatred of his fellow man. God makes sure that he is afflicted with leprosy, i.e., that he is forced to confront what he hates in himself. In order to do so, he must be banished from society. [He must leave the camp and dwell away from others.] He must realize that, until he is able to uproot the cause of his own leprosy from his heart, until he experiences the same pain he inflicted on others, he does not deserve to live in close proximity with others. "His place is outside the camp."

Kol Negidim 111b

עַל חֵטְא שֶׁחָטָאנוּ לְפָנֶיךָ בְּתִמְהוֹן לֵבָב
"For any error we may have committed before You through mental perplexity."

Faith in God is the foundation of Judaism. For this reason, one should avoid useless metaphysical speculation and philosophical sophistry which tend to undermine one's faith. The path to true faith is through the observance (*na'aseh*) and study (*v'nishma*) of our religious teachings. Even if one feels his faith wavering, he should continue his observance and his studies, and they will bring him back to God. If one is confronted by questions and doubts concerning our religious fundamentals, he should have faith that these questions are answerable. There is nothing that can stand before absolute faith, as the prophet taught us, "The righteous person *lives* by his faith" (*Chavakkuk* 2:4).

When we allow doubts to undermine our faith, on the other hand, this is called *timhon levav*—"mental perplexity," "wavering faith," or, literally, "a dismayed heart." The sin of wavering faith includes becoming trapped in the nets of those whose philosophical sophistry makes them doubt certain details about the commandments of the Torah. This is especially true when their doubts lead them to adjust the commandments to their own liking or altogether deny the authority of their Author. The Maggid of Warsaw explained this with a parable.

A man was once extremely ill, but none of the doctors whom he consulted could help him. Acquaintances suggested he go to the famous Academy of Medicine in Paris—perhaps they could find a proper treatment there. He took all his money with him and traveled to Paris, where he paid the doctors and professors a handsome sum. After they had examined him and met together to discuss the case, it was unanimously agreed that he required treatment with the oil of an especially rare herb which could only be procured on certain distant islands. Despite the difficulty, the herb was procured, the oil prepared, and the treatment begun. It was a success. Slowly the patient began to recuperate, until he finally regained all his strength.

The doctors warned him: "Remember that you are not yet cured. You still have the disease, but this medication has the power to weaken it and prevent it from getting out of hand. You may return home, but do not forget to take one spoonful of your medicine every six hours."

The man thanked the doctors and returned home with his medicine. Once there, he felt healthy enough to begin working again. He soon became so involved in his daily business affairs that he didn't pay attention to the clock, and so he was unable to take his medication regularly, every six hours. He came up with a solution to the problem, however, which he considered ingenious: Why should he spread out the medication in four doses over a twenty-four-hour period? He would take four spoonfuls every morning, all at once! But there still remained the problem of getting it all down, for the medication was extremely bitter. So he came up with another ingenious solution: he put all four spoonfuls in a cup of wine and drank the entire cup down in one gulp. Now he could stand the taste, and all his problems were solved. Only one thing diminished his euphoria. The disease returned with full force...

The man traveled back to Paris and once again assembled all his doctors. They were shocked that the miracle medication had failed.

"Did you take your medication, as we told you to do?" they inquired.

"Certainly," he replied. "And what is more, I took all four spoonfuls in one gulp. I also mixed the entire amount with a little wine. It tasted better that way. You never thought of that, did you?"

"Do you realize what you have done?" they rebuked him, horrified. "With your own hands you have destroyed the precious medication we gave you. Did you really think that the doctors and professors of the Paris Academy of Medicine would prescribe something arbitrarily? Did you think you could change their instructions to suit your whims? The medication was chosen only after extensive research..."

The commandments of the Torah are not arbitrary. They were given by the Creator of the world, and are to be performed in the way He prescribed, without alteration. David Ha-Melech said, "O God, my heart was not haughty, nor my eyes conceited. I did not speculate about things too great and too wondrous for me" (Tehillim 131:1). That is, I did not philosophize about Your Torah! On the contrary, I believed in You. I relied on You as my doctor, as it is written, "I am God who heals you!" (Shemos 15:26).

Chomas Ha-Da'as v'Ha-Emunah 14b

וְעַל חֲטָאִים שֶׁאָנוּ חַיָּבִים עֲלֵיהֶם כָּרֵת
"For errors punishable by spiritual excision."

What is spiritual excision (*kares*)? What is it meant to accomplish? In the Torah, it is written, "If any person, whether a born Jew or a proselyte who joins the Jewish people, offers any of his children to Molech, he must be put to death... I will direct My anger against that person and excise him [spiritually] from among his people" (*Vayikra* 20:2-3), and "If a person turns to mediums and oracles to prostitute himself to their ways, I will direct My anger against him and excise him [spiritually] from among his people" (*ibid.* 20:6). The Sages' enigmatic comment on the words "from among his people" is "so that his people will have peace" (*Sifrei ibid.*). What does this mean? The Maggid of Dubno answered with a parable.

A man's leg was hurting him, so he went to the doctor, who bandaged the leg and prescribed certain medications. The pain did not subside, however; in fact, it became even stronger. Examinations showed that gangrene was spreading throughout the man's leg to the point of endangering his whole body. The doctors consulted among themselves and decided to amputate the infected limb, in order to save the man's life.

The Jewish people is likened to a single organism, all of whose parts are interconnected. This is the meaning of the *midrash* (*Vayikra Rabbah* 4:6): One Jew transgresses, and all of them suffer!... Rabbi Shimon bar Yochai likened [the nation of Israel] to a large ship filled with passengers. When one of them began drilling under his seat, his fellow passengers became alarmed and demanded, "What are you doing?!" He replied, "What do you care? I'm only drilling under my own seat, not yours!" They cried, "But can't you see that the water is seeping in and the whole ship will sink? We'll all drown!"

The lesson is that there are some sins which are so grave, and the one who commits them becomes so contaminated, that he is liable to infect others directly or indirectly as long as he remains part of the organism. His judgment is therefore clear: "His soul shall be *hikares tikares* and his sin shall remain upon him" (*Bemidbar* 15:31). The oral tradition explains the double verb form thus: *hikares,* cut off or amputated in this world, *tikares,* cut off or amputated in the World-to-Come. Why? To protect the organism from becoming infected as well. This is the meaning of the statement quoted above: Cutting a person off "from among his people" guarantees that "his people will have peace." The people (the organism) will have peace only when the infected limb is amputated.

In this sense, *kares* is not only to be construed as a punishment for the individual, but also as a preservation of his surroundings and of the entire nation.

Now, if a doctor were suddenly to arrive on the scene and announce: "Wait! Do not amputate the limb! I have a special wonder treatment which can destroy the infection and regenerate the gangrenous areas! It will restore the leg to its full strength, and guarantee total recovery!"—this man would be welcomed as an angel of grace sent from Heaven.

The doctor exists and so does the treatment. Hashem is offering us the cure: "'As I live,' says God, 'I have no pleasure in the death of the wicked, but that he return from his way and live. Return! Return from your wicked ways! Why should you die, O House of Israel?'" (*Yechezkel* 33:11).

Who would not be thankful to such a doctor? Who would refuse to undergo his treatment?

Ohel Ya'akov, *Kedoshim*

הֲרֵינִי לְפָנֶיךָ כִּכְלִי מָלֵא בּוּשָׁה וּכְלִימָה

"Behold, I stand before You as a vessel filled with shame and humiliation."

The Maggid of Kaminetz asked: What does it mean to describe ourselves "as a vessel"? Why not just say, "Behold, I am filled with shame and embarrassment"? He answered with a parable based on a true story.

At the World's Fair in Paris, a wonderful wooden cabinet was placed on exhibition. The craftsman had worked on it for months, inlaying it delicately with intricate carvings of flowers and other designs, which were astonishing in their detail. As much as the cabinet's external appearance aroused admiration, its interior aroused even more. It had hidden drawers as well as visible ones. It had pull-out shelves as well as revolving ones. It was the talk of the fair, and its creator won himself a gold medal.

The cabinet was purchased by a wealthy merchant from Vienna, for thousands of gold coins. He placed it in his reception hall, where he derived great pleasure from it, praising and displaying its hidden wonders to all his guests.

With time, the wealthy merchant's fortunes changed, and he lost everything. When his creditors came to seize his estate, they sold everything he had. The cabinet, too, was put up for sale, but because its true value was not realized at the time, it was sold for just a few marks.

As the years went by, the cabinet was passed from owner to owner. It became scratched and chipped; its finish wore thin and dull; a number of carved flowers fell off; one leg broke. Finally a cobbler bought it; he found all its shelves very useful for his tools. He hung swatches of leather in the glass window case which had once been used for gold and silver ornaments. He placed different sized nails in the various drawers, and glue and wax in the velvet-lined cubbyholes.

Many years later, the carpenter who had made the wonder cabinet was visiting Vienna, and as he was touring the city, the sole of his shoe became loose. He stepped into a shoemaker's shop to have it repaired. While he was waiting, he looked around, and his eye fell upon what had once been his wonderful cabinet! It stood propped up in a corner, missing one leg, leaning crookedly against the wall. Gone were its embellishments and adornments, its carved inlays and gleaming finish. It was dusty and filthy, covered with scratches, chips and breaks.

The craftsman saw it, and fainted. When he came to, he began to cry and pull at his hair. "Look what's happened to my beloved cabinet!" he cried. "Look what they've done to it!" And he began to show the cobbler and his family: "This was supposed to be a drawer for silver. This was for gold. This was for precious jewels. Look—this hidden drawer was for important documents." He told them how much he had labored to create such a fine piece of craftsmanship, how much time he had spent designing it and executing it, how thousands of people had admired it at the World's Fair in Paris, how they awarded him with a gold medal, how a wealthy man from Vienna had purchased it for thousands of gold coins. And now... how could he not weep? His precious cabinet had been transformed into a storage closet for leather and worn-out shoes. Instead of gold and silver, its drawers now held shoelaces and nails! What was left of all its former beauty?

The moral: God made man with wondrous wisdom. He created him in the image of the Divine. Moreover, He placed within him, within his head and brain, numerous compartments, cubbyholes, and hidden drawers. A compartment of wisdom, a compartment of understanding, and a compartment of knowledge. He equipped him with drawers for memory storage and drawers for new information. He equipped him with the ability to experience humility, fear, shame, empathy, pity, love, and concern for others. In short, He crafted him as a superb creation, a vessel to receive blessings and share them.

Now, however, what can we say? Not only did we not sanctify ourselves, we misused and sullied our inherent holiness. Instead of utilizing our mind to think good thoughts and our heart to feel His presence, we tarnished them both by entertaining negative and unproductive thoughts and succumbing to every passing whim and fancy. Instead of humility, we felt pride; instead of awe of Heaven, rebellion; instead of shame, insolence. Instead of intelligence, we cultivated ignorance.

Now we stand before our Creator and acknowledge: "You created us as wondrous instruments to receive Your blessings. Behold, we stand before You as vessels filled with shame and embarrassment..."

Ateres Tzevi, *Derush* 19

שֶׁלֹּא אֶחֱטָא עוֹד

"May it be Your will, Hashem my God and God of my ancestors, that I sin no more."

We have resolved to return and better our ways. Our first request is for Divine assistance to "sin no more," that is, to stand strong in our resolve, to be freed from the compulsion to sin. As the Talmud (*Sukkah* 52a) states, "A man's Evil Inclination becomes stronger every day and wishes to kill him. Were it not that the Holy One comes to his assitance, he would never be able to overcome [such a mighty opponent]." This is the meaning of our request, "May it be Your Will [i.e. may it please You to assist me in my resolve] that I sin no more."

The inverse of this is expounded in the Mishnah (*Yoma* 8:9): "He who says, 'I will sin and repent, I will sin and repent,' will be prevented [by Heaven] from repenting." As the Talmud (*Yoma* 87a) explains, the double expression, "I will sin and repent, I will sin and repent," teaches us that once a person commits a sin and then repeats it, he begins to rationalize and perceive it as permissible. His declaration that he intends to "repent" after the sin is thus not a resolve to better himself. On the contrary, it is an excuse to do the opposite. Such intent disqualifies him from receiving Divine assistance.

And, as we have said, without Divine assistance, our chances of overcoming the inclination to sin are nil. The Maggid of Lublin explained with a parable.

There was once a merchant in a large city who purchased all his stock at the great fair in Danzig. He would then sell his merchandise to store owners in the surrounding areas. Each year before the fair, he would write to all the store owners, requesting that they pay their outstanding bills without delay so that he would have sufficient cash to buy new merchandise at the fair.

Once, one of his customers who received the letter had just suffered a great misfortune. His store had burned down, and everything he owned had gone up in smoke. Upon receiving the letter, he did not know what to do, for he had nothing left with which to pay. He turned to his friends for advice, and they told him, "You have no choice but to travel to the merchant and tell him the whole story. Perhaps his mercy will be aroused and he will give you time to get back on your feet."

The store owner traveled to the city, staying with an old acquaintance. He had come all this way to tell the merchant of his misfortune, but now that he was there he felt incapable of going through with it! His friend gave him encouragement, however. "You are already here," he pointed out. "Just go and get it over with. What have you got to lose?"

The store owner went. As he stood at the merchant's door, he was unable to control himself and broke down crying. The merchant heard him and came out to see what was happening. "Please come in, and tell me what is bothering you!" he said kindly, recognizing his old customer.

Sobbing, the man went in and, with a trembling voice, recounted the story of his misfortune. He described how his store had burned down; how his life savings had gone up in smoke; how his children were starving for bread. More than everything else, though, he was pained by the fact that the merchant had trusted him and given him merchandise on credit, and now he felt like an ingrate for lacking the funds to pay his debt. "I am ruined. My world has collapsed around me. How can I not cry?!"

The merchant's mercy was aroused, and he took the bill of credit from his desk drawer and tore it up before the poor man's eyes. "Look!" he said. "I have canceled your debt. You don't owe me a thing. Go home to your family, and may Hashem replenish all your losses so that you will once again be able to purchase your merchandise from me as you used to!"

The store owner wiped his tears away and thanked the merchant with all his heart. When he returned home, his friends met him and asked what had transpired. "The merchant was truly generous, compassionate, and gracious. When he heard me crying, he tore up the bill of credit!"

"How much was the debt?" one of his friends asked.

"Approximately three thousand gold coins," he answered.

The man immediately traveled to the city and hurried to the merchant's house. He stood outside his door and began to weep bitterly. The merchant heard and went outside. "What's the matter?" he asked. "Why are you crying?"

"I need three thousand gold coins. Can you give them to me?..." he sobbed.

The merchant was taken aback. "How dare you ask me for such a fortune!"

"But why not?" the man countered. "You gave So-and-so the same amount!"

"What does one have to do with the other?" the merchant replied. "I have sold merchandise to him for years on credit; I was certain he would repay me as he always has. He suffered misfortune and lost everything. What would I gain by not absolving him? After all, he has nothing with which to pay me. I only pray that Hashem will help him in the future! You, on the other hand, are asking for an outright gift—tell me, what right do you have to do so? Why would I even consider such a thing?"

The moral: A human being can trip and stumble, and even completely veer off course. Still, when he pleads to Hashem to be accepted back again, why should he be refused? What is done is done. He is now sorry; he regrets his mistakes. Out of His love for man, Hashem therefore acquiesces and absolves him of his sins. He assists him in overcoming any compulsion to sin. A charlatan, on the other hand, who thinks that he can fool God by saying, "I will repent after I sin a few times..." disqualifies himself from such assistance. He is not is even given the chance to repent!

Kochav Mi-Ya'akov, note to *Haftarah* of *Tzav*

Seudah Mafsekes

The Mitzvah of Eating on Erev Yom Kippur

The Torah states, "The *tenth* of the seventh month (Tishrei) shall be the Day of Atonement for you; it is a sacred holiday on which you must fast..." (*Vayikra* 23:27). Immediately following this, however, the Torah states, "It is a Sabbath of Sabbaths to you, [a day on which] you must fast; from the evening of the *ninth* of the month to the following evening, you must observe this Sabbath" (*ibid.* 23:32). Noting the contradiction between these two verses, the Sages (*Berachos* 8b) asked: "Do we fast on the ninth of the month? No! We fast on the tenth, as stated. Rather, [the Torah teaches us that] when we eat and drink on the ninth, which is the eve of Yom Kippur, it is considered as if we fasted on the ninth and the tenth!"

The Maggid of Dubno was not satisfied. If Hashem wants us to eat and drink on the ninth, he asked, why didn't He state it explicitly? Why did He use the word *v'inisem* ("fast," from *ta'anis*) which is reserved for Yom Kippur itself? Why did He command us about something so important in such an enigmatic and obscure way? He answered with a parable.

A wealthy man had an only son. The boy was his father's and mother's sorrow. He was wild, intractable, and completely impetuous. Every day on his way to school, he would pass by the marketplace and wreak havoc: he would turn tables over, make fun of the shopkeepers, and steal apples. In short, he caused upheaval and destruction wherever he went.

The shopkeepers came to his father and complained. He graciously remunerated them, but could not find a solution to the problem. All his warnings, pleadings, and beatings had not helped in the least. Perhaps...

One morning, the father told his son in that he wished to speak to him. The boy knew why he was being called, of course, and prepared himself for the usual lecture. To his surprise, however, his father greeted him with a smile. "My dear son," he said in a pleasant voice, "since you are about to leave for school, where you learn Torah, I want you to know what our Sages said: that the world stands on the merit of children who learn Torah. Do you realize how fortunate you are, that the entire world rests on your studies? Now tell me, would you say that the running of the city depends on the mayor doing his job? Possibly... but at any rate, he never leaves his office alone without an honor guard. You, then, upon whom the continued existence of the entire world depends—should you go out alone? I will call my servants to accompany you, as is fitting for a Jewish child who is going to learn Torah!"

The boy's eyes lit up. The servants were summoned. They accompanied the boy through the streets with pomp reserved for a prince. Surrounded by his guards, the boy strode with pride, eager for everyone to see how a Jewish boy makes his way to learn Torah!

In this way, not only did the shopkeepers in the marketplace gain, but the boy excelled in his studies as well. Knowing that the world depended upon his being pure and free of vice, he became a different person.

The same is true of us. Our baser desires, including the desire to eat and drink, exert a powerful hold on us. If we were commanded explicitly to eat and drink on the ninth of Tishrei, Yom Kippur eve, we might feel justified in discharging our duty by eating delicacies fit for a king. We might even eat and drink to the point of wildness and drunkenness. In order to prevent this, Hashem expressed this commandment in the language of "fasting." In this way, we would appreciate the value and significance of eating on this day in a completely different way. We would eat and drink with the seriousness and respect due to Yom Kippur. We eat and drink as if we were eating holy food before Hashem! And it would be accounted to us as if we had fasted!

Ohel Ya'akov, *Emor*

Preparing for Kol Nidrei

On This Day...

Before Kol Nidrei, all the God-fearing Jews gathered in the old synagogue. The year was 5536 (1775), and the holy Rebbe Shmelke of Nickolsburg was about to address his congregation. Rabbi Pinchas, his disciple, described the scene:

An hour and a half before the prayers began, the synagogue was already filled to capacity. My Master came to the door of the synagogue enveloped in his *tallis*. As he made his way from the door of the sanctuary to the holy ark, he slowly recited the verse, "For on this day, [Hashem] will atone for you, so that you may be cleansed. Before Hashem you will be cleansed of all your errors" (*Vayikra* 16:30). As he continued, he slowly chanted the *mishnah* (*Yoma* 8:9): "Rabbi Akiva said: Fortunate are you, O Israel! Before Whom do you purify yourselves? And Who purifies you [when you are unable to purify yourselves]? Your Father in heaven!"

Everyone present broke down and cried. Their tears flowed at the sound of his voice and his sobbing.

When he stood in front of the ark, he began reciting verses to arouse us to *teshuvah* and tear open our closed hearts.

"Be gracious to me, O just God, with Your love.
With Your generous mercies, wipe away my sins.
Cleanse me of my wrongdoing, purify me of my mistake.
I know my crimes. My mistakes are ever before me.
My private sins are [known] by You alone. I have done that which is evil in Your eyes...
Purge me with hyssop that I may be pure. Cleanse me so that I can become whiter than snow.
Let me hear of the joy and gladness [that You have in store for those who return to You]. Then the bones You have crushed will rejoice.
Hide Your face from my mistakes, and wipe away all my sins.

O God, create a pure heart for me. Renew an unswerving spirit within me.
Do not cast me away from before Your Presence. Do not take Your Holy Spirit away from me.
Restore the joy of Your redemption to my [weary soul]. Let [Your] spirit of generosity sustain me.
I will then teach wrongdoers Your ways. Even incurable sinners will return to You..." (*Tehillim* 51:3-15).

"I am prone to suffer, and my pain is continually before me. I declare my sin [before You]; I am troubled by the error I have made" (*Tehillim* 38:18-19).

He continued reciting many verses to arouse us to *teshuvah*. He interspersed these verses with moral teachings (*musar*) and clarification. Due to his great outpouring of tears, however, and the powerful sound of weeping that filled the synagogue, I was unable to understand clearly what he was saying. Until he began speaking about the awesome holiness of the Day, that is. Of Yom Kippur. Of how simple it was for a person to hasten redemption and reclaim his soul from nonexistence on this Day! And he told a parable.

There was once a king who had an only son. He appointed a man who was wise and clever to tutor the boy and accompany him in all his activities. To rise with him in the morning, sleep near him at night, and be with him during the day. To show him how to be upright in all his ways as a prince. To teach him the ways of life. To educate him.

But the young prince did not heed his tutor. He refused to walk in his ways...

The tutor informed the king that his son was veering from the proper course, refusing to listen to his advice and follow his counsel.

The king became angry with his son and refused to see him, which caused the young prince great anguish. He requested to be admitted to his father's presence, to plead before him. But his tutor acted strictly with him, and blocked the boy's entrance to his father. Moreover, he made sure to bring all the boy's wrongdoings to the king's attention, and thereby fuel his anger toward his son.

One day the tutor had to leave on an errand. The prince took immediate advantage of his absence: running to his father's chamber, he burst in and fell at his feet, crying and pleading. He acknowledged all the wrong he had done from the day of his birth till that day. He apologized. The fire of youthful passion had burned within him. He took it upon himself to abandon the path of wickedness and follow the path of goodness. "Father, forgive me!" he wept bitterly.

The king's mercy was immediately aroused, for he loved his son dearly. He drew him close tenderly with his right hand, sat him on his lap, and showered him with affection.

The Talmud (*Yoma* 20a) tells us that the name "Satan" has the numerical value of three hundred and sixty-four. There are three hundred and sixty-five days in the year, and Yom Kippur is the one day that the Satan may not denounce and accuse. It is the one day that he is forced to absent himself long enough for us to fall at our Father's feet and beg His forgiveness. Without a doubt, if we take advantage of this day and seek Hashem, He will answer us. There will be no accusation and no evil.

Divrei Shemuel, Yom Kippur

To See Ourselves as We Are

The Talmud (*Yoma* 20a) states that the Satan has no power to accuse on Yom Kippur. This being the case, said the Maggid of Lublin in his discourse prior to Kol Nidrei, let us take advantage of the situation. Listen well to the following parable.

A man once had a son who continually drank himself into a stupor. At every opportunity, he would make his way to the local tavern and drink until he lost his senses. Sometimes the father would be told that his son was lying drunk in the street. With a broken heart he would rush to carry his son home, take his filthy clothes off, wash him and put him in bed to sleep off the effect of the wine. When the son had slept his full, he would awaken and hurry to the tavern, to once again drink himself into oblivion. This went on night after night and day after day. The father was at his wit's end: What should he do? How could he wean him of his habit?

His friends advised him: "The way you are handling it now, he will never change. Think about it: you bring him home, take off his filthy clothes, and wash them. He sleeps like a baby, and wakes up in his own bed, on his clean sheets. He does not know and cannot imagine what he looks like when he is at his worst, sprawled out in the gutter. As long as drinking is a pleasant experience for him, he will never want to stop it! What you should do is this: The next time they come and inform you that your son is sprawled out in the gutter, leave him there. Let him sleep it off. When he awakens and sees himself, he will realize what his friend, the bottle, has done to him! He will see how far he has fallen, and be ashamed of himself. You can then support him in his decision to renounce his ways."

Is it not the same with us? asked the Maggid. All year round, the Satan does his utmost to blind us to his insidious tricks. He is smart enough to prevent us from taking stock of ourselves, from looking at ourselves in the mirror. This blindness allows us to feel that everything is well. Hashem rebuked us through His prophet for the sin of complacency: "Behold, I will enter into judgment with you because you have said, 'I have not sinned'" (*Yirmeyahu* 2:35). As a result, we are all guilty throughout the year of the first half of the verse, "Each man perceives his own way as correct" (*Mishlei* 21:2), and we forget the second half, "but God weighs the heart" (*ibid.*). We therefore find it hard to abandon our ways, and we continue to descend from one lapse to another, with no end in sight.

On this day, however, the Satan has no power. We can open our eyes and see reality, and be ashamed of how far we have strayed. If our regret is sincere, we can be assured that we will never return to our foolish ways!

Ohel Ya'akov

Tefillah Zakah—Forgiveness

Settling Our Accounts

What is the nature of the confession in the *Tefillah Zakah* prayer? The holy Rebbe Shmelke of Nickolsburg explained with a parable. [What follows is an updated version of what he said.]

A certain man bought his groceries in the local store on credit. Every morning he would send his children to the store with a shopping list of all kinds of nice things. They would return with their sacks filled to overflowing with expensive items of all kinds. The bill soared—three hundred... six hundred... one thousand... fifteen hundred... The shopkeeper sent the man a reminder to pay his bill. Eighteen hundred... two thousand... The grocer asked the children to remind their father. Just when the bill passed the three-thousand mark, the man held a celebration, a family *simchah*. Because he had to buy large quantities of food and drink, he would have to go to the store himself. The problem was: How could he show his face?

You may say: Well, let him pay his bill! But, I am sorry to tell you, he has no money just now. He is pressed at the moment.

What does he do? He sends one of his children to request a complete accounting of what he owes. In return, he sends a number of post-dated checks to cover the account. He can then enter the store and buy all he needs, despite the fact that he has not paid one cent!

All year, we buy on credit. And the bill soars. On Yom Kippur we must come to the synagogue ourselves to place our huge orders for the coming year. How will we show our faces if we do not first settle our accounts?

Divrei Shemuel, *Bechukosai*

מִשַּׁשְׁתִּי אֶת כָּל אֵיבָרַי, וּמְצָאתִי אוֹתָם בַּעֲלֵי מוּמִין

"I have examined all my limbs and discovered them to be impaired."

The Maggid of Dubno told the following parable about *Tefillah Zakah:* A man once fell ill. After some time, he became bedridden, suffered terrible pain, could neither eat nor drink, and was terribly weak and emaciated. But by the grace of Heaven he eventually recovered, and within a few weeks he was able to leave his sickbed. He thanked God for giving him back his health and strength. He felt as well as he had before he was sick...

Until he went to his clothes closet to get dressed, and discovered that all his clothes were huge on him. He then realized how emaciated he still was, and that he had a long way to go until he would be fully recovered.

Hashem sanctified us with His commandments. He gave us two hundred and forty-eight positive commandments, paralleling the same number of limbs and joints in our bodies (*Makkos* 23b). The commandments are likened to precious garments (*Zohar* 3:101a): When man is healthy, the commandments fit perfectly, and have the power to suffuse his limbs with holiness and light.

But when man forgets why he was born, and he turns to his business dealings, oblivious of what the Torah has to say to him, he becomes spiritually emaciated.

Then come the month of Elul and the Ten Days of Repentance. Hashem offers us a cure if we will only turn to Him, examine our lives and our deeds, return in *teshuvah*. We begin traveling the road to spiritual health and well-being, and it feels to us as if we have already become whole, upright as Hashem created us, healthy, strong and able to overcome all temptation.

On the eve of Yom Kippur, however, we must make another accounting. This is the purpose of *Tefillah Zakah*. With its help, we examine every aspect of our lives. We review the condition of our character traits. We remind ourselves how we misused the limbs we were given to serve God. We try on the precious commandments, and realize that we are still emaciated. We are distraught, and admit: "I have examined all my limbs and, to my disappointment, discovered them to be impaired."

Ohel Ya'akov, *Emor*

"I have examined all my limbs..."

The Maggid of Rotzky likened this to a doctor who was roused in the middle of the night to make a house call to a patient who had lost consciousness. The doctor examined all his limbs, and they were cold; he felt his head, and there was a slight warmth; he felt his hands—cold; he felt his legs— freezing. Seeing that the doctor was having trouble finding body warmth, the members of the family began to cry as if in mourning.

"Do not give up hope," the doctor reassured them. "I still have not felt his heart."

And thus it was. When he felt the man's heart, he detected a quick butterfly-like palpitation and a slight warmth.

"Quick!" he called out. "Hurry and bring hot water to warm his limbs. There is hope that we can revive him!"

We are weak and faint, the Maggid concluded. Our heads are cold; our thoughts are cold; our lips are cold from speaking slander; our hands are cold from having assisted others in crime, our feet from hurrying to do harm. Still, we must not despair! As long as there is the slightest sign of life in the heart, there is hope! Bring hot water, hot tears, and you will return to your full strength!

Serigi Nefishi, *Derush* 13

וּכְשֵׁם שֶׁאֲנִי מוֹחֵל לְכָל אָדָם, כֵּן תִּתֵּן אֶת חִנִּי בְּעֵינֵי כָּל אָדָם
שֶׁיִּמְחֲלוּ לִי בִּמְחִילָה גְמוּרָה

"And just as I pardon all my fellows, let me find favor in their eyes so that they can completely forgive me as well!"

On one level we seem to be willing to pardon and forgive our fellow human beings in the hope that they will pardon and forgive us. The reason for this is that Yom Kippur does not atone for sins between man and God until a person appeases his friend by making amends and asking his forgiveness.

The Maggid of Rotzky found another level in this, which he illustrated with a parable.

A man went to visit his friend, but he was not careful to wipe the mud off his shoes before he entered the house, and he dirtied the polished floor. His friend was so upset, that he yelled at his guest with sharp words, getting more and more aggravated, until he grabbed him by the shoulder and forcibly ejected him from his house. "This is what a person who has no consideration for his friend's property deserves!" he thought to himself.

Witnessing all this, his neighbor reprimanded him: "What are you making such a fuss about? Why are you so upset? Just take a pail of water and wash the mud off the floor!"

"This is none of your business!" the man replied. "Besides, you have to teach insolent people like him to have manners. You have to show them that they can't get away with such behavior!"

The neighbor shrugged his shoulders and went back into his house. The next day, the man needed to borrow something from this neighbor, and as he entered his home, he accidentally knocked over a precious glass vase, which fell and shattered into hundreds of pieces. He turned white and begged his neighbor's forgiveness.

"Why should I forgive you?" the neighbor replied. "After

all, just yesterday you punished your friend for having the nerve to step into your house with muddy shoes, despite the fact that he did not cause you any damage. Why shouldn't I hold you accountable for causing me actual damage?"

On Yom Kippur, we ask forgiveness and pardon for all the wrongs we have done. These wrongs damaged our Godly souls, our precious vases. Their effect reverberated up to the highest heavens and caused Hashem's light to be hidden from the world. How can we now ask forgiveness if we have refused to forgive our fellow human beings for the tiny wrongs they may have done us?!

Serigi Nefishi, Derush 16

"...so that they can completely forgive me as well!"

Rabbi Chayim of Volozhin told the Maggid of Dretshin what happened once when his brother, Rebbe Zalman of Vilna, was sitting in the great Beis Midrash in Vilna. A fellow approached him and said, "Let me share with you a good and convincing explanation (perush) of a mishnah in Maseches Demai." [Demai is produce of the Land of Israel which was picked by an ignorant man who cannot be trusted to have taken off a tenth for tithes, and which therefore requires tithing.] Now, this fellow had a slight lisp, and it sounded to Reb Zalman that he said, "Let me share with you the good fruits (peros) of Demai."

He began his discourse, but Reb Zalman could not make much sense of it. It sounded to him like a lot of silly talk, and suddenly he grew irritated over the fact that this fellow was grossly distorting the Torah, and wasting his precious time as well. He therefore turned him away with the insulting remark, "It seems to me that your fruits are demai," meaning, the produce of an ignorant man...

The fellow fell silent and went his way.

The moment he disappeared, however, Reb Zalman regretted what he had said: What have I done?! I have caused pain to another Jew! Even if his explanation to the *mishnah* was slightly askew, or even completely unfounded, so what? I should have spoken to him amiably and led him gently towards the proper explanation. I should never have made fun of him and insulted him!

Reb Zalman wept genuine tears over what he had done. He went out to the street to look for the fellow, but he could not find him. He went searching from one synagogue to another, from one study hall to another—all for naught. Each day he would go to every single one of the tens of study halls in Vilna. He would go from person to person, and look each one in the face, all on the chance that he would find the person he had insulted. He wanted only to ask his forgiveness.

A month passed, two months. A year. Reb Zalman could find no repose for his soul. He was so depressed about not finding the man that he almost became bedridden.

His brother-in-law, Reb Michel Pesles, saw this and had an idea. He spoke to a friend from a neighboring city and asked him to appear before Reb Zalman as the fellow he had insulted and forgive him for his sin.

The friend agreed. He came before Reb Zalman and said, "Don't you recognize me?"

"No," he replied.

He smiled, and said with a lisp, "Everyone says that you have a phenomenal memory. Don't you remember how I told you an explanation of a *mishnah* in *Maseches Demai*? You insulted me by telling me my fruits were *demai*!"

Reb Zalman jumped up in joy. But then he immediately suspected that the man in front of him was not the same gentleman. He held his hand warmly and said, "Swear to me, now, and tell me the truth. Are you the same fellow? I beg you not to do me a false kindness. Do not console me with vain consolations. Are you really he?"

The man could not stand up before Reb Zalman's powerful words. He admitted that he was not the man.

"I thank you for you wanting to help me," Reb Zalman said, "but how could it have worked? I insulted another person. I sinned against a fellow Jew... a sin for which neither repentance nor Yom Kippur can suffice to bring atonement, until forgiveness is granted..."

Reb Zalman cried. He decided that he had no choice but to continue to go from synagogue to synagogue, and from study hall to study hall, searching for the man. He would stand up and tell his story before the people. He would ask that the man he had insulted forgive him if he was among the people he was addressing.

The story finally reached the Gaon of Vilna. He sent a message to Reb Zalman, asking him to come to him. Reb Zalman appeared before the Gaon.

"Our Sages say (*Sukkah* 52a)," began the Gaon, "that a man's Evil Inclination becomes stronger every day and wishes to kill him. Were it not that the Holy One comes to his rescue, he would never be able to overcome such a mighty opponent. It is thus written, 'The wicked man watches for the saint and seeks to kill him. Hashem will not allow him to fall into his clutches' (*Tehillim* 37:32). But there is a difficulty here. Why did the Psalmist, and the Sages in his wake, deem it necessary to inform us of this? What difference does it make, that is, whether we overcome the Evil Inclination with Hashem's help or on our own?" The Gaon paused and then continued. "Rather, they informed us of a great thing with this. If a man does everything in his power, and still does not succeed, Hashem will finish the job for him. You, Reb Zalman, have done everything in your power to find the man you insulted and ask his forgiveness. You did not succeed, but Hashem will finish the job for you!"

"How?" asked Reb Zalman.

The Gaon opened the book *Duties of the Heart* and showed him what was written there in the tenth chapter: "And if he harmed his fellow either bodily or monetarily, the blessed Creator will fill the wronged person's heart with good will and love, so that he will forgive the wrongdoer for the offense committed, as it is written (*Mishlei* 16:7), 'When a person's ways please God, He even causes his enemies to make peace with him.'"

Reb Zalman was relieved.

At that time, Reb Zalman was fourteen years old.

Toldos Adam 45b

The Confession of Rabbenu Nissim

אֲשֶׁר הִתַּרְתָּ אָסַרְתִּי, וַאֲשֶׁר אָסַרְתָּ הִתַּרְתִּי

"I declared forbidden that which You permitted; [moreover] I declared permitted that which You forbade."

While it is certainly not advisable to declare forbidden that which God has permitted, it is infinitely more serious to declare permissible that which He has forbidden. This involves the majority of our wrong actions. It is for this reason that *Rabbenu* Nissim placed this confession in an ascending order of gravity: (1) "I not only declared forbidden that which You permitted; much worse, (2) I declared permitted that which You forbade."

This order also parallels the order of the verse which states, "Do not add to the word I am commanding you, and do not subtract from it. You must keep all the commandments of God your God" (*Devarim* 4:2). ["To add" parallels (1) forbidding what God permitted, i.e., adding unnecessary stringencies; "to subtract" parallels (2) permitting what God forbid, i.e., detracting from the stringency of the Torah.]

The truth is, the Maggid of Dubno said, that by paying attention to the verse itself we will see that 1 even leads to 2. Adding our own stringencies leads to doing away with God's; forbidding what He permitted leads to permitting what He forbid. He illustrated this with one of his most celebrated parables.

There was once a famous miser, known far and wide for his stinginess and greed. His neighbor, who was a great joker, once decided to make fun of the miser and teach him a lesson he would never forget. He knocked on the latter's door and announced, "I'm in the midst of a *sheva berachos* celebration for my daughter, who has just gotten married. I need two wine goblets, one for grace after meals and one for the seven blessings. I have only one—my *Kiddush* cup. Could you perhaps lend me an extra one of yours?"

Before the miser had a chance to refuse, the neighbor produced his gold watch from his pocket and said, "I'll give you this gold watch as security; if I don't return the goblet in ten minutes, the watch will be yours!"

The miser's eyes lit up with avarice. He took the watch and brought out an old silver *Kiddush* cup.

Seven minutes later, the joker knocked on the miser's door. When the miser saw him, he turned pale with disappointment and, with a heavy heart, he returned the gold watch and held out his hand to receive the goblet. To the miser's surprise, the joker handed him not only his goblet, but another smaller one, of gleaming new silver.

"What is this?" the miser asked.

"Unbelievable!" the joker exclaimed. "Did you know your goblet was expecting? While it was in my house, it gave birth to this tiny silver goblet. Cute, isn't it? So, *mazal tov*, and may you have *naches* from them..."

The miser was at a loss for words. He took the two goblets silently and closed his door.

The next day the joker came to him again, gold watch in hand. "I'm making another *sheva berachos* today," he said, "so I'd like to borrow the goblet again... if it has recuperated from the birth!"

"Yes, fine," the miser replied, and he hurried to bring the wonder goblet.

"I'll leave my watch here again as security," the joker declared. "Oh, and you know how it's the custom to light candles at the table. Do you happen to have some extra candlesticks?"

"Just some inexpensive bronze ones," the miser replied suspiciously.

"My candles aren't picky," the joker assured him, and he took the goblet and the candlesticks.

An hour later, he returned them, together with a tiny

bronze candlestick, brand new. "Your house must be blessed," the joker declared. "The left candlestick just gave birth! I'm certain that this little one will grow to be very big," he added, paraphrasing the blessing given at a *bris*. "And may he travel only on straight paths!"

"Amen," the miser said with great concentration. "And what about *sheva berachos* on Shabbos? Guests are bound to show up, and you'll need a lot of candlesticks." In his heart, he was already calculating the number of births he could count on.

"Yes, you're right," his neighbor replied. "But I'm sorry to say that I can't leave my watch with you this time—I have to wear it on Shabbos to impress the new in-laws."

"No problem," the wealthy miser replied. "No problem at all—I have already seen that you are trustworthy. You could have conveniently forgotten to tell me about the births and not brought the babies back to me.... on second thought, in order to really impress the guests, and so that there will be enough light in the house, it would be worthwhile for you to take my *menorah.* It's a large, rare *menorah* made of silver, the work of a master craftsman. It is worth its weight in gold. In my house," he added in a whisper, "it has been barren."

The joker agreed to take the precious *menorah* along with the goblet and the other candlesticks. At the departure of the Sabbath, the miser hurried to his neighbor's house and knocked on the door. "Well?" he called. "Is there anything new?"

"Yes, without a doubt," the joker replied, and the miser's eyes glittered in expectation. The joker left and came back to the front door. In his hand were the goblet and the candlesticks.

"And what about the *menorah?*" the miser asked, hardly able to conceal his anticipation of another birth.

The joker's face suddenly became very somber. "To my sorrow," he began, "ah! to my chagrin... the precious *menorah*... died." His voice was choked with tears.

The miser was struck dumb for a moment. Then, "How could that be?" he cried out. "Who ever heard of such a thing? A *menorah* that dies! You're a liar and a scoundrel. A thief! Give me back my belongings immediately. Who ever heard of a *menorah* dying?"

"Enough," the joker said. "I suggest you hold your tongue. Who ever heard of a goblet and a candlestick giving birth? If you've made some strange profit, you must accept the strange loss as well..."

The authorship of the Torah is Divine. It is from beyond this dimension. As an expression of God's Mind, it cannot be fathomed. Worlds upon worlds depend upon the fulfillment of its commands. And for one reason: God is the commander. Man is therefore not at liberty to accept or reject. If he thinks he can add to the commandments, improve on the Torah, as it were, he will eventually come to think that he is the boss. If he adds at a whim, he will also come to detract at a whim. He will decide what is to be done and what not. For this reason, Hashem established the guidelines, "Do not add... and do not subtract!" If you add, you will come to subtract. If you forbid what is permitted, you will come to permit what is forbidden.

Ohel Ya'akov, *Va-Eschanan*

Kol Nidrei

אוֹר זָרֻעַ לַצַּדִּיק, וּלְיִשְׁרֵי לֵב שִׂמְחָה

"Light is sown for the righteous, and joy for the upright of heart."

The Maggid of Kutno stood before his congregation just prior to beginning the Kol Nidrei service. He began his discourse with a question: Of all the verses in the Bible, why do we say this verse from *Tehillim* immediately before Kol Nidrei? He answered with a parable.

A group of merchants embarked on a sea voyage to purchase goods in distant lands. Suddenly, a powerful storm began to brew. The waves rose up like mountains and then plunged down upon them with mighty force. The ship ascended to the heavens and sank down to the depths. The storm ripped the sails, broke the mast, and shattered the rudder. Passengers and crew held on for their lives, reeling and staggering, crying out to God in their distress. When the storm finally subsided, the vessel drifted rudderless every which way. They had no control over it, no way to navigate.

At first simply grateful at being alive, they soon began to realize that their water supply was rapidly diminishing. They were staring death in the face. Again, they began to pray, to cry out, to hope for some salvation. Suddenly one of the sailors cried, "Look! There, in the distance, is a ship!"

"We've been saved!" they cried out. "If only they see us, we've been saved!"

With renewed strength they did everything in their power to attract the attention of the other vessel before it disappeared on the vast sea. They sounded the ship's siren over and over again. Finally the scout at the helm shouted, "The ship has changed course. It's coming towards us!"

In a short while everything would be all right. They would be drinking all the water they wanted. They would be steered home, escorted to their destination. But it seemed their troubles were not over. A dense fog came down, wrapping the entire area in a white blanket. They felt as if they were submerged in a cloud. What would become of them now? The other ship would flounder in the fog and then, not finding them, resume its course...

Crew and passengers rushed to light the ship's beacon, to pierce the fog, to shine through the thick curtain, to indicate their location, to ensure their rescue...

The moral: After the Days of Awe of the past year, we sailed for the new year. We knew our way, the direction to follow towards our ultimate destination. We were resolute in our decision to bring our New Year's resolutions to fruition, but the winds of time and change then began to blow. The fleeting desires and unrelenting pressures built up and forced us off course, destroyed our ability to navigate, pulled us here and there...

As the year neared its end and Elul came upon us, we searched our souls. We were rudely awakened to the fact that we had strayed off course. Our fresh drinking water—the Torah we had been so resolute in wanting to learn—was almost gone. With broken hearts we came to *Selichos* and hoped for salvation. In order to arouse Heavenly compassion, we sounded the shofar, our siren.

Now, at the very moment the Satan sees his prey about to escape his clutches—when our salvation is at hand—he manages to darken our worlds in a thick fog. All of a sudden our minds and hearts are made insensitive; we find it difficult to concentrate when we pray; the tears should flow but they don't. But it is all a test. This is the darkness before the dawn. We must gather all our strength to pierce the thick curtain that separates us from our Source. We must light the beacon in our hearts, the light of prayer, until it bursts into a burning flame. This is why we light so many candles on *Erev Yom Kippur:* to remind us to ignite the flames in our hearts.

And now we call forth the words of *Tehillim*, "Light is sown for the righteous, and joy for the upright of heart!" The candles we have lit remind us to sow the light of *teshuvah* in our hearts. In the merit of this light we will be judged worthy of more light and blessing. And if our thoughts are concentrated on this light from the onset of the holiest day of the year, we are assured that we will merit great joy and success.

Our Sages promised us: He who comes to purify himself will be assisted from Above (*Shabbos* 104a). If we shall then light the beacon, the Heavenly throne will find us and dwell in our midst. This is what Rabbi Akiva meant when he said (*Yoma* 8:9): "Fortunate are you, O Israel! Before Whom do you purify yourselves [and enflame your hearts in the passion of your prayers]? Who purifies you [when you are unable to purify yourselves]? Your Father in Heaven!" Our Father in Heaven Who turns to you and seeks only your salvation!

Gefen Yisrael, *Derush* 14

סְלַח נָא לַעֲוֹן הָעָם הַזֶּה כְּגוֹדֶל חַסְדֶּךָ,
וְכַאֲשֶׁר נָשָׂאתָה לָעָם הַזֶּה מִמִּצְרַיִם וְעַד הֵנָּה

"With Your great love, please forgive the sin of this nation just as You have forgiven them from [the time they left] Egypt until now!"

Why did Moshe, the faithful shepherd of his people, include in his request for pardon a reference to their former bad ways? The Chasam Sofer answered with a parable.

There was once a king whose older children were so spoiled by the life of pleasure and ease that they ended up following an evil path. Seeing this, the king wished to save his youngest son from such a fate, so he sent the boy to a village, where he would grow up in the house of a poor man and where simplicity, moderation, and humility would become ingrained in him.

His plan succeeded. The prince grew up to be an extremely modest and humble young man. When the king then brought him back to the royal palace, he followed his father's instructions faithfully, serving him with fear and trepidation, as a servant serves his master.

But this very thing turned out to be the prince's problem, and the success of his village education was also his undoing. In the villager's home he had learned to tremble with respect before anyone dressed in an official uniform. (This was how the villager had behaved before the tax collector and the local policeman.) As a result, when the king's ministers sat down with the king in council, the prince would begin trembling and perspiring. He would stand and bow before them and completely lose his dignity...

The king shared his disappointment with one of his ministers: "What should I do with this boy? How will he ever wear the crown? How will he ever bear his royalty with dignity?"

The minister replied: "Your Majesty, your son is graced with many good qualities. He has wisdom and understanding, and a regal glow shines from his face. True, when he was in the village he became accustomed to bowing and effacing himself before any sign of authority—but this is merely acquired behavior, and not his intrinsic nature. In the course of time, when he becomes accustomed to the ways of the palace and adjusted to his new rank, his heart will understand the ways of royalty and he will make you proud!"

The moral: The Creator saw the children of men becoming increasingly arrogant and destructive. The generation of the Flood said to God, "Depart from us. We do not wish to know Your ways!" (*Iyov* 21:14; *Sanhedrin* 108a). The generation of the Tower of Bavel intended to storm the heavens (*Tanchuma, No'ach* 18). The people of Sedom "had arrogance, [because of] an overabundance of bread, leisure, and repose..." (*Yechezkel* 16:49).

What did God do? He sent His young son, Israel, to

Egypt, in order to break his spirit of arrogance, to have moderation and humility ingrained in his character.

God's plan succeeded. In the desert, Israel responded willingly to His invitation to receive the Torah, with "We will do and obey all that God has declared!" (*Shemos* 24:7). On the other hand, they also acquired an inordinate sense of worthlessness. They learned to bow down to His ministers—the stars and constellations—and worship them.

Moshe then arose and declared: The Children of Israel are good at heart. These are merely habits of behavior they have acquired. Once they have lived for a while in close proximity to holiness, they will automatically cast them off. "O God, why unleash Your wrath against Your people whom You have brought out of Egypt with great power and a show of force?" (*Shemos* 32:11). They became so accustomed to being in Egypt that a show of force was needed to bring them out! But when they become accustomed to their new rank, You will see how quickly they abandon their old ways and reveal their intrinsic goodness. Then, "I and your people will be distinguished from every nation on the face of the earth" (*ibid.* 33:16). "You will grant them ascendance above all the nations You made, for praise, fame, and beauty" (*Devarim* 26:19).

We also mention this verse now, with awe and trepidation, as we stand poised at the onset of the holiest day of the year. "With Your great love, please forgive the sin of this nation, just as You have forgiven them from [the time they left] Egypt until now!" (*Bemidbar* 14:19). That is: It is known and revealed before You, that our desire is to do Your will. What prevents us? The yeast in the dough (the Evil Inclination) and our subjugation to the ideologies of foreign nations (*Berachos* 17a). If You will only mend our hearts to love and fear You alone, and remove the yoke of our subjugation to the nations, we will divorce ourselves from our former wrongs and make You proud of us!

Kesav Sofer 1:40

כְּגוֹדֶל חַסְדֶּךָ... וְשָׁם נֶאֱמַר: וַיֹּאמֶר ה' סָלַחְתִּי כִּדְבָרֶךָ

"With Your great love, please forgive... You therefore told him: 'I will grant forgiveness as you have requested.'"

The Sages warn us: "Whoever thinks that God waives [punishment for sin], his life will be waived" (*Bava Kamma* 50a). "God is patient and long-suffering, but He collects His own [in the end]" (*Bereshis Rabbah* 67:4). How is it, then, that we have the audacity to ask Him to be lenient and grant us forgiveness even when we may not deserve it? How dare we stand before Him and say, "Forgive the sin of this nation"?!

The question becomes even stronger when we examine the circumstances surrounding our verse.

When the spies returned from the land of Canaan, they delivered an evil report: "The land we crossed to explore is a land which consumes its inhabitants. All the people we saw there were gigantic..." (*Bemidbar* 13:32). Hearing this, the entire Israelite camp began to complain, "We wish we had died in Egypt! We should have died in this desert! Why is God bringing us to this Land to die by the sword? Our wives and our children will be captives! We had better return to Egypt!" (*ibid.* 14:2-3).

At this point, God said to Moshe: "How long will this nation continue to provoke Me? How long will they refuse to believe in Me, despite all the miracles I have performed in their midst? I will kill them with a plague and annihilate them, and make you into a greater, more powerful nation than they" (*ibid.* 14:11-12).

Moshe understood that God was affording him a chance to challenge Him and argue for his people. He therefore began his request for forgiveness with the following argument: "And what will happen when the Egyptians hear about it... and tell the inhabitants of this land? They have heard that You, merciful God, have been with this nation [Israel]! You, merciful God, have revealed Yourself to them eye-to-eye, and Your cloud stands over them... Now, if You kill this [entire] nation like a single man, the nations who hear this news about You will say, 'God was not able to bring this nation to the Land He swore to them, so He slaughtered them in the desert!'" (*ibid.* 14:13-16).

Moshe continues: "Now, merciful God, is the time for You to exercise even more restraint! You once declared, 'God is slow to anger, great in love, and forgiving of sin and rebellion...' [Therefore] with Your great love, please forgive the sin of this nation, just as You have forgiven them from [the time they left] Egypt until now!" (*ibid.* 14:17-19).

God's immediate answer: "I will grant forgiveness as you have requested..." (*ibid.* 14:20). Moshe won!

Or at least it seems as if he won. Not so, the Maggid of Dubno countered. And he explained with a parable.

The daughter of an extremely wealthy merchant became engaged to the son of an aristocrat from another city. The wedding date was set. A short time before the wedding, the wealthy merchant visited his future in-law and said, "I am sorry, but when we set the date of the wedding, it completely slipped my mind that the fair was set for the same day. All the villagers stream to the fair to make their purchases, and my store will be packed from morning to night. I simply will not have a second to spare. Could we possibly change the date of the wedding?"

The aristocrat was uncompromising. "I'm very sorry," he said, "but an agreement is an agreement, and a date is a date. The wedding is more important than the fair. It will therefore take place as scheduled, and if not, I will understand this as an indication that you are backing out on our agreement. This will involve a penalty!"

The merchant was taken aback. "Why should we argue?" he said. "Let us go and speak with a rabbi. He will help us arrive at a just settlement. Whatever he says, we shall do!"

The rabbi heard both sides. "You are both right," he said. "Still, let us see whether one of the events cannot be put off an extra day. Now, it is true that the wedding must take place on the day agreed upon by both parties. The date of the fair, on the other hand, is set. The villagers will come on that day, and if the store is not open, the merchant will suffer heavy losses. In view of all this, the appropriate thing to do is to postpone the wedding by one day, and not consider this a cancellation of agreement."

[The aristocrat is God; the merchant is Israel; the rabbi is Moshe.] Moshe said to God: "You say, 'I will kill them with a plague!' If You do so, however, the loss will be irreplaceable. When the nations say, 'God was not able to bring this nation to the Land that He swore to them, so He slaughtered them in the desert,' Your Name will be profaned. I therefore beg You, 'With Your great love, please forgive the sin of this nation!' In this way, not a single one of Your words will be cancelled. The 'wedding' (punishment) can be postponed and spread out over the next forty years. Justice itself requires that You acquiesce to my plea!"

God then answered Moshe: "I will grant forgiveness *as you have requested*," that is, "I will postpone the punishment and extend it over a longer period of time."

This is exactly what the Talmud means: God is not compromising. Of course, He is patient and long-suffering, but He is not compromising. He will postpone punishment, but He will collect what is His over an extended period of time.

And yet, there is an extra benefit in His being patient and long-suffering: We are given the chance to return in *teshuvah*. Our *teshuvah* then makes it highly possible that the judgment against us will be mitigated and the punishment cancelled completely!

Ohel Ya'akov, *Shelach*

Yom Kippur Night

מְחֹל לַעֲוֹנוֹתֵינוּ בְּיוֹם הַכִּפּוּרִים הַזֶּה

"Pardon our sins on this Day of Atonement."

The *Shulchan Aruch* (*Orach Chayim* 582:9) declares: "Although the *Amidah* prayer must be said silently during the entire year, on Rosh Hashanah and Yom Kippur it is customary to raise one's voice [slightly in order to increase concentration]."

The holy Rabbi David Moshe of Tchortkov explained this with a parable.

A man once opened a wine store, and the customers flocked to him. "Tell me," an interested bystander asked some of the customers, "why is everyone flocking to this new store, when there are several older wine sellers in town?"

They told him: "A bottle of wine sells for more or less the same price everywhere—but here, the storekeeper fills the bottles up to their brim until the wine spills out and overflows!"

The bystander heard this and had a great idea. Why, I can make a mint! he thought to himself. He immediately set off to buy a barrel of wine and dozens of empty bottles. He then stood on the street and called: "Come and buy! Wine for half the price!"

While customers gathered, he took an empty bottle, corked it, and opened the spout of his wine barrel. Lots of wine flowed down and around the sides of the bottle...

People laughed at him, but the fool did not understand. "Look how the wine spreads over the whole bottle!" he argued. "Isn't that what you liked about the other wine store? Isn't that why you bought there?"

They laughed again. "Don't you see the difference? He fills the bottle first! When it overflows and spills over the outside of the bottle, that is a sign of abundance and blessing. But what good is it for wine to spill all over the outside of the bottle if inside it's empty?"

Prayer is the service of the heart. When is it appropriate for us to lift our voices slightly in prayer? When the heart is full to overflowing and the prayer bursts forth. But one who first stops his heart up, and whose prayers are merely from the lips and outward, has missed the whole point!

Ner Yisrael 2:161

כִּי הִנֵּה כַּחֹמֶר בְּיַד הַיּוֹצֵר
"As clay in the hands of a potter."

The source for this liturgical poem is found in God's instructions to the prophet: "God's word came to Yirmeyahu saying, 'Arise, go down to the potter's workshop and I will speak to you there.' I went down to the potter's workshop. There he was making pottery on the pottery wheels. The vessel the potter was making was ruined in his hand. So he made it again into another vessel in a way that seemed good to the potter to make. God then spoke to me saying, 'O house of Israel, can I not do with you as this potter has done?' says God. 'Behold, as clay in the hands of a potter, so are you in My hand, O house of Israel!'" (*Yirmeyahu* 18:1-6).

The Maggid of Rotzky asked: What did God intend to teach Yirmeyahu by showing him the potter in the process of ruining and remaking his pottery? What exactly is the meaning of the simile, "As clay in the hands of a potter"?

The potter cannot always decide to begin again if a vessel is not to his liking. The clay must still be soft and fit to be molded. If he has already placed it in the kiln, however, and baked it, the only choice is to break it...

The same applies to the people of Israel. If our hearts are soft, we can return in *teshuvah* and be transformed into new vessels. If our hearts are hardened and stubborn, however, God has no choice but to break them with suffering...

Serigi Nefishi, *Derush* 11

Ne'ilah

"Woe to us, for the day is ending."

The source for this is the verse in *Yirmeyahu*, "Woe to us, for the day is ending, and the shadows of evening are stretching..." (*Yirmeyahu* 6:4). In one of his discourses before *Ne'ilah*, the closing service of Yom Kippur, the Maggid of Dubno explained this prayer with a parable.

An innkeeper once fell behind in his rent payments to the local squire. One year, two, three years passed, and still no payment. The squire warned the innkeeper numerous times, and when his patience came to an end, he had the innkeeper thrown into the dungeon.

This dungeon consisted of a covered pit in the squire's backyard. The pit was deep and dark, smelly, damp and airless. Pity anyone locked up in this dungeon! Hour after hour, day after day, the innkeeper felt less and less hope of ever emerging into the light of day. Death was preferable!

Suddenly, one day, the hole was opened. The heads of the Jewish community had entreated the squire, and he had agreed to allow the innkeeper to leave the dungeon for the Days of Awe. They helped him out, washed and dressed him, fed him and gave him drink. "Oh, the sunlight and the fresh air!" the innkeeper exclaimed. He couldn't get enough sun. He appreciated every breeze. He enjoyed sleeping on a comfortable bed and eating to his fill.

Rosh Hashanah passed. The Ten Days of *Teshuvah*. Kol Nidrei. Yom Kippur morning. *Musaf* and *Minchah*. The time for *Ne'ilah* had come.

He knew it. In another hour, when the sun had set, the squire's police would come to take him away, and he would be thrown back into the dungeon. Again, as if he were among the dead... Can we imagine how he felt?

This is exactly how our souls feel! They descend into the

darkness of this world, into the constricted imprisonment of a physical body, to learn Torah and perform good deeds, to illuminate the darkness, to know God's Presence even in this world... But we spend the entire year sunken in material pursuits. We fall asleep and forget how to illuminate our lives with the light of the soul.

During the Days of Awe, we awaken to the task. We learn, pray, and go about performing good deeds with zest and passion. We make an accounting, a moral stocktaking— *cheshbon ha-nefesh*. This is like opening the dungeon. Our souls rejoice once again and bask in the light of day. But Yom Kippur is about to end. Soon we will return to our customary behavior, fall asleep again, pursue things which have no value. The light will be extinguished, and darkness will surround our souls.

It would be a mistake, however, to think that our souls alone will suffer. This can be clarified with another parable.

When the king's daughter reached marriageable age, many princes asked for her hand in marriage. She found something lacking in every one of them, however. After some time, the king saw that his daughter was not getting any younger, and he decided to accept the next match offered to him.

A young ignorant village boy happened to be next. The king agreed.

The princess cried and cried, and refused to be consoled. But the king would not budge—the villager married her and took her to his mother's house.

The "house" was a tiny village hovel with a mud floor, rough planks for walls, and a thatched roof. The extended family squeezed into it along with the goats, sheep, chickens, and geese. The young man's mother put her new daughter-in-law to work milking the goats and making cheese, baking and cooking, sewing and weaving, and all the other household duties. The princess' delicate hands became covered with blisters and callouses; her back ached, and her entire body felt sore. Life was bitter indeed.

In her despair and suffering she wrote to her father complaining to him about her life. In time his answer arrrived, written on the finest paper and sealed with the royal seal. The letter said that in another forty days the king would visit his daughter.

Hearing this, the whole household busily prepared for the arrival. Goats and sheep were cleared out of the hovel and put in a pen at the edge of the courtyard. Fine clay was brought to pave the dirt floor. The walls were whitewashed with fresh lime. Tables and benches were repaired. The family began pampering the princess, and she was freed from all drudgery. Instead of black bread, she was given fine white bread. She began to regain her health and gained back the weight she had lost. Color returned to her face and light to her eyes.

On the day that her father arrived, she welcomed him joyously. The king found her living quarters quite acceptable, and he spent an entire day rejoicing with his daughter as well as with her husband and the entire family.

Night approached, and the king prepared to depart. Suddenly, his daughter fell on his shoulder and began to weep. "Father, Father, don't leave me! How can you abandon me, your beloved daughter?"

"But what is wrong, my dear one?" the king asked in surprise. "I see how you are treated here with the utmost honor. I see how happy you are here!"

The princess began to cry bitterly. "Oh, Father, don't you see, this is only a show! They are just fooling you, trying to pull the wool over your eyes! The moment they heard you were coming and would see my condition with your own eyes, they feared for their lives. They started easing my workload and making this hovel a little more presentable. But *I* know how terribly my mother-in-law has treated me. How many difficult chores she forced me to do! Father, the moment you leave, I fear that I will be made to work doubly hard!"

She finished speaking and fell silent. Everyone stood as still as a stone.

The king turned to his son-in-law. "Is it true?" he demanded. Silence answered him. "Why have you treated her so?" he went on. "Did you not realize that she is the daughter of the king? She is sensitive and delicate. She must be appreciated according to her station!"

Her husband also began to sob. "Yes, my king!" he cried. "I also knew how much honor she deserved. When I asked to marry her, I knew how much I would be expected to honor and revere her. However, I said to myself, the king knows that I am a poor simple villager. If he chose me as his son-in-law, he will certainly provide me with an estate, with a castle and dozens of servants to provide for my wife's needs. If his majesty allowed me to return to my poor hovel, how can I possibly honor his delicate daughter as befits her?!"

Our Sages have taught us that God wished to give the Torah to the first man, Adam. When he ate from the Tree of Knowledge, however, the Torah refused. God then wished to give the Torah to No'ach. When he became drunk after the Flood, she refused this match as well. In much the same way, generation after generation, the Torah found something wrong with every proposed match.

Finally God gave the Torah to Israel... But we make light of the Torah's honor throughout the entire year, and she complains bitterly to the Almighty of this shameful treatment, as the Mishnah (*Pirkei Avos* 6:2) states: "Every day a prophetic echo emanates from Mount Chorev, declaring: 'Woe to mankind because of the disgrace of the Torah.'"

Only when the month of Elul comes do we begin taking stock of ourselves. We are told that in another forty days the awesome Day of Atonement will arrive. God will take account of all we have done. He will make us answer for the disgrace of the Torah. We therefore begin improving ourselves, learning more, praying more, and respecting the honor of our fellowman with greater sincerity. For forty days, we elevate ourselves, until on Yom Kippur we are elevated to the level of the angels. We dress in white and don our prayer shawls. For twenty-six hours we live and breathe holiness. And the King accepts our *teshuvah*.

Now, the sun is setting, the day is ending. The holy Torah turns sobbing to her Father, the King. "Father, Father, how can You leave me? How can You abandon me, Your beloved daughter! In a short while, everything will revert to its former condition. They will take away my crowns. Every man will return to his false ways."

The King, the King of the world, turns to us and asks: "How did you dare to treat My daughter thus? Do you not understand that the soul I placed within you is pure? It is the daughter of the King. It is an extension of the Divine. Do you not realize the same is true of the holy Torah, emanated from the highest heavens?"

What is our answer? "Our Father! Merciful, compassionate Father. You know our condition. We earn a living with the sweat of our brows, with our very souls! The pressures and hardships of our livelihood, detract from the time it takes to pay attention to our souls. We therefore turn to You and ask: All wealth and honor are Yours. Please bestow goodness and blessing upon us so that we will be able to honor the daughter of the King as befits her—so that we will be able to devote ourselves to a life of Torah and mitzvos!"

Ohel Ya'akov, *Emor*

The Last Arrow

The Maggid of Lublin told the following parable about *Ne'ilah*. A hunter once became lost in the forest. He walked along with trepidation, his bow readied in his hand, lest he have to defend himself. Suddenly he saw something among the trees. Was it perhaps a lion? A leopard? He sent an arrow flying, but the object did not move. He approached it and discovered it was a dry tree stump.

But now, a sound behind him! He whirled around, and in a split second another arrow was flying to its mark. But this too proved to be a false alarm. Perhaps it had been the rustling of leaves.

What was that? He sent forth another arrow, but when he approached the spot, he discovered it was a rock.

He now realized that he had only one arrow left. Suddenly, he heard the bloodcurdling roar of a lion... a real lion. His heart pounded. He held his bow tightly, prepared. He knew how much depended on this; how much his life depended on the single arrow in his hand...

The Books of Life and Death are open. Danger lurks everywhere, and we have already shot most of our best arrows. We have cried out and pleaded, but we do not know if we hit the mark—if our prayers have had any effect. Now we have only one arrow left: *Ne'ilah!* How our lives depend upon this one arrow! How careful we must be to aim...

Ohel Ya'akov

שַׁעֲרֵי אַרְמוֹן, מְהֵרָה תִּפְתַּח לְבוֹאֲרֵי דַת אָמוֹן

"Hasten to open the palace gates to those who elucidate the teachings of the Master!"

The Maggid of Vladislav told a parable about a wealthy prince who ruled over many provinces. On the eve of departing on one of his annual tours of his domain, he called to his chief servant and administrator and said, "Tomorrow I embark on a journey to oversee my affairs. I leave the estate in your hands. Be especially attentive to my wife's needs. Make sure she lacks nothing. Honor her according to her station."

The administrator promised and the prince departed.

The administrator immediately began to see himself as lord of the estate. His heart puffed up, and he acted like a tyrant. He made light of the princess' dignity, refused to do her bidding, angered her, and generally made her life miserable.

One day, news arrived that the prince was on his way home and would return in a month's time. Upon hearing this, a radical change took place in the administrator's conduct. He became extremely attentive to the princess' needs. He honored her, flattered her, and did her every bidding. When the prince returned from his journey, he found his trusty servant submissive and ingratiating. His wife did not have a critical word to say about him.

The prince rejoiced and said, "I knew I could trust you. And now, I am about to depart on another journey. I'm sure that I do not need to caution you again: Be attentive to my wife's honor. Do her every bidding."

The prince set off again, and history repeated itself. Before long, the trusty servant began acting as he had before. He made light of the princess' dignity; worse, he often disregarded her completely.

Time passed, and news arrived of the prince's return in another thirty days. This time, however, the servant was too busy with his own newly established business concerns to prepare for the prince's return. Even when he appeared before the princess in response to her summons, he arrogantly belittled her and tormented her by ignoring her supplications.

One day, as he haughtily strode out of her suite, the world turn dark around him. In the distance a cloud of dust could be seen. The prince's coach was approaching! Now, he thought, I will be required to deliver a complete report. I will be compelled to explain my behavior towards the princess—why I belittled and humiliated her.

He remembered how he had had thirty days to better his ways, to serve her loyally and thereby cancel out his previous misconduct. But he had failed to take advantage of that precious time. Just a few seconds ago he had arrogantly defied her to her very face!

But now he thinks to himself: True, the prince is about to arrive. True, he has already entered the gates of his estate. But he hasn't seen the princess yet! He hasn't heard the whole story from her. I still have a few seconds!

So the servant quickly turns on his heels, enters the royal suite again, and begs forgiveness from the princess. With tears in his eyes and a broken heart, he promises he will never ignore her again or refuse to do her bidding. He promises to honor her from now on, to do everything she asks... If only she will not hand him over to his master. If only she will not expose the way he acted...

She graciously replies, "If you keep your word, I will not denounce you, and moreover I will request that your salary be doubled—but on one condition. Your regret must be heartfelt and sincere. Your heart must feel what your lips say."

As she finishes speaking, the door opens and the prince enters. "Hello, my beloved, I'm back! How has the servant conducted himself towards you? Did he respect your wishes?"

The Holy One has transferred His beloved, the holy Torah, into our care. He has instructed us to obey her commandments, to heed her pronouncements—in short, to honor, esteem, and revere her.

During the entire year we debase the Torah. We defy its teachings and neglect its injunctions. We are lax in setting up fixed times for Torah study and we are lethargic and apathetic even when we do take time from our busy schedules to learn. The blowing of the shofar on *Rosh Chodesh Elul* informs us that the Holy One is going to judge us in thirty days. Rosh Hashanah comes, and we are found sorely lacking. We are then given ten more days, between Rosh Hashanah and Yom Kippur, to seek Hashem's mercy, before it is too late. The prophet alludes to these ten days when he says, "Seek God when He can be found, call out to Him when He is close at hand" (*Yeshayahu* 55:6; *Rosh Hashanah* 18a). It is at this time that all Jewry is bestirred, and studies Torah with added vigor, while paying extra attention to fulfilling all the commandments according to the strict letter of the law...

But there are still a few of us who are apathetic and who fail to perk up during Elul. Either we neglect our studies completely or we are lax in setting aside specific times each day for Torah learning. As a result, we are ignorant and therefore incapable of observing the commandments with the proper care and consideration.

Now, when *Ne'ilah* approaches, we begin to worry. Our hearts melt in the face of Hashem's imminent judgment. And the Torah cannot testify in our defense; on the contrary. So we begin now to pray the *Ne'ilah* service, and we say, "Hasten to open the gates of the palace to those who elucidate the teachings of the Master!" This alludes to those who study, explain, and clarify the Torah, which is called God's master plan for creation.* And God asks the Torah, "Does he really

---

* This is based on a sequence of verses in *Sefer Mishlei* (the Book of Proverbs) in which Shelomo *Ha-Melech* has the Torah speak of itself (herself) as the conceptual blueprint that God used, so to speak, in creating the universe: "God created me [the Torah] as the genesis of His way, the first of His works of old. I was set up from eternity, from the beginning, before the earth was conceived. When there were still no depths, I was brought forth... Before the mountains were imprinted, before the hills [were conceived], I was brought forth... When He established the heavens, I was there... When He established the foundations of the earth... I was with Him. He was my Nurse. I was [His] delight each day. I was always frolicking in His presence, playing with the universe, His earth. The children of men were my delights" (*Mishlei* 8:22-31).

Commenting on Shelomo *Ha-Melech*'s masterful use of metaphor, the Midrash (*Bereshis Rabbah* 1:1) begins: Rabbi Hoshayah began his discourse: "I was with Him. He was my *Amon*—Nurse. I was [His] delight each day." The Torah says: God was my *Omen*—Pedagogue... He was my *Oman*—Master Craftsman. I was the instrument with which He created the world. This is similar to a builder. He does not erect a building without consulting an expert architect. The architect does not build without consulting his blueprints. The blueprints inform him how each room and hall is to be made. In the same way, God peered into (consulted) the Torah and created the world. It is thus written, "God created the world *B'reshis*, 'with beginning, with me.'" For nothing deserves to be called *reshis*—beginning like the Torah. Truly, it is as the Torah says: "God created me [the Torah] as the genesis of His way, the first of His works of old."

clarify You? Does he think of You constantly, throughout the day? Does he find all his values in you, and place all his aspirations in You?"

Before these questions are asked, and before we come before God to seek His mercy in the merit of having learned His Torah... we can plead our case before the Torah itself, asking her to overlook the fact that we arrogantly belittled and tormented her by ignoring her supplications. Our last resort, the one way to ensure the opening of the palace gates before our prayers, is to declare our honest resolve to protect and defend her dignity in the future, to fulfill our due obligations towards her, and to learn her wisdom with true persistence and perseverance, thereby proving ourselves worthy of her mercy.

Siach Eliezer 8

יַעֲזֹב רָשָׁע דַּרְכּוֹ
"Let the wicked man forsake his way..."

What does it mean to "forsake" one's way? It is possible to "change" one's way, but how does one "forsake" and "abandon" his way? The Maggid of Lublin explained with this parable:

A smuggler once loaded a wagon full of taxable merchandise. He set out at night, through the forest, slowly making his way along narrow and crooked paths in order to cross the border unseen. As he was moving along, he was suddenly caught in a surprise ambush by the border patrol. They fell upon the wagon, and he knew at that moment that if he were caught he would be imprisoned for many years. What did he do? He abandoned the wagon with all its merchandise and escaped while there was a chance.

This is the meaning of "Let the wicked man forsake his way." It is time for *Ne'ilah*. Yom Kippur is ending. Leave the entire wagonload of contraband and forbidden pleasures behind! Escape while you can!

Ohel Ya'akov

"Let the wicked man..."

The Maggid of Dubno told a parable with a similar lesson: A villager went to the city to sell his wares on market day. By the end of the day, he had sold everything and made a nice profit. Satisfied and in a good mood, he went strolling around town. Chancing upon a clothing store, he decided to buy a new suit. The salesman sized him up at a glance, brought him a suit and said, "You can step into the changing booth here and try this on."

The villager took the suit, stepped into the booth and closed the curtain. The salesman went about his duties, and then, all of a sudden, angry grunts could be heard coming from the booth. The salesman hurried to see what was wrong. He pulled the curtain aside to behold an almost comical scene —comical, that is, to the salesman, not comical to the villager. His right arm had gotten caught halfway through the sleeve, and the poor man was struggling vainly with his left hand to push it through. He looked as though he were in a straight-jacket. The suit was bursting at the seams!

"Stop!" the salesman cried out. "You are ripping the suit. You will pay for this!"

"What kind of suit did you give me?" the villager complained. "It isn't big enough for a child!"

The salesman hurried to disentangle the villager from the suit. "Where are your brains, you simpleton?" he scolded him. "Whoever heard of anything so ridiculous! Did you think you could try the suit on over your thick sheepskin coat?"

He helped the villager take off the sheepskin, as well as several other layers of clothing beneath it. The villager then tried the suit on again—and it fit!

We desire to come close to God, to return to our Father, to be accepted back Home again. And God's hand is open to receive all who wish to return unto Him. There is only one condition: We must take off our old clothes. "Let the wicked man forsake his way and the immoral man his [impure] thoughts. Let him return to God who will show him compassion, to our God who forgives generously" (*Yeshayahu* 55:7). Let him not resemble the man who tries to put on a beautiful new suit over a sheepskin coat...

This is the meaning of the verse, "Love Hashem your God with all your heart" (*Devarim* 6:4). We wish to ascend to this level, and yet it seems to lie so far above us, so far off in the distance. We stand amazed: How could Hashem command us to do something which seems so far beyond our present capacities?! But He gives us the answer in the next verse: "Let these words that I command you today be on your [mind and] heart!" (*ibid.* 6:5). If we divest ourselves of our old clothes, our worn-out habits and character traits, discontinue our immature ways and discard those useless and negative thought patterns which presently clog our minds and hearts—we will find that loving God comes as easily as slipping our arms into a suit that was tailor-made for us!

Ohel Ya'akov, *Va-Es'chanan*

"Let the wicked man..."

The Maggid of Dubno taught: A person sometimes comes upon a fork in the road and chooses the wrong path. He may travel an hour, or two hours, before he realizes his mistake. At that point he has no choice but to turn back and retrace his steps. He must travel back to his point of departure and begin again on the right road.

A person who has chosen the wrong spiritual path, however, and becomes aware of his mistake, need not retrace his steps. Rather, right where he is, on that very spot, he must change his direction and continue forward! He will already be on the right road!

Kochav Mi-Ya'akov, *Haftarah* of *Shoftim*

At the End of the Day

At the end of the Day of Atonement we must realize that we are no longer the same. Our sins have been pardoned and our repentance accepted.

Rabbi Shneur Zalman of Liadi thus writes: "One's heart must be firm and trusting that God desires [to do] lovingkindness. He is gracious and merciful, and generously forgiving the moment one pleads for pardon and forgiveness from Him, may He be blessed. It is thus written, 'With Your generous mercy, wipe away my crimes. Cleanse me of my wrongdoing, purify me of my mistake... and wipe away all my sins' (*Tehillim* 51:3,4,11). Not the slightest doubt should remain to dilute this conviction. For this reason, in every *Shemoneh Esreh*, after we plead, 'Forgive us...' we conclude, 'Blessed are You, Hashem, the Gracious One Who generously forgives.' Without the certainty of pardon, this would be a case of a doubtful blessing, which we would never recite lest it be a blessing in vain. Rather, there is no doubt here whatsoever, for we have asked, 'Forgive us... pardon us'" (*Iggeres Ha-Teshuvah* 11).

After Yom Kippur, we turn over a new page in our lives, as Rambam writes about one who has repented: "I am another person, not the same one who committed those deeds" (*Hilchos Teshuvah* 2:4).

What if we do not feel different? The possibility exists. Days and weeks after the holidays have passed, we might look back and feel that all the change has faded... In fact, this very question once bothered a very special man. His name was Dr. Guardia.

Dr. Guardia was an assimilated Jew, the personal physician of the king of Prussia. Under the guidance of the Maggid of Mezrich, he totally changed his life and returned in complete repentance. He became one of the Maggid's devoted followers and drank from the wells of his deep wisdom.

During the initial period following his return, however, Dr. Guardia became confused and disturbed. He asked the Maggid, "How can I free myself of negative thoughts and memories from my former days, which torment me?"

The Maggid answered with a parable.

A Jew named Moshe who lived in a faraway village ran the local tavern. The gentile farmers would assemble there, drink themselves into a stupor, and wreak havoc. The more alcohol they consumed, the more debased their speech became. But that was just the beginning. They would argue and fight with each other. Tables and chairs would be broken, bottles and mugs smashed. This would go on every night. They would drink until they lost consciousness and wallow in their own filth until morning. Disgusted with running such a vulgar establishment, Moshe decided to change his line of work by transforming the tavern into a food market.

The farmers, however, accustomed to spending their nights drinking in his tavern, paid no attention to this change! Their feet inevitably led them to their old haunt. They would bang on the door and shout: "Moshke, open up. Give us whiskey! Give us vodka!"

"You've got the wrong address!" he would shout back from within. "I no longer run a tavern but a food market!"

"Do you see?" the Maggid asked Dr. Guardia. "This is how you should answer those distressing thoughts when they knock on your door: Leave me alone! I am not the same man I used to be! I have repented and changed my life. My repentance has been accepted. I have turned over a new leaf. I am traveling on a different road. Leave me alone. You have the wrong address..."

Dor De'ah

We Are Not the Same!

The greatest stumbling block that lies before us after Yom Kippur is that we tend to judge ourselves as if we were the same person we were the day before. "Nothing has changed," a shadowy voice whispers from within us. As a result, we might become depressed, God forbid, and feel that the whole thing wasn't worth it! But it simply is not so. And this parable by the holy Rebbe Chayim of Tchernovitz delightfully illustrates this.

A young boy fell deathly ill. He sank into a deep coma and seemed on the brink of death. A specialist who was rushed in from the city administered a strong medication. A few minutes later, he took the boy's hand and checked his pulse. "That's that," he announced. "You needn't worry, he'll be fine. He's healthy!"

The distraught parents looked at their son, who was still lying there unconscious. His face was white as a sheet. They turned to the doctor, so sure of himself. Disbelief was on their faces.

The specialist smiled. "You aren't familiar with this illness and how it works. You don't know how it is cured. I realized at once how serious your boy's condition was, and therefore I understood which remedy would cure it. As soon as I administered the medication, I detected an improvement in his pulse rate. So, although he is stretched out on his bed just as he was before I arrived, and he is still pale and weak, I can assure you that he will continue to improve until he is completely recovered. The improvement may not be apparent today, nor tomorrow or the day after. However, it will come. As far as I am concerned, he is already healthy!"

One who repents and decides to make a major change in his life generally does not feel a tremendous improvement on the spot. He might, as well, still be inclined to do things he thought he had left behind. He should not give up, however, but know with a certainty that he is on the right path. In essence, he is already cured, for within, in the inner recesses of his soul, he is healthy, despite the fact that the improvement will only become outwardly apparent farther down the road.

A Heavenly voice can therefore be faintly heard at the end of Yom Kippur: "Go and eat your meal in joy!" (*Koheles* 9:7), for you are already another person! You are already good! You are already pure!

Be'er Mayim Chayim, *Tahorah*